Dr. Barbara Fournier is an Assistant Professor of Psychology at Curry College where she lectures on developmental psychology. She consults with schools, community groups, and research organizations about learning problems in children and has a clinical practice that specializes in children and young adults.

Dr. George J. Fournier is an Assistant Professor of Psychology at Emmanuel College where he lectures on experimental psychology. He is Director of Health Resource Associates in Boston, where his research and clinical work focuses on the prevention and alleviation of stress and anxiety.

Pre-Parenting
A Guide to Planning Ahead

Barbara Fournier

George J. Fournier

A SPECTRUM BOOK

PRENTICE-HALL, INC., Englewood Cliffs, New Jersey 07632

Library of Congress Cataloging in Publication Data

Fournier, Barbara.
  Pre-Parenting.

  (A Spectrum book)
  Includes index.
  1. Parenting. 2. Family life education.
I. Fournier, George J., joint author. II. Title.
HQ755.8.F68   613.9'4   80-11961
ISBN 0-13-694877-4
ISBN 0-13-694869-3 (pbk.)

To Mom and Dad

Interior design and production by
The Book Department
52 Roland Street
Charlestown, MA 02129

© 1980 by Prentice-Hall, Inc., Englewood Cliffs, New Jersey 07632

A SPECTRUM BOOK

10 9 8 7 6 5 4 3 2 1

Printed in the United States of America

PRENTICE-HALL INTERNATIONAL, INC., *London*
PRENTICE-HALL OF AUSTRALIA PTY. LIMITED, *Sydney*
PRENTICE-HALL OF CANADA, LTD., *Toronto*
PRENTICE-HALL OF INDIA PRIVATE LIMITED, *New Delhi*
PRENTICE-HALL OF JAPAN, INC., *Tokyo*
PRENTICE-HALL OF SOUTHEAST ASIA PTE. LTD., *Singapore*
WHITEHALL BOOKS LIMITED, *Wellington, New Zealand*

Acknowledgments

We would like to thank some of the many wonderful people who helped make this book possible. Thank you to those who so openly shared their time and personal experiences with us. Thank you to our friends, to Dr. Bruce Steinberg, to Ms. Mary Faas–Gorman and Dr. Arthur Gorman, to Ms. Kristine Dever, and to the many others who gave us support and encouragement. Extra special thanks to Ms. Bonnie Moore, our typist, who deciphered our hieroglyphics and gave up her Sundays. Thank you also to Elizabeth Kudzma, M.S., Associate Professor of Nursing at Curry College, Milton, Mass., for her review of the chapter on health considerations. We would also like to thank our editors, production staff, and all the supportive people from Prentice-Hall, especially Margaret Kearney, our copy editor.

Contents

Introduction

This book was written because we have shared with many family members, friends, and clients the difficulties associated with deciding to have or not have children. We hope that we can help those of you who are debating whether or not to have a child to make the decision intelligently, with all the pertinent information at your disposal. We also hope that the book will help those who have already decided to have a first or another child to prepare for the consequences of that decision so as to increase your chances of having a positive experience.

The availability of contraception and abortion requires that we must make decisions about having children that were once dictated mostly by chance. We must now decide whether or not to have children, how many to have, and when to have them. We address these decisions under various circumstances: when we contemplate marriage ("What kind of parents would we be?"), when we are childfree ("What changes would we experience if we were to parent now?"), when and if we are already parents ("Would my family and I benefit from having another child now?"), and even if we are single or divorced ("Could I handle parenting on my own?").

Most of us recognize that these times are very difficult ones in which to parent—more so for some of us than for others, and more so during certain periods of our lives. Yet there are few useful guidelines to assist and advise us in making a good parenting decision. Other family members are likely to be biased, friends are often as confused and ambivalent as we are, and professionals often direct us to get in touch with how we *really* feel (a good but not particularly useful idea). We believe that the best way to decide and/or prepare for parenting is to become informed about three factors that critically affect the parent experience: knowing yourselves and how you are likely to behave as parents, knowing about children and how they change as they develop, and knowing what is involved in being a good parent. We have entitled this book

Pre-Parenting, because it emphasizes an active process in which we try on and learn about parenting to see how well we enjoy and handle it.

In order to help you predict how you and your partner (if you have one) are likely to behave as parents at this time in your lives, we have included personalized questions and exercises. While this kind of prediction is far from perfect, it is more reliable and useful than you might imagine. We focus on what you have done in the past, are doing in the present, and are likely to do in the future. We have tried to avoid talking in generalities and abstractions, which most of us have difficulty applying to ourselves and each other.

We have also included information about adult development. Most books on parenting neglect to adequately consider adult needs and changes, even though these are critical to a parent–child experience. In making a long-range decision like parenting, we need to be able to look ahead and anticipate our future needs and priorities. Thus, the growing body of research on adult change can be very useful to you.

We also need to know something about children. Parenting is considerably different from being pregnant or even from having a baby. We need to know how children change as they grow, and what their needs and strengths are likely to be, so that we can better evaluate how well we can enjoy and handle the experience. Even those of us who are already parents can benefit from knowledge about children because they are all different. It is important that we recognize that another child will not be a carbon copy of our first and that we can, and should, anticipate differences.

In order to make an informed decision about parenting, we should not only know about children and about ourselves as adults, but also about what is involved in good parenting. Many experts have many, frequently differing, opinions about how to be a good parent. We have summarized the data on which these views are based and have tried to separate the information from the prescriptions. As experimental and developmental psychologists, we are in a unique position to both know the relevant data and to select the most reliable conclusions.

We think the best time to find out about parenting skills and commitments is before you decide to parent and certainly before you have a child. By knowing what you and your partner ought to do as parents, you can better decide whether or not you enjoy, or are comfortable, doing these sorts of things. If not, you can elect not to parent or to prepare, in advance, to parent well. Preventive parenting, like medicine, is better than waiting for problems to develop. It is easier to set the occasion for a good relationship than to repair a poor one, and easier to improve your behavior and to change destructive habits before you parent than afterward.

We have also taken great pains to address those issues and questions that are especially important to men contemplating parenting. Too often men have been excluded from or unprepared to participate in what should be a cooperative venture.

Along with the formal sources of information (research articles, developmental patterns, clinical examples), we also present material from interviews we conducted with over 200 couples and singles. We did not attempt to do this scientifically, nor to control our subjects for race, social class, and so on. We did, however, interview a variety of people of different ages, races (white primarily, but also black and Oriental), cultures (in addition to Americans, we also interviewed people in and from France, England, Germany, Italy, Israel, Switzerland, China, Iran, and Africa), and family sizes (ranging from one to fourteen). The majority of people were middle class with a minimum of high school education. Most of the Americans were from the Northeast and lived in the Boston area. We have interspersed their feelings and recommendations throughout the book.

There are a few possible objections that can be raised about the purpose of this book, and we would like to address them. One objection may be that we should all parent because procreation is a biological and developmental need necessary to humanity's survival and to our own personal development. We disagree. There are many ways of serving humanity other than, or in addition to, parenting. We think this is a personal decision and that we all have a right to opt to be childfree. We would even argue that we may serve humanity better as nonparents than as unhappy parents.

Parenting may be a source of personal anguish for us, our children, and society. A recent Ann Lander's survey reported that 70 percent of the parents who wrote in said they regretted having had children, and if they could live their lives over, would not have them. A major surprise in the interviews we conducted was how many parents were ambivalent, even regretful, about being parents—even those with healthy, beautiful children. "We had no idea what was involved" was the common theme. Even if we were to eliminate childfree couples, we would still have to address how to best limit our family size so as to maximize our own and our children's development (as well as that of the rest of our overpopulated world). We would still have to address when to have a first or another child, and to decide at what point in our lives parenting is most likely to be positive. The best way to avoid regrets and poor decisions is to make the most informed, prepared, and realistic decision you can about parenting before you become one, either again or for the first time.

Some people also believe that it is not necessary to be prepared for parenting because there are maternal and paternal instincts that will ensure that you adequately cherish, nourish, and rear your child. However, millions of children over thousands of years have been tortured, murdered, mutilated, starved, beaten, raped, and sold by their parents, often with the approval of their culture. This reality is hardly encouraging evidence that children naturally elicit proper caretaking behavior from their parents.

Under present conditions, it is especially important to be well prepared for parenting. Increased mobility and the breakup of the extended family have left to parents the responsibilities once shared by family members and neighbors. At the same time, institutions and the media have allowed parental values to be compromised more easily; even a middle-class child, in the security of suburbia, can cooly observe murder, rape, and sex and be sold sugar, toy guns, sex roles, and profiteering. The world is changing so rapidly that children take for granted what their grandparents believed miraculous.

The majority of parents now work outside the home as well as in it (or for it!), some voluntarily, some desperately. In either case, parenting becomes something one does in addition to, and different from, what one does in work. This dual role is considerably more difficult than when parenting was woven into the fabric of one's daily activities, as in agrarian societies.

To make the task even more difficult, parenting now involves helping children prepare for (and consequently put off) being useful and independent citizens. The number of years children are dependent on their families has increased markedly, and it is no longer uncommon for a child to reach 30 without being self-sufficient.

There are numerous other reasons why parenting is so difficult now, many of which have probably occurred to you before. These difficulties and the agonies associated with them have precipitated the writing of this book in the hope that it can help prospective parents to evaluate and improve their parenting skills *before* they decide whether or not to parent.

Some people believe that there is no such thing as "good" parenting because standards and values vary so greatly in the melting pot of America. We disagree. There is parenting that fosters learning and loving, and there is parenting that promotes fear and mistrust. While cultures and customs do vary greatly, those of you who care enough about your children to have read this far would prefer to raise productive, happy, and intelligent children, rather than indolent, depressed, and defeated children. Researchers, educators, psychologists, physicians, developmentalists, clinicians, and statisticians have compiled much information that will be useful to you. The best time to avail yourself to all of this is before you have a child so that you can decide either not to parent or to prepare to parent well.

In order to help you make an informed, thoughtful decision based on the present and future welfare of you, your partner, and possibly a child, this book has been divided into the following chapters:

1. *Health Considerations:* In this first chapter we present those issues relating to health that should be addressed when considering whether or not to have a child. Included are discussions on contraception, pregnancy, personal health habits, genetics, and the physical consequences for men and women of having, or not having, a child.

2. *Birth Considerations:* What is childbirth really like? What birth styles are

available to today's parents and how would you select a compatible and safe one?

3. *Economic Considerations:* What are the costs, obvious or hidden, of parenting? What expenses can you anticipate as a child grows up? What might you have to give up, if anything, to parent in the manner you wish?

4. *Lifestyle Considerations:* How would having a child, the first or another, alter your lifestyle? What kind of commitment would parenting require in the coming years? How much parenting would you and your partner share? What child-care resources are available, and what impact do they have on a child's development?

5. *Interpersonal Considerations:* How might you relate to your child? How well might you and your partner handle the many issues raised by parenting? How many differences are you likely to encounter? How would having a child affect your relationships with your family, friends, and neighbors?

6. *Competency Considerations:* What kind of parenting fosters health, intelligence, love, and confidence? Would you be likely to encourage these qualities in your children? How could you maximize the likelihood of doing so?

7. *Considering Your Options:* What do you do if you remain undecided? If you have decided to be childfree, how do you handle going against the mainstream? If you have decided to parent, either again or for the first time, how should you prepare for it?

It is our sincere hope that this book will encourage and serve all who recognize that parenting is something you do, not something you become. It should be considered and be prepared for as thoughtfully as we prepare for marriage or a career. By doing so, we will be more likely to increase our own happiness and that of future generations.

1

Health Considerations

In this chapter, we describe various birth control methods, so that you can select a reliable and appropriate one. This will give you more time for pre-parenting. We also discuss some of the usual reasons for so many unplanned pregnancies and how you can avoid them. If you do become pregnant, when is the earliest you can tell and how? What is pregnancy like, for both parents, and for the developing fetus? What abortion options are available and how do you feel about employing them?

We also look at the ways in which pregnancy and birth may affect your health, appearance and sex lives. What are the health risks and benefits of not having children or of having another? Few people realize that men are often physically affected by their wives' pregnancies, and that their health, even drug use, may affect the health of the baby. We examine how likely you are to have a healthy baby, and what, if anything, you can do to better your chances. Under what conditions might genetic counseling be advisable? How can you influence the sex of a baby? Last, but not least, we present some health-related questions that both men and women can discuss with their doctors before deciding whether to have a child.

CONTRACEPTION

In order to decide, let alone plan, on parenting, you need time. You gain time by using birth control. There are numerous methods of contraception, many of which have important consequences for your health. Therefore, you should keep in mind two questions.

First, how long are you likely to use contraception? Certain contraceptives, like the birth control pill, cannot be used indefinitely without increasing the risk of health problems. Others that are more unreliable may work for a while, but the more often you use them, the more likely you are to have an "accident." And contraceptives that must be used during each intercourse demand a consistency of motive and self-control that few of us possess for extended periods of time.

Second, how do you and your partner feel about a pregnancy at this time? For some of us, the possibility is acceptable. It may even seem to be a relief from indecision (we say "seem" because most expectant parents remain indecisive throughout most of the pregnancy —and afterward as well). Those who are comfortable with abortion can elect that option just in case they decide against parenting at that particular time. But if even one of you is not yet ready to parent or parent again, and abortion would be difficult for you, contraceptive reliability becomes exceedingly important. It is a good idea for both of you to explore the pros and cons of the different contraceptive methods we will discuss. You have to find, for you, the right balance between safety, reliability, ease of use, and expense.

The Birth Control Pill

The pill works by preventing the release of the egg and by thickening the mucus produced at the neck of the womb so that the sperm can't get by. There are several kinds of pills, each varying in the proportion of two female hormones: estrogen and progesterone. The pill is taken orally—the woman who told her doctor that the pill couldn't possibly work because it always fell out was misinformed!

A major advantage of taking the birth control pill is that it does not interfere with sexual behavior. Also, it is virtually foolproof if taken properly. But the woman must remember to take it every day. Pregnancy can occur if it is not taken for two consecutive days; therefore, it pays to use a back-up method of contraception if this should occur (a woman doesn't want to be pregnant and take the pill at the same time).

A medical examination is required to obtain a prescription for birth control pills. Additionally, constant medical supervision is recommended for pill users because of numerous possible side effects. Over 20 percent of all pill users experience headaches, backaches, and other problems common to the early stages of pregnancy (if you or your partner have had a bad reaction to the pill, pregnancy may also be a little difficult). A British study reported pill users to have a ten times greater risk of thrombosis (internal blood clotting that may be fatal) than nonusers, but recent American studies have not replicated these findings.

Many women are advised *not* to use the pill if they have family histories of cancer, diabetes and thrombosis; if they are over 40 years old (the chances of heart attacks are slightly increased); if they are nursing (milk production and content are affected); and if they have already been using the pill for several years. Pill use also increases susceptibility to venereal disease and vaginitis by changing the acidic balance of the vagina.

How safe is the pill? We really don't know. Certainly, long-term biochemical intervention is likely to produce a broad range of physical reactions, some of which may be unpleasant, even dangerous. The kind and extent of these changes would be greatly determined by the woman's physical makeup and her medical history. Before deciding to use birth control pills, women should discuss with their doctors possible side effects and risks of pill use in relation to their specific medical histories. They might also consider how likely they would be to systematically and conscientiously employ any of the other contraceptive methods discussed. Whatever the possible risks of pill use, they are substantially less than the known risks associated with pregnancy and childbirth. Both of these risks to your health need to be carefully weighed.

The IUD (Intrauterine Device)

This device, made mostly of plastic, has to be inserted in the uterus (womb) by a gynecologist. The success rate for the IUD is very high, but it requires frequent checking since it can move out of position. A few threads hang into the vagina to permit the user to make sure that it's still in place; this should be done each time before intercourse. The IUD *appears* to work (we're not really sure how it works) by not allowing the fertilized egg to attach itself to the uterus; thus, the egg gets "flushed out." This means that the IUD, unlike the pill, does not stop conception from occurring, just from continuing. If you believe that human life begins at conception, an IUD may ,make you uncomfortable.

Another disadvantage of the IUD is that the insertion may be painful for some women. The IUD also carries a small (1 percent) risk of infection or perforation of the uterus unless the physician is well trained in the insertion procedure. Its side effects may be so unpleasant—usually cramping, backache, and excessive bleeding—that about 15 percent who try cannot tolerate the device, especially nonmothers.

The Diaphragm

The diaphragm also must be fitted by a doctor, usually several times, to ensure a perfect fit. The diaphragm is a rubber cup that covers the cervix (the lower part of the uterus) and, therefore, prevents sperm from getting to the egg. When used properly with spermicidal jelly, it is very effective and has no biochemical side effects. Unfortunately, it must be put in no more than a few hours before intercourse, and it is sometimes difficult to plan ahead or to stop sexual behavior in order to insert it. It also cannot be removed until six to eight hours after intercourse so that some hardy sperm won't be able to slip by (spermicidal jelly must be used if intercourse occurs again before removal of the diaphragm). Other disadvantages are that some sexual positions (especially the position with the woman on top) can jostle the position of the diaphragm; and some people claim to be able to feel it (even though you are not supposed to). A rare minority (only 2 to 10 percent) have such strong internal muscles that the diaphragm is either popped out of position or, during orgasm, the cup is suctioned so hard that the device cannot be removed without the aid of a physician.

The Condom

The condom (also known as a rubber or safe) is a sheath that fits over the penis and, therefore, prevents the sperm from entering the vagina. There are no side effects, and the condom helps prevent communication of venereal disease. Condoms come in different brands, colors, shapes (some have tips on the end), and materials (from plastic to intestinal tissue, some lubricated). There is a story about a young man in a drugstore who, for the first time, abashedly asked for some condoms. The clerk, watching the lad redden, asked, "What size, young man?" The boy looked down and mumbled, "A medium, I think." The clerk was, of course, asking for the box size since condoms come in one-size-fits-all.

Condoms are very effective—if used properly, they fail only about 3 percent of the time, and then the cause is breakage due to improper storage or application. There are many advantages to using the condom: it is nonchemical and noninvasive, highly portable, and readily obtained (in the Midwest they are available from dispensing machines; in the East they are in open display in drugstores). Many men like the fact that the condom offers them participation in contraception and may even delay orgasm by cutting down on sensation (like showering with a raincoat on, some say). Obviously, not all men find this a positive effect. Condoms also add some measure of protection against venereal disease and can be lubricated (do not use vaseline with condoms because it tends to make rubber disintegrate). One of the primary advantages is that its failure or nonuse is obvious, which allows you to consider abortion options or pregnancy precautions immediately. It also comforts those who are unsure of the contraceptive habits of their partners.

Of course, the condom also has disadvantages, the most obvious one being that it interrupts intercourse. The penis must be erect and the sheath must be put on prior to entry into the vagina since early secretions are often spermladen. Pausing at a critical moment has saved many a woman's virtue, and not pausing has produced many a sleepless night. Condoms must be put on carefully so that there is room at the tip for the ejaculate. Additionally, care must be taken that an unwanted package is not left behind. People who fall asleep still entwined may find themselves either expectant parents or stuck to the sheets—or both!

Foams, Creams, and Jellies

These preparations are put in the vagina immediately before intercourse and are supposed to kill sperm on contact. They are especially effective when used in conjunction with such methods as the diaphragm and condom. Although they are easily obtained in drugstores without prescription, they have several disadvantages. They have to be put in right before intercourse and can get very messy (since they cannot be washed out until at least 12 hours later, morning or afternoon lovers need to wear sanitary napkins). Also, they may cause irritation, too much lubrication, or a sensation of heat, which some people find unnatural and unpleasant.

The Rhythm Method

Most women are fertile for only a short time each month. The female cycle is critical to conception. Men ejaculate about 100 million sperm each time that swim toward the egg with varying degrees of speed, stamina, and strength. But the egg must be either in the proper position (called ovulation), or else the sperm must get there first and wait to fertilize the egg (they can wait only 48 hours or so before they die). This means that most women can get pregnant only during a 72-hour period each month—for 24 hours when the egg is in the proper position and for 48 hours before that since sperm might still be alive and waiting for the egg. It's somewhat inefficient to use contraception constantly, given the short time it is really necessary. The problem, however, is determining when those 72 hours are. The fertile period varies from woman to woman and within each woman from month to month.

We recommend that a woman and her steady partner be familiar with her menstrual cycle and use the rhythm method, if not alone, then in conjunction with another method. If you do want to conceive after reading this book, it certainly will help to know your fertility peaks. This information can also help you to influence the sex of the child (more on this later). And if you don't want to conceive, you have to know when you are most at risk. For example, some men delay putting on condoms, even though they know they're not supposed to. But if you both know which day you are likely to ovulate, you may want to be careful for those few days. Knowing your cycle will also enable you to spot pregnancy early so that you can take whatever measures are necessary.

Using the rhythm method by itself is somewhat risky since there is considerable variability in the fertile period from month to month. Most users, therefore, employ several rhythm techniques together. Another disadvantage is that it may require relatively long periods of abstinence or contraceptive use. Because we don't know which 72 hours are the fertile ones, most conservative estimates will recommend precautions for 240 hours—that is ten days, or more. We will now discuss the major approaches to the rhythm method.

Keeping Temperature Charts. Since most women's body temperature rises slightly when fertile, a daily temperature chart is sometimes used to predict and measure ovulation (when a woman is fertile). Once you realize you have ovulated, you know that after 24 hours or so you are likely to be infertile. To do this, you must take your temperature (using a special thermometer, like the Ovulindex) right after getting out of bed in the morning (before eating or smoking) *every day.* If accurately recorded, your temperature will rise slightly (several tenths of a degree) when you ovulate. Your temperature will remain elevated until menstruation starts. Since your temperature may rise a little prematurely, wait for *three days* after your temperature rises. You should be infertile from then until, and during, menstruation. We say *should be* because you may have had an increase in temperature if you were sick or fatigued. Usually, women who use this method also use the calendar method.

The Calendar Method. This approach is based on the fact that, generally, women ovulate 14 days before menstruation begins (plus or minus 2 days are usually added to this time because of human variability and because sperm can wait around for 48 hours until the egg is ready). You must record your menstruation cycle (that is, how many days between the *start* of one menstruation and the *start* of the next menstruation) for at least 6 months, and you can calculate safe and unsafe times.

Take your shortest menstrual cycle, as measured from the first day of bleeding to the day before your next menstruation started. Subtract 18 from that number of days.

EXAMPLE: Shortest menses
                      First day menses: April 1
                      First day of next menses: May 1
                      Length: 26 days; 26 – 18 = 8

This number is your first unsafe day—that is, the day on which you may become pregnant.

EXAMPLE: I start to menstruate on July 1. I may be fertile by July 9.

Now take your longest cycle and subtract 10 days from that. This is your first "safe" day, by which time ovulation should be passed.

EXAMPLE: Your longest cycle is 30 days. 30 – 10 = 20. If you start menstruating on July 1, and start contraception on July 9, you can stop contraception again on July 20.

The Billings' Natural Family Planning Method.   Dr. John J. Billings has claimed that women can easily be taught to tell when they are about to ovulate by feeling the texture of their vaginal secretions. He and his followers claim a high success rate (which is questioned by some) and have applied their techniques to poor populations in many countries. They have considerable economic support, have established many inexpensive or free classes in different cities in the United States and frequently use nurses and/or nursing nuns to run these classes.

Women (and their husbands) learn to check their mucus secretions every day by inserting their fingers or a long Q-tip deep into the vagina. By examining the changes in the amount and the feel of their secretions when rubbed between their fingers, women can tell when ovulation is occurring. During infertile days, mucus is either almost nonexistent (dry days) or cloudy, thick, and tacky. During fertile days, the mucus is likely to be plentiful (wet days), clear, slippery, and stringy (it will form strands if put between thumb and first finger). Used in conjunction with the temperature and calendar charts, this method is very helpful.

The Ovutimer and the Ovulometer. These recent inventions, which should be on the market soon, also measure changes during the menstrual cycle. The ovutimer tests the viscosity of cervical mucus, supposedly more accurately and reliably than the Billings' Method. The Ovulometer measures changes in the electrostatic currents of the body that, according to the developer, become negative in a woman 3 to 6 days before ovulation. Both ought to be commercially available at relatively inexpensive prices. Hopefully, subsidies will assist poorer women in purchasing the devices since, unlike other contraceptives, there is little reason to anticipate resistance from any religious group.

Sterilization

Sterilization is the fastest growing contraceptive technique in the United States. In fact, according to Princeton's Population Research Center, a quarter of all married couples using contraception have chosen sterilization of the husband or wife. And the *New York Times* (May 6, 1976) reported that among married women over 30, sterilization is the leading form of contraception. In most states, sterilization can be performed only when both husband and wife sign consent forms (whether this is legal has yet to be tested).

Sterilization should be seriously considered if, after careful consideration of all the issues, you are certain that you want no more, or any, children. It should also be considered if you decide to have one last child. You may want to discuss with your doctor the possibility of an operation upon the delivery of this last child, so that once you have completed your family you will not have to deal with the worries and risks of contraception.

How do people decide to become sterilized? Dr. Stephen Mumford, author of the book on sterilization decisions referenced at the chapter's end, studied 235 men and 187 wives who were considering sterilization. He reported that they seemed to go through five distinct stages in their decision process: (1) becoming aware of the sterilization procedure; (2) deciding not to parent any more; (3) talking to someone who had had the sterilization procedure performed; (4) going through a pregnancy scare or an unwanted pregnancy; and (5) seriously considering surgery. Although Dr. Mumford studied only those people considering male sterilization, it is likely that these same experiences precede voluntary female sterilization. Reading his books and others on the subject, talking to each other and to your doctor, and speaking to couples who have had the procedure can assist you in making a wise decision.

Male Sterilization. Male sterilization is less expensive, complicated, and dangerous than female sterilization. The usual procedure is called a vasectomy and is usually performed by a urologist in his or her office in about 15 to 20 minutes. The physician will inject a local anesthetic into each side of the testicles (hold on!—the worst is over because now you are numbing). After the testicles are numb, the urologist makes an incision into each testicle and removes a small section of the tube that carries sperm from the testicles into the penis (called the *vas deferentia*). The remaining ends are tied off, and the incisions are sewn up. As the anesthetic wears off, some soreness may be experienced, and there may be discomfort for a day or two. Some men take a day off from work or have the procedure performed on a Friday, while others continue working with minimal discomfort. Within a week, most men will probably feel like resuming intercourse. There will be no physical signs or changes indicating a vasectomy other than the small scars on the top section of the testicles (just in case someone is suspicious). The ejaculate will appear unaltered because sperm make up less than 10 percent of the fluid normally ejaculated.

How effective are vasectomies? Failures occur only in a small fraction of 1 percent of all vasectomies. When they do occur, it is because men have unprotected intercourse *before* having a sperm test done. Sometimes, sperm hide out in the ducts beyond the incision. They may stay alive, in waiting, for several weeks and "jump" into some ejaculate as it goes by. Thus, it is recommended that contraceptives be used until a laboratory examination certifies that the ejaculate is spermfree. In rare cases, the severed ends may "untie" and rejoin, or there are, unbeknownst to the urologist, more than one tube per testicle carrying sperm to the penis.

Attempts have been made to make the operation reversible by putting in a "spigot," instead of tying off the ends. (Technically, this is called a "stop-cock.") One could turn the stop-cock on when and if one changed one's mind at some point. Unfortunately, scar tissue tends to form and seal the stop-cock shut, so that up to now reversals have been successful only about 75 percent of the time. Even when reversals are successful, pregnancy rates are surprisingly low (about 35 percent), for unknown reasons. Sperm banks were developed as an alternative. Before the vasectomy, sperm is quick-frozen and stored. If, at a later date, a child is wanted, the sperm could be defrosted and artificial insemination employed. Recent data suggest that frozen sperm can retain their potency for as long as ten years.

What side effects are there from a vasectomy? The only thing that has been directly disturbed is the tube carrying the sperm—sperm production itself is unaffected, as well as the production of male hormones. What then happens to all the little sperm who can't get out of the testicles? They swim around for awhile and then die; they are then reabsorbed into the body from whence they came. Do these reabsorbed sperm have any effect? Preliminary evidence in rats shows some reduction in the amount of male hormone, testosterone, and a slightly higher than expected incidence of rheumatoid arthritis among some vasectomied males has suggested that the men's own bodies may be attacking these sperm as though they were foreign invaders, like bacteria. The data so far are very meager. At present, vasectomies appear to be as safe as any other style of contraceptive and considerably more convenient and reliable than most.

Female Sterilization. Female sterilization is more complex. The two kinds most commonly done are the hysterectomy and the tubal ligation (or "having your tubes tied"). Quite literally, this is what is done in a tubal ligation, as in a vasectomy for a male. The tubes, called the fallopian tubes, that carry the egg from the ovaries to the uterus are severed and tied off. The procedure also fails in a very small fraction of 1 percent of all cases for the same reasons vasectomies fail—the ends untie and rejoin or other pathways are employed.

There are actually hundreds of techniques for performing tubal ligations. Frequently, the physician goes through the vagina—this is often done after birth. A preferred procedure when there is not a birth is called a laparoscopy. The gynecologist gets to the tubes by going through the navel (no scars, no general anesthesia, no hospital).

The hysterectomy is one of the most hotly debated of surgical procedures, along with circumcisions, mastectomies, tonsillectomies, and appendectomies. It is estimated that one out of every three American women will have a hysterectomy by the time she is 65. What is a hysterectomy? It is the removal of the uterus. The Greek word for uterus is *hustera*—the ancient Greeks believed that hysteria was a condition brought on by a woman's uterus wandering around her body in search of a child. (As you can see, our attitudes toward sterility reflect centuries of culture!)

Neither tubal ligations nor hysterectomies affect the secretion of female hormones. These secretions are altered only when the ovaries (which control the secretion of many female hormones) are removed (done only in cases of pathology). As with a vasectomy, there are no physical changes produced by these procedures except that without a uterus, pregnancy is impossible. Rarely, however, is a hysterectomy performed for solely contraceptive reasons; rather, there has usually been a diagnosis of tumors, fibroids, cancer of the cervix, and so forth. Sometimes these diagnoses are inferred from a woman's pelvic discomfort, and some people have questioned the reliability as well as the effectiveness of the procedure in eliminating complaints of this sort. As one feminist said, "What doctors are telling us is if you have a problem with being a woman and you are too old for babies, then take out whatever female parts you can. You know, just in case." Most women are now consulting with at least two independent physicians when a hysterectomy is recommended. (This should be standard procedure when any surgery is recommended.)

Psychological Consequences of Sterilization. The psychological consequences of sterilization vary. Most people report some shock immediately afterward, some a sense of loss and doubt and then, ultimately, relief. Said Ida, age 37, "I felt just like I had in my pregnancies—oh, shit, this is forever, what have I done? And then—I felt terrific. I had decided at last. Once and for all. No more pills, no more leaky rubbers, looking for tissues, worrying whenever my period was late—no more anxiety." For some, sex has never been better and more free of restraint and fear. Occasionally, some people feel as through they are no longer "whole." This is especially true when the procedure has been medically mandated. For some, not being able to have babies (even by accident) takes the point out of sex. It is important to plan carefully before deciding upon sterilization. Additional questions on dealing with the decision to have no more (or any) children are raised in the last chapter.

Why Accidents Happen

There are many reasons why contraceptives are not used effectively, even when couples do not wish to parent. Sometimes only one partner wishes to have a baby and may deliberately or subconsciously undermine contraception. One woman admitted she stopped taking her birth control pills without telling her partner. Another would exclaim, "Oh no, I forgot my diaphragm!" just as her husband started to ejaculate. One male confessed sticking holes in his wife's diaphragm, and another would hide his condoms. If you think your partner is trying to manipulate you unfairly or deceive you about contraception, you ought to have a very serious discussion, perhaps with the help of a therapist or counselor. While people may learn to love an unwanted baby (though many never do), it is far more difficult for them to forgive a partner who has used deceit to accomplish conception.

Sometimes neither partner takes precautions, and pregnancy is left to chance. They run out of contraceptives and never quite get to a serious discussion. Or, they figure "one time—what the hell!" One young couple told us, unhappily, that they were expecting. Since we knew she had been using birth control pills, we asked whether something had happened to them. The young man replied, "We decided it wasn't good for Jane to be using them—so she stopped a few months ago." "Oh," one of us said, "what did you use then?" There was an awkward pause. "Nothing," said the young man. "Oh. So I guess you don't mind having a child now?" "Well," said the husband, "now is the worst time possible. I wish we had waited a couple of years." "What did you expect?" we asked. "I know," said the wife, "but we thought it wouldn't happen until we tried to have one—you know, *wanted* it." She, by the way, was a nurse, and he was in school as a paramedic.

It might be helpful to ask yourself some questions. For example, do you forget to use contraceptives occasionally? If so, do you or your partner remind and help each other with contraception? One solution is to place a reminder someplace where you are likely to see it. One couple with a four-poster colonial bed has adorned each of the four bedpost knobs with a half-rolled condom—it may not be your style, but it works for them! Do you find yourself arranging things so that contraception is difficult—making love on the living room carpet when condoms are upstairs, or perhaps drinking too much? If so, reconsider your feelings. Are you trying to avoid making a decision and leaving it up to chance?

Sometimes one or both partners question their ability to have children. Some couples who are not really trying to have a baby find themselves worrying if after a few "accidents," nothing happens. Most of us have experienced this sort of ambivalence and know it is not easy to dismiss lightly. There is the "whew" feeling associated with not being pregnant, but there is also a tinge of "I wonder why I'm not?" Such couples often begin to use contraceptives less and less frequently and await what will happen with a mixture of dread and disappointment.

Many pregnancies result from people "testing" their abilities to propagate. It is considerably less expensive, however, if you test yourself when you really do want a child. A man can simply have a sperm evaluation done by a urologist. If you identify with the concerns raised here, it might be useful for you to recognize that an unwanted baby is a costly consequence of proving yourself in an area in which proof is more readily obtained. If you can't help feeling this way, at least recognize its self-destructive possibilities and take *special* precautions so that in a weak moment you won't put yourself to the test.

Sometimes people select the wrong contraceptive for their needs. Their choice may not be pragmatic—it may take too much time, effort, and planning and may be messy, inconvenient, and a "turnoff." However, remember that contraceptives are not nearly as time consuming, messy, or inconvenient as an unwanted infant. These issues can be minimized by carefully selecting an appropriate contraceptive (many free birth control clinics are available to assist you) and by placing it in an appropriate, accessible place *before* you need it.

"Accidents" sometimes occur because people have misconceptions about birth control. They misuse contraceptives or rely on ineffective methods. Douching, for example, is more likely to facilitate pregnancy than prevent it since the force of the douche will speed up the sperm's journey to the egg. Salt, bleach, pendants, garlic, prayer, and various odds and ends will *not* prevent pregnancy. Many people believe that women cannot get pregnant soon after they have given birth. This is *not* true. Recent studies indicate that women who do not breast-feed resume menstruation, on the average, two months after birth. However, certain individuals may resume menstruation considerably earlier. Mothers who breast-feed generally resume menstruating later than those who do not breast-feed; however, the length of time varies considerably and seems to be affected by many factors such as nutrition, stress, age, and genetics. It is therefore possible for both lactating and nonlactating women to become pregnant very shortly after birth. It is also important to remember that it is unwise to wait for the return of menstruation as a sign to begin using contraception because fertility usually begins 14 days *before* menstruation, whether it is the first after birth or not. In other words, by the time a woman resumes menstruating, she has probably already been fertile.

As you can see, to work effectively, contraception has to be part of your life, actively planned and shared with your partner. Under those conditions, you exercise control over your body and over the creation of another life.

HOW TO TELL IF YOU'RE PREGNANT

Many women are not sure how to tell whether or not they are pregnant. A few believe they can tell immediately after intercourse, but it takes at least two hours for the sperm to swim to the egg. Others believe they know within days; while some do, over 60 percent of all pregnancy tests are negative (not pregnant), so many women *mistakenly* believe, or fear, or hope, they are pregnant.

Pregnancy Tests

The earliest time to positively determine pregnancy is seven days after conception by getting a pregnancy test that analyzes the hormone levels (doctors measure the amount of human chorionic-gonadotropin, HCG, in the blood). This relatively new procedure was developed by two Boston-based doctors, Dr. Tom Kosaya and Dr. Melvin Taymor, and is called a Beta Sub Unit pregnancy test. While accurate, the test is expensive (around $15 plus a clinic or doctor's fee) and usually must be done at a hospital, laboratory, or upon a physician's request. The test is available in the Boston area at the Screening Clinic of the Peter Bent Brigham Hospital. Unfortunately, it is not yet widely available across the country. You can check with your local gynecological clinic for referrals in your area. If pregnancy is confirmed, there are measures that can be taken that would not be available to the woman who waited the usual six weeks.

The common pregnancy test in most areas is a urine analysis that usually can be done free or for a minimal charge. A sample of the urine (the first one in the morning, having not eaten or drunk for 12 hours beforehand) should be brought in a *clean* bottle. The menses should be at least six days late so that the test will be accurate. It is always a good idea to check results whether positive or negative—some women have claimed that clinics have told them they were pregnant when they were not, and others have reported getting some-one else's results by mistake. These cases are *very* rare, and most clinics are honest and careful, but it doesn't hurt to be sure by having the test redone whether positive or negative when a period has not come within a week

What substance in urine indicates pregnancy? The same hormone, HCG, that was measured in your blood can also be detected in your urine. Laboratories used to use the so-called "rabbit tests," in which rabbits, mice or toads were injected with the urine of women who might be pregnant. If HCG were present, the animals would respond in predictable ways. Male toads, for example, would ejaculate, and the ovaries of a female rabbit would fill up with blood. Of course, test-ing for this required killing the rabbit. Therefore, the common ex-pression for being pregnant—"the rabbit died"—is inaccurate; in the rabbit test, all the rabbits die, regardless of pregnancy. Few labs now use such tests. Today, urine tests involve chemical rather than animal reactions to HCG.

Chemical testing is also used in the over-the-counter home preg-nancy testers. These handy kits are obtainable in most large drug-stores, are easy to use and relatively inexpensive ($9–$12). They are reliable six to nine days after a missed period (depending on the type of test) and will give you results within two hours. The kits contain clear instructions, a dropper to be used for your urine, and a vial containing chemicals. A drop or two of urine in the vial will produce two different chemical reactions, depending upon whether there is HCG in your urine. The kits include pictures so that you will easily recognize a positive (pregnant) reaction.

Early Physical Symptoms

The early physical symptoms of pregnancy vary enormously from woman to woman, sometimes from pregnancy to pregnancy. Usually, the first telltale sign is a failure to menstruate at the usual time. Most pregnant women do not menstruate, and a missed or late period is the reason most women get the usual pregnancy test. However, there are many other reasons for being late (miscalculation, stress, climate changes, and so forth), so lateness is not necessarily a dependable sign.

Occasionally women do bleed while pregnant, but the flow is generally less heavy than usual. Other symptoms are tenderness in the breasts, increased frequency of urination, and sometimes a darkening of skin around the face or down the body to the pubic hair. About 50 percent of all pregnant women experience morning sickness (nausea, even vomiting, in the morning and at other times as well) by the second month, but this usually passes by the third or fourth month. The only way to be sure of pregnancy is to have a pregnancy test and to be examined by a physician. The physician looks for Hegar's sign, a softening of the uterus just above the cervix and a purplish color in the inner lips of the vagina. These signs are generally not present until six to eight weeks after conception.

FRUIT OF THE WOMB
(The Experience of Pregnancy, the Development of the Fetus, and Abortion Options)

A woman who thinks or has test results indicating that she is pregnant may either continue the pregnancy full term or terminate it. The following section will detail the major changes that generally occur for the pregnant woman, the expectant father, and the fetus, as well as the abortion options available at these stages.

When we consider the issue of terminating a pregnancy, we often feel confused. This confusion may arise because we were all fetuses at one point in our development (and share their vulnerability), and yet we all recognize that bearing an unwanted child may be a great handicap for many people. We also realize that it is often chance that controls life's very beginnings. Many of us are products of an extra glass of wine, a chance meeting, a weak moment. At what point can we interfere with the creation and development of human life? This question was raised at an abortion rally in Boston a few years ago. A priest approached a heavy-set woman who was holding a large sign reading, "Abortion is a woman's right." "Tell me," said the priest, "how would you like it if your mother had aborted you?" The woman paused and then replied angrily, "How would you like it if your father had been a priest?"

Few of us are comfortable with how we define the beginning of human life. Both the sperm and egg are alive before conception, and if they merge, the multiplication of the fertilized egg is a continuous unfolding. It is most difficult to point to a moment during these changes and say, "Ah! Now this is human and before it was not." Is there such a time for you and your partner?

Conception

Conception is the merging of the sperm and the egg. Some people believe that mechanically interfering with this merger or depositing sperm in a nonfertile area is immoral since the egg and sperm have life potential and are designed exclusively for procreation. The only acceptable birth control procedures for this group are chastity, the rhythm method, and sterilization.

Once conception has occurred, the fertilized egg (now called a zygote) implants itself into the uterine wall so that it cannot be easily dislodged. Before the implantation occurs (usually 10 to 14 days after conception), the zygote is not fixed to anything and can be removed by several methods.

Abortion Options Immediately Following Conception. The IUD. As previously mentioned, the IUD prevents implantation, not conception.

The Morning-After Pill. This pill prevents the zygote from implanting in the uterine wall. Most gynecologists now prescribe heavy doses of estrogen (instead of Diethylstilbestrol, DES, as in the past), which involves taking a series of pills (not one pill) every few hours for three days. The pills may produce severe nausea and cramping in some (not all) women. Each series has as much estrogen as 40 years' worth of birth control pills. The advantage of this treatment is that it is begun as soon after intercourse as possible (it will not work reliably if you start more than three days after the intercourse in question and will, if not effective, possibly damage the embryo). It is recommended in cases of rape, incest, or if a woman is likely to be psychologically "damaged" by waiting a little longer and taking a pregnancy test to be sure of pregnancy.

Menstrual Extraction. Before the zygote has implanted itself securely (10 to 14 days after conception), a minor type of abortion may be employed known as menstrual extraction. This procedure is done in a doctor's office and costs between $50 and $100. It is usually done around the time menstruation is due (no more than eight days after the earliest possible date) and is trickier when periods are irregular. The doctor will insert a catheter (a thin tube) into the uterus and extract the menstrual fluid (and the egg, fertilized or not). While it is not a pleasant procedure, it is less uncomfortable than a full abortion, less traumatic physically and psychologically, less expensive, and has fewer complications. Some women have learned the procedure and do it for each other monthly as a form of contraception. As yet, there is no data as to whether any harm might result from using the procedure so frequently. The major limitation is time: this procedure must be performed within a week of the menstrual due date; otherwise the catheter will not exert enough force to dislodge the fertilized egg. Hence, the urine analysis test results are received too late to enable use of the menstrual extraction method. Any woman who thinks she might be pregnant should check with her gynecologist to schedule a Beta sub-unit pregnancy test and should ask if he or she performs menstrual extractions (many do not).

Is Conception the Start of a Human Life? There is no easy answer to this question—perhaps there is no answer at all. The fertilized egg now has 46 chromosomes and if left alone will generally develop into a baby. Do you and your partner feel a zygote is human? Some people say yes because it is alive, but then so is the egg and sperm. Therefore, many who support the view that one cannot interfere with the development of human life do not use contraception. Others believe that once conception has occurred, a complete, separate organism is brought into being that should be considered human because it is capable of developing independently in the right environment. Others say the zygote is not yet human since it is a simple, as yet unspecialized, unconscious mass of cells. They believe that under natural conditions a high percentage of zygotes (25–50 percent, some estimate) are spontaneously aborted because of abnormalities;

they argue that no one mourns the death of a zygote (thus the widespread use of the IUD), and that the only time it is considered human is when a woman wishes to get rid of it. Aborting a zygote, they claim, is exercising intelligent control over what occurs naturally. Opponents, however, claim that although death also occurs naturally, we still consider murder to be immoral and that, convenience aside, conception is the start of a biologically separate and complete human being.

As you can see, there is no "right" answer. There is a right answer for you, given your personal history, and it is one based on emotion, reason, and, like it or not, practicality. One woman taking the morning-after pill said, "I'm sorry I have to go through this, but I don't feel guilty at all. This thing in me was just an accident, and it's only the size of a pin head. It doesn't think or feel. If I abort it now, it's no different than if I hadn't gotten pregnant." Another woman who would not take the pill said, "I really don't want this baby, but that's what it is to me. I know it's real tiny now, but it'll grow into a full baby unless I kill it." And yet another woman confessed after a menstrual extraction, "I don't care about these verbal games. It's my body and I didn't want to have a child right now. I could moralize and justify what I've done, but why should I? A baby is a responsibility I can't handle, and I feel that is what is important—not some theoretical debate about the sanctity of life."

The First Trimester (conception to three months)

After the zygote is firmly implanted in the uterus, it is now called an embryo until it is eight or nine weeks of age. At three weeks, a primitive heart begins to beat; the embryo is about one-quarter inch long and has a head (the first part to develop), sides, and a tail. Some people feel this primitive heartbeat marks the start of a human life and would not abort after this time. For others, the human life marker occurs around eight or nine weeks. At this time, the embryo is about one inch long and has developed all human structures in some basic, simple form. This includes hands, feet, palm and foot prints, well-shaped outer ears, mouth, and lips, the start of bone cells, and the ability to move. It is now called a fetus.

For the pregnant woman, the first trimester might be called a period of indecision as her feelings swing back and forth between joy and despair. Studies indicate that 80 percent of all mothers regret their pregnancies, even planned ones, during this time—probably because pregnancy is producing vast hormonal changes that may increase one's tendencies toward mood swings and because there are not yet the "goodies" of pregnancy to compensate for some of the changes that are now occurring.

Many women are nauseated in their first trimester (eating something like graham crackers in the morning before rising is helpful to some), but nausea usually disappears by the fourth month. It is difficult to assess how many of these symptoms (and those we'll be discussing later) are related to psychological factors, such as expecting yourself to have morning sickness. In fact, it is not uncommon for women who think they are pregnant to experience morning sickness until they discover that they are not. Janice, a college freshman, told me, "My roommate thought she was pregnant, and every morning she would get up and vomit. When she found out she wasn't, she was fine." More interestingly, Liebenberg reported that 65 percent of 64 expectant fathers also reported "pregnancy symptoms" in the first trimester, such as fatigue, nausea, backache, and so on.*

Other women report being fatigued. They may either lose weight (because of a poor appetite) or gain considerably (water retention may become a problem). They may feel as though they have to urinate constantly. It is the most common time for miscarriages and the time in which the fetus is most susceptible to becoming deformed by drugs, diseases, and so forth. Many women begin exercise and diet programs at this time, although, of course, it is wisest to prepare before pregnancy occurs. A visit to the dentist is a good idea. Evidence indicates that pregnant women are more prone to cavities and gum infections. A visit may save a toothache and an infection that may affect the fetus, but care must be taken not to use any drugs or X-rays. (Be sure to tell the dentist you are pregnant.)

*Liebenberg, B., "Expectant Fathers." *Child and Family* 8 (Summer 1969):264-267.

Abortion during First Trimester. It is during the first trimester that people often consider abortion. Nearly half of all abortions are performed by the eighth week of pregnancy, and nearly 90 percent by the twelfth. It is also the preferred time, medically, for an abortion to be obtained. The courts have given women the right to abort without legal interference or knowledge up to the end of this first trimester. The abortion procedure is done in a clinic, hospital, or in a specially equipped doctor's office. Some clinics have general anesthesia available for an extra charge. While some women find abortion quite painful ("Having a baby was easier," according to one woman), others say it is relatively painless. Pain is so personal and so affected by culture and emotion that there is great variability in the experience.

Abortions are relatively speedy, usually five to ten minutes. Most clinics have free counselors to help the woman explore her feelings about the procedure before having it done and to help her avoid a future abortion. There has been concern about repeat aborters (estimated as between 13 to 24 percent). Preliminary data released from a five-year study sponsored by the March of Dimes Foundation suggest that repeated abortions may cause some increase in miscarriage or premature delivery. There is no evidence of birth defects, stillbirths, or other kinds of complications. The study will be completed in 1981, after having examined approximately 25,000 pregnancies, and the data should be more definitive at that time. Abortions, if done properly, are relatively safe, the most common problem being a 2 percent risk of infection or excessive bleeding and an only 1 percent chance of uterine perforation. Abortion in the first trimester is considerably safer than is pregnancy.

The most common type of abortion, used in 75 percent of induced abortions in the United States, is the suction method, where the fertilized egg is sucked into a catheter, as in a menstrual extraction (only more powerful). Usually, clinics prefer women to be between six and eight weeks pregnant (again, dated by the time since last menstruation) so that the embryo is large enough, but not too large, for the catheter. Sometimes women are aborted via curettage (scraping of the uterus), but this procedure requires general anesthesia and hospital facilities and presents a greater risk of complications and considerable expense (upwards of $500). Therefore, it is only used about 5 percent of the time. Clinic abortion costs are usually around $150 without anesthesia and $175 with anesthesia. Few clinics and physicians would refuse to help poor women.

Some common misconceptions about how to self-abort still persist and should *not* be attempted by the woman, her partner, or her friends. The following remedies do *not* work except by killing or very seriously injuring the woman:

Falling down stairs

Eating salt

Drinking lye, bleach, 100 percent alcohol—anything!

Saying prayers or incantations

Stabbing the fetus with a coat hanger or some sharp object

Extreme exercise

Hot or cold baths

Pills (other than those prescribed by a physician for abortion purposes)

Potions, plants, or vegetables

Compresses

Black cats, frogs, or any other animal in any form

None of these desperate (and futile) efforts are necessary now that abortion is legalized. A woman who believes that she is pregnant and knows no one should look up either a gynecologist or abortion clinic in the Yellow Pages and then call the state medical licensing board (also listed in the white and yellow pages of the telephone directory) and ask about the physician's or clinic's credentials. In this way she will be assured of competent and legal assistance.

Ambivalence toward Abortion. How do you and your partner feel about abortion? How you *think* about an issue may or may not fit with how you *feel* about it. We often assume that reason and emotion go together, but this is not always so. A woman may desire sex, but her reason may tell her it would not be a good idea to engage in it. Another woman's reason may provide excellent arguments for enjoying sex, but her emotions do not agree. Some studies have found that a majority of women who obtain abortions think that abortions are wrong. Most women abort because they feel they have to; few are cavalier about the experience. The severe measures women have used to self-abort attest to the intensity of these feelings.

For some, being pregnant is an irreversible life crisis. Whether or not they elect to abort, feelings about themselves may change profoundly. We interviewed many people who had profound ambivalence about their decisions. Some regretted having aborted. Said Jean, childfree at 32, "I had an abortion several years ago. Every 'anniversary' I get so depressed I cry. It was so easy. Nobody even tried to talk me out of it. I wish they had. Of all the things in my life I most regret—that is it." But, of course, many women also regret not having aborted. Listen to Joyce, "If abortions had been legal, I would have had one, no doubt. Even if my doctor would have done an illegal one, I would have, but he wouldn't hear of it. Now I look at my son, at how wonderful a person he is and how I would miss him. But my whole life changed. Even though I love him dearly, if I could go back to that point in my life, I would never have had him."

It seems to us that the best alternative to abortion is to avoid pregnancy carefully until such time, if ever, you and your partner are prepared to parent. But we all know accidents can, and do, happen. We recommend, therefore, that you and your partner discuss your feelings about abortion now, when your own pregnancy is not an issue. When, for each of you, does human life begin? Under what conditions would you elect to have an unplanned baby? Keep these questions in mind as you read this book. But don't be irrevocably bound by this discussion if and when you do discover pregnancy. Some people's feelings change when it happens to them. You have a right, even a responsibility, to be honest and respectful of your own feelings and the changes initiated by pregnancy. But you also have a responsibility to your partner, especially if you have changed your mind about an agreed-upon abortion option.

What are the legal rights of fathers in cases where there is a disagreement about abortion? After all, the fetus is half his, even if it is in the woman's body. Don't you, as a potential father, have a legally protected voice in the abortion? No, at least not thus far. Even a legally wed husband has not been able to enjoin his wife from aborting. Some men are understandably angry because they feel they have been trapped in the middle of a Catch-22. "If my girlfriend gets pregnant and wants to abort *our* baby, I have no say except to pay half of the costs. But if she refuses to abort, even if I want her to, I can be held liable for child support. It's not fair." He is right, but so is the woman who claims, "It's my body, and I have a moral right to decide whether I will bear a baby or not." Financial responsibility for that decision should also be her right, argue some people. Practically speaking; the issue is legal as well as ethical, and it is likely that our courts will have to grapple more substantially with the father's interests in the near future.

The Second Trimester (three to six months)

This phase of pregnancy could be called "lively." There is often an increase in energy, and by the fourth month the nausea has usually disappeared. The breasts will start to secrete a small amount of yellow fluid (called colostrum) that will increase during pregnancy, until after birth when the mother will be able to nurse if she so desires. Veins in the breasts and the bumps around the nipples will become more noticeable. This change is also part of preparation for nursing.

Body shape during pregnancy varies greatly from woman to woman. One important factor in how much a woman will "show" is the condition of her muscles around the lower abdomen. If she is in good physical shape and has strong abdominal muscles, she will not show as much. Muscle strength is likely to be greater for a first advanced pregnancy if the woman is young (or exercises very frequently), and if her stomach was flat before conception. It has also been found that women who hold their abdomens in during pregnancy rather than puff them out, strengthen these muscles and show less. The size of the fetus is also important. Size is, in part, determined by heredity; the birth weight of you and your partner will give some indication of the probable size of your fetus. Firstborns tend to be somewhat smaller than later-borns. (More factors affecting birth size will be dealt with later.) Body build is another factor in determining how visibly pregnant a woman looks—how well does she carry the extra weight, particularly in the stomach area? And finally, does she wear loose clothes to accommodate her expanding waistline? (Some women don't need to alter their clothes until their fifth or sixth month.)

The fetus is undergoing rapid development now. By sixteen weeks, it is about four and one-half inches long. This is often the time of *quickening*—that is, the time when the mother can first feel the fetus moving. Some women do not feel movement quite this early, but the many who do say it is this movement that produces a glowing "I did the right thing" or a desperate "oh, my God" kind of response. For many, this is the start of human life—in fact, Thomas Aquinas believed, during the fifteenth century, that abortion was permissible until quickening. He felt that when the fetus moved, it was reacting to the entrance of a human soul and thereafter could not be aborted.

At 20 weeks of age, the fetus's hands can grip, hair is sprouting, and its eyes (though fused) can blink. Within the next four weeks, the eyes will be completely formed, and taste buds will appear. If the fetus should be born at the age of six months, it might be capable of a breath or two and a weak cry, but not of sustained life.

Abortion during the Second Trimester. Abortion is still legal during the second trimester, with the additional qualification that the state may regulate the procedure in ways reasonably related to maternal health. Abortion is more dangerous, painful, and upsetting than it would be in the first trimester, however.

The customary abortion employed between 16 and 20 weeks of pregnancy is done in hospitals, with the usual stay of two to three days. A saline solution is injected, and within one to two hours the fetus and placenta die. Labor begins within 48 hours, with most women aborting within 72 hours. As you can imagine, this can be physically and emotionally exhausting. It is also dangerous, for women risk a 20 percent chance of complications (the most common being hemorrhage and infection), the same as with full pregnancy. Some hospitals, doctors, and/or nurses will not perform an abortion in the second trimester. It is also very expensive and rarely covered by insurance, unless it is mandated by a physician for the mother's health.

Some, but not all, doctors (and few, if any, abortion clinics) will perform a suction-type abortion during the fourth month. During this procedure, called a D & E (dilation and evacuation), the cervix is gradually dilated, and the fetus is extracted with an aspirator. The suction is stronger and longer than used in first-trimester abortions. Recent research suggests that this method can be used safely and effectively later into the second trimester than once thought. However, Dr. William Cates, chief of abortion surveillance for the National Center for Disease Control, cautioned that overstretching of the cervix may become a factor in premature delivery in some women who have had repeat abortions. Nonetheless, D & E's are considerably safer than the usual late abortion procedure.

Usually, women who have not aborted by their fourth month are encouraged to carry the fetus full term and place it for adoption if they do not want it. However, abortions are still legal at this time and there are physicians and hospitals who will perform them, though you may have to search a bit.

Why do some women wait until the second trimester before aborting? Some of the major reasons are ignorance, fear, indecision, and knowledge of deformities.

Ignorance. Some women just don't know they're pregnant until past their third month (some even later). This is particularly true of young (and probably naive) women, many of whom may have no idea of how one gets pregnant and what can be done about it. (They may attribute the passing nausea, if they experience it, to a virus and the weight gain to increased appetite.) Even if they think they might be pregnant, they don't know or are afraid to get tested. Some women have very irregular periods and may not show very much or recognize other symptoms. One educated woman, the wife of a dentist, was being examined for infertility when the doctor discovered she was six months pregnant! If you have intercourse, you should *always* record your menses so that you can tell when you are late; if you are irregular, you should be on the alert for the other symptoms mentioned earlier. Even if abortion is not an issue, early detection can help you take proper care of yourself and avoid possibly serious complications.

Fear. Some women are so afraid of being pregnant that they ignore the symptoms, in the futile hope that the problem will just "go away." We do this sort of thing in many areas of life, so the fact that it is done with pregnancy should not be surprising. Mrs. Archibald Adams, a social worker who has done much work on breast cancer, reports that many women refuse to check their breasts regularly. Furthermore, many who find lumps "ignore" them until the disease has become fatal. Other women "ignore" the cheating of their husbands, and many of us "forget" examinations, leaky roofs, and taxes. This ability to deny problems is useful because it is difficult to deal with many simultaneously. However, in pregnancy, the "problem" becomes more and more obvious to the expectant mother and everyone else.

Some women are terrified by the prospect of the abortion itself (some for moral, others for pain-related fears). And teenagers are often terrified that their parents will discover the pregnancy. In some states, girls under 18 must have the signature of at least one parent for any medical procedure, including abortion. However, teenagers may have urine tests without parental permission, and if they are pregnant, they can speak in confidence to anyone they choose. Planned Parenthood, legitimate abortion clinics, hot lines, gynecologists, and psychologists all are able to assist teenagers in dealing with both the pregnancy and the parents. Larger communities often have facilities similar to the Crittenton-Hastings House in Boston, which specializes in teenage pregnancy. As a society, we are growing more tolerant of illegitimacy, and there are increasing numbers of options available to the unmarried woman, both teenaged and older.

Indecision. Some people still can't make up their minds and continue the indecision of the first trimester in the second. Whether or not to bear a child is never an easy decision, and it is particularly difficult when you are already pregnant. When abortions were illegal, married women had less of a problem because alternatives to having the baby were considerably more unsavory than they are now. At the same time, the option of an unmarried woman to keep her child was entertained less often. Now, with more options available, decisions are harder. Some women make appointments for abortions, cancel and buy maternity outfits, then reschedule. They vacillate their way into the second trimester where, now, undeniably with child, the feared consequences occur. Other times, it is clearly circumstantial; a husband may ask for a divorce and a wanted baby becomes unwanted; a woman may lose her job, and so on.

Possible Genetic Defects. Sometimes one or both parents are found to be, or are considered likely to be, carriers of certain genetic disorders. Amniocentesis is a test performed during the thirteenth to sixteenth week of pregnancy to determine whether the fetus has these disorders. Some of the fluid surrounding the fetus is withdrawn by inserting a long, thin needle through the mother's abdomen (local anesthesia is used) and into the amniotic sac. Analysis of the chromosomes in the fluid indicates whether there are certain specific genetic defects—and can also reveal the sex of the fetus. Amniocentesis will reveal if the fetus has any of the following genetically determined defects:

1. Tay-Sachs disease, an enzyme deficiency common to Jews of Russian and Polish descent.
2. Sickle cell anemia, a deformity of red blood cells, occurring frequently among blacks.
3. PKU, an enzyme deficiency that can produce severe mental retardation.
4. Muscular dystrophy, a slow deterioration of the muscles, characterized by muscle convulsions.
5. Down's syndrome, an extra chromosome that produces stunted growth and mental retardation. A risk if either parent is a carrier of the trait, Down's syndrome is also threatening when the mother is over 35 or the father over 45. The older you are, the greater the risk of Down's syndrome and the greater the advisability of amniocentesis.

Amniocentesis carries an increased risk (2 to 5 percent) of miscarriage and is expensive (costs run over $500 and may not be covered by all insurance policies). Because it is not reliable if done much earlier than the thirteenth week, prospective parents who run a risk of passing on any of the previously listed disorders must wait until the second trimester to determine whether they have a defective fetus. And then they may have to decide whether to abort or carry the fetus full term. The test cannot reveal, however, the more common sorts of fetal deformities that are caused by harmful environmental agents, like powerful drugs or diseases. Thus, amniocentesis will not be useful for most of the prospective parents who are frightened by the possibility of giving birth to a child that is in some way "defective."

Many parents, particularly first-timers, experience a lot of anxiety, thinking about endless possibilities of endless complications. Others have had problems before: the parents of a retarded child may worry about their next child, even when assured that the disorder was due to a lack of oxygen, not a chromosome. These concerns, while real, are not unusual and may be intensified by the publicity accompanying the birth or existence of a deformed child. Additionally, some people have an almost "Dorian Gray" feeling about their offspring, as if their children might reflect all the "bad" things about them. If you are very anxious about having a defective child, talking over your fears with a physician or psychologist might reassure you and aid you in dealing with these thoughts. It might be comforting to know that despite all the risks, approximately 95 percent of all babies born are normal or have very minor physical problems.

Although amniocentesis is only a diagnostic test, there is much controversy about it. In 1975, some members of the Catholic Church picketed the March of Dimes because of its support of the use of amniocentesis. They argued that when couples find out they have a defective child they will be encouraged to abort it; if they lovingly accept their child as he or she is, checking would not be necessary. The March of Dimes replied that, yes, many prospective parents have serious concerns about whether or not their children will be born defective. But they argued that finding out is not equivalent to aborting. Many women would have aborted unnecessarily if they had not had such a test available. Others may choose to bear a defective child and have the time to pre-parent knowingly.

Yet another area of controversy is the issue over whether or not a fetus should be aborted because it is an undesired sex. While there are ways in which parents can influence the sex of a fetus (and these are discussed later in this chapter), only amniocentesis can accurately tell what sex the fetus is prior to birth. However, most amniocentesis reports do not specify sex, and some physicians refuse to release that information, even if the parents request it. Whether they have the moral or legal right to do this is unclear. Some parents feel they should have the right to decide the sex of their child. "If I have five girls and want a boy," said one father, "why can't I try until I get one? I mean, either abortion is murder or it's not. Why should one reason be better than another?" Some physicians claim they would refuse to abort a normal fetus because it is the "wrong" sex, but others say that the reason for abortion is always to be viewed as the woman's right until the law says otherwise. Some people, then, do not abort until the test indicates they have a defective or wrong-sexed fetus. They then must undergo a late abortion if they decide not to carry the fetus full term.

The Third Trimester (six to nine months)

This phase of pregnancy may be described as one of *acceptance (or rejection)*. Most pregnant women report that at this time they virtually "turn themselves over" to the fetus. There is a feeling, sometimes a fear, of abandoning control over one's body. Many women lose the energy they had during their second trimester and become very sleepy and lethargic. They may experience significant mood shifts. They often report heartburn and indigestion because of the changes in their digestive system. Appetites become very large, and women must exercise a lot of control over how much they eat. They are growing rapidly now, and in most cases, it is difficult to hide pregnancy (there have been some exceptions, of course, particularly when the baby was a firstborn or small and the woman was very large-boned and/or heavy in the stomach area prior to pregnancy and wore loose, baggy clothes).

Fetuses now have definitive time patterns of movement, and often mothers- and fathers-to-be have devised ways of communicating with the unborn. One young mother said, "Whenever I pushed, he would push back. It was wonderful!" Studies support the fact that during the last few months of pregnancy fetuses are responsive to events outside their own bodies. Their taste buds are operative by six months of age, so they are probably tasting the fluid surrounding them (the fluid is sweet, and from birth, infants prefer sweet-tasting food). It is likely that they hear the workings of the mother's body. When a microphone was placed in the uterus of a pregnant woman, it recorded the whooshing sound of pulsing blood, the mother's heartbeat, and the rumbling of gas. A Japanese recording of these very sounds has been found to be very effective in soothing newborns! (This finding may also help explain why babies seem to relax when they are rocked or sung slow, rhythmic lullabies.)

Studies have also found that babies respond to strong maternal emotions such as anger and high levels of anxiety and grief, which is not surprising since considerable biochemical and physical changes accompany strong emotions and would directly affect the fetal environment. Some researchers (Sontag and his colleagues)* have claimed that mothers who experienced considerable emotional trauma during the last trimester of pregnancy had very active and irritable fetuses; furthermore, these fetuses were irritable and hyperactive after birth, and some had serious feeding problems. These data should be viewed cautiously, however; the infants could have been responding to many factors, including the mother's continuing (rather than past) emotional upset.

Babies respond not only to events outside their own bodies, but to events outside the mother's body as well! Studies have shown that fetuses will respond to strong lights directed at the mother's womb and will move quite measurably to loud noises (and thus probably react to loud parental arguments!). Some tentative data from Japan

---

*Sontag, L. W., "Differences in Modifiability of Fetal Behavior and Physiology." *Psychosomatic Medicine* 6 (1954):151–154; Sontag, L. W. et al., "Status of Infant at Birth as Related to Basal Metabolism of Mothers in Pregnancy." *American Journal of Obstetrics and Gynecology* 48 (1944):208–214.

is correlating loud noises during pregnancy (as would be experienced by those living close to airports) with increased risk of birth difficulties. Even more amazing is a study that demonstrates that fetuses can learn while in utero. A researcher named Spelt presented eight- and nine-month fetuses with a vibrator placed on the mother's belly.* The vibrator was followed by a loud noise that elicited strong fetal movement. After ten or so trials, the fetuses responded to the vibrator just as they responded to the noise! It is possible that even younger fetuses also can learn such responses, but Spelt could not test for it because of the immaturity in their hearing systems at earlier stages of development. Also, no one has yet shown that this learning was remembered after birth, but the implications for further research are exciting.

Reactions of the Mother-to-Be. By the third trimester, being an expectant parent is now a central concern, especially for the pregnant woman who cannot avoid having to deal with it all the time. Researchers have found that people tend to stand farther away from pregnant women and to stare at their stomachs. This response may be due to the relative "novelty" of the sight. When people were encouraged to look all they wanted to, they very shortly began to behave in a pregnant woman's presence as they did in the presence of nonpregnant women. Being treated differently produces strong feelings about being pregnant. Some women adore pregnancy and all that accompanies it. They feel whole and complete and may behave with newfound confidence and independence. They may become surprisingly assertive, some even "bitchy," in part because hormone changes are producing mood swings and, in part, because such behavior is usually tolerated more in pregnant women! In fact, society is, in general, more tolerant of the behavior of pregnant women. This acceptance may be one reason why we see more extreme variations in behavior at this time, from the amount and types of food consumed to the kind and intensity of emotions displayed.

Additionally, some women can justify behaving assertively in the

*Spelt, D., "The Conditioning of the Human Fetus in Utero." *Journal of Experimental Psychology* 38 (1948):338-346.

interests of their babies when they couldn't bring themselves to do so for their own benefit. A classic example is a woman in her seventh month who told us that her baby couldn't stand certain people. "Whenever Alice comes over, the baby goes wild!" she confessed. "It kicks and jumps and gets upset! So I had to make excuses not to see Alice for a while! Thank God—she always upsets me!" It is reasonable to assume that the fetus was responding to its mother's response to Alice, not Alice herself (who was a somewhat jangly but not sinister woman). For her future baby, the mother could do what she could not do for herself—terminate an undesirable acquaintance!

For many women, being pregnant is an end in itself. As one pregnant woman confessed, "I was never very attractive, or smart, or anything. When I'm pregnant, I am special. I'm proud of my body. People smile at me and treat me nice. Even my family. And I love to feel the baby growing. And I get to sleep and eat a lot. I wished I liked babies after they were born because I would be pregnant all the time!" While other women display their breasts or legs, or degrees, or husbands, some women display their swollen bellies. For some it is the accomplishment of a lifetime. Lawrence Durrell once observed that the beauty of pregnant Jewish women was related to the fact that the people were still awaiting the birth of their Messiah and that each woman thought she might be carrying him. We don't think this is uniquely Jewish. Pregnancy is potential.

Other women hate being pregnant. They feel their bodies are out of control (perhaps as they felt during adolescence when each morning, upon awakening, they would find some part of their bodies altered). They feel fat and unattractive. (This was more true ten years ago when women were encouraged to gain 30 and 40 pounds during pregnancy than now, when 24 pounds is considered the optimal gain.) Some pregnant women gain weight very easily because of changes in both metabolic and eating rates. One woman told us she put on 90 pounds in her first pregnancy! Others resent the priority given their bellies over themselves and regard the solicitous behavior of friends as insulting. They miss being looked at sexually and want more sexual reassurance. They worry about being "mom-ified" in the eyes of others and themselves. They are already planning how to minimize the baby's effect on the family, and they're worried over whether it can be done. They are often concerned about the changes that will occur in the father-to-be.

Adopting a "sick role" is not uncommon among pregnant women. We have all seen examples of the doting husband who, upon hearing of his wife's pregnancy, responds as though she were fatally wounded ("Are you all right?" "Sit down!" "What can I get you?"). This role is strengthened by a woman's increased contact with health professionals and the difficulty in finding a comfortable way to behave while pregnant. The sick role is also compatible with the decreased mobility and lower center of gravity the pregnant woman experiences throughout the last part of the third trimester. She is limited in what she can do, how quickly she can do it, and how well. She may have to stay off her feet as much as possible, and daily events like climbing out of a bathtub or climbing a flight of stairs may be difficult. A particularly active woman may feel a little bit like an invalid.

The sick role is compatible with feelings of dependency many women experience when a baby is coming, and with some of the fears of being abandoned that frequently accompany pregnancy ("Will he love me looking like this?" "Will he want to stay home with a screaming baby? Do I?" "What will I do if he leaves?"). The sick role also enables the pregnant woman to get attention, even if it is solicitous, and it can effectively control other people's behavior; it gives them a better defined way of behaving also! Interestingly, researchers have found that women who respond to pregnancy as a "sickness" are likely to be socially mobile (either upward or downward). It may mean that the woman is no longer surrounded by an intimate group of helpful friends and family. Midwives (who are discussed in chapter 2, p. 87) may be particularly helpful in such situations.

Reactions of the Father-to-Be. While fatherhood is not as visible as motherhood, its consequences are still profound. Men react strongly to becoming parents. For example, some studies have found that men whose wives are pregnant report greater numbers of physical symptoms than do men whose wives are not pregnant. Among the chief complaints are headaches, backaches, weight gain or loss, insomnia, and depression. These symptoms may be a response to the wife's "sick role" or it may be a result of increased stress or work output.

One sociologist interviewed 29 university couples who were about to have children.* He found that the fathers fell into three broad categories of feelings about the approaching birth:

Romantic: These men were emotional, intense and idealistic. They were frightened by the prospect of fatherhood.

Family-oriented: As you might suspect, these men were active and happy in planning for the baby.

Career-oriented: These men were resentful and unhappy. They perceived the coming child as an economic burden.

Unfortunately, we don't know whether these feelings persisted. We do know that sometimes men who don't want children or who are frightened by the prospect have more intense feelings (both positive and negative) than those who are more relaxed. After the child is born, the positive feelings may outweigh the negative ones, especially when conditions are optimal.

Several studies have found that the majority of men respond to impending parenthood with economic worry. The prospect of becoming a father triggers crises about careers and financial capacity. One sad consequence of economic pressure is that while the woman is seeking emotional support, the man may be out seeking economic security. While both share similar concerns, they may behave incompatibly. Ellen, age 30, stated: "My husband is never home any more. I'm so depressed—it's like he hates me now, he never wants to spend time with me. He's always at work. Even when he's home, he's working on papers or he gets this distant look on his face, and I know he's thinking about work. At least, I hope that's what he's thinking about. It's certainly not me or the baby! He's avoiding dealing with us!"

*McCorkel, R. J., "Husbands and Pregnancy: An Exploratory Story." Unpublished Master's thesis, University of North Carolina, 1964.

But Ellen's husband has a different perspective. "I am so excited about the baby! I can't wait! I want him to have the best of everything. You know, when I was a kid, I didn't have the money to go to the movies with other kids. And my mom worked so hard, always counting pennies and dragging us kids miles to buy things on sale across town. I want my kid and wife to have it easier. But I haven't had a raise in over a year. Costs are going up. How am I going to afford staying even, let alone getting ahead? . . . I don't want to bother Ellen with this, but I am concerned." No one can minimize these concerns (a whole chapter will be devoted to them). But if Ellen and her husband had talked openly, Ellen wouldn't feel abandoned, and her husband might not see her as clutchy or dependent, which in turn might lighten his perceived economic burden.

Communication is especially important during the last months of pregnancy because unlike parenthood after birth, men are physically excluded from the pregnancy process. This exclusion can amplify the fear that the child may become more important to the wife than himself, that he may be emotionally abandoned as he tries to cope with new or added responsibilities. He may be disturbed by the very sight of the pregnancy, which he, unlike his wife, can avoid. Without adequate communication between the two of them, his wife's nausea, fatigue, or physical awkwardness may impinge upon him in many ways: they may play less together, and he may have to, or be expected to, assume some of his wife's responsibilities.

Sometimes men fight back indirectly, especially if they did not want the child. For instance, many men use nicknames for their wives or child-to-be that are derogatory or double-edged. One father-to-be called his wife "Blimp," and another dubbed his forthcoming baby "Houdini" because it had not been planned. Other men resent medical personnel, especially if they are not participants in the office visits. While some fathers are deliberately excluded from the pregnancy experience, others behave as though they were. Some men try to take over; they order their wives around by selecting foods and listing mandates.

Obviously, balancing concern and separateness is difficult, both before and after birth, and each partner must explore different balances at different times in their lives. The happiest expectant parents seem to be those who balance their needs with those of the coming baby, rather than assuming that either they or the baby must fit some preordained pattern. They also share and support each other, rather than assuming that the father-to-be has no needs since he is not physically pregnant. Pregnancy is considerably more than carrying a fetus in one's body. While most pregnant women need support, so do men. Yet men do not physically change, nor are they likely to express their feelings. Their needs can be easily overlooked. This situation is less likely to occur if we recognize the importance of the changes that are happening to both men and women and encourage them to share their reactions with each other.

Abortion During the Third Trimester. It is still possible to obtain a legal abortion during the last trimester, up to a fetal age of 24 weeks. Legally, a fetus becomes a human being, entitled to protection, when it is viable—that is, when it can live on its own. In 1973, the Supreme Court established the age of viability as 24 to 26 weeks. After this age, the state may regulate or prohibit abortion except when necessary to preserve the mother's life or health.

One problem with the Supreme Court's definition of human life is that it is very difficult to accurately assess fetal age. The age is almost always estimated from the time of a woman's last menstruation, which is probably a week or more before conception actually occurs. Also, it is hard to distinguish a small, weak but mature fetus from one at an earlier stage of development, especially toward the end of gestation. Thus, it is difficult to agree on exactly when a particular fetus is to be legally protected.

An additional issue is whether abortion necessitates the death of the fetus or whether it is simply the removal of the fetus from a woman's body, in which case the physician might be required to maintain the fetus's life. This issue will become a more pressing problem as the age of viability moves forward. It may soon be possible to maintain the lives of younger and younger fetuses, even zygotes. Should abortions ever be allowed if a zygote can develop independent of the mother's body? And, if so, can the mother request the destruction of the fetus? What would happen to the use of the IUDs? Of spontaneous abortion? Most people feel that at some time before birth the fetus is an independent human being. However, few can pinpoint, let alone agree upon, when this happens.

SEX AND CHILDBIRTH

At one time people in our society believed it was dangerous to have sexual intercourse when pregnant. Conversely, other societies have believed that continued intercourse during pregnancy was necessary in order to nourish the developing fetus. The truth appears to be that it is considered safe to have intercourse well into the third trimester and, for most women, up until birth.

A recent study reported that one-quarter of the women studied reported decreased sexual interest in their first trimester.* This decreased interest may be related to nausea, tenderness, or fear (unfounded) of hurting the fetus. During the second trimester, sexual interest picks up, but the frequency of orgasm declines slightly. Many women find that they are very often sexually aroused, in part because of increased pelvic blood flow and in part because they may desire to be loved and cuddled. However, orgasms are usually more difficult to achieve and less satisfying because the increased blood flow to the area does not dissipate as it usually does after orgasms. This, of course, does not mean that lovemaking is less pleasurable, emotionally or physically, especially when you know that these changes are not a result of psychological withdrawal but of temporary physiological alterations.

During the third trimester, frequency of sexual intercourse tends to decrease with each month. One of the main reasons is physical awkwardness. There may also be incompatible scripts between being a parent and being sexual. The very pregnant woman frequently feels as though sexual behavior is inappropriate, and her partner may feel the same way. Said one woman, "I want to make love, but I feel so— contained. It's like there's three of us— it isn't private enough any

*Hobbs, D., "Transition to Parenthood," *Journal of Marriage and the Family* 30 (1968).

more." It is more of a problem when both partners don't feel the same way, in which case there is often misunderstanding and tension.

The major medical concern about intercourse late in pregnancy is the risk of premature labor. An orgasm in the third trimester is usually accompanied by strong contractions of the uterus (sometimes for as long as a minute). Is this dangerous? One study reported a 15 percent risk of premature labor and/or fetal membrane rupture in orgasmic women after the thirty-second week. Yet, a more recent study did not find any correlation between sexual activity and prematurity. Most couples can probably participate in sexual activity throughout the third trimester without risk. Of course, particular caution ought to be exercised if there has been vaginal bleeding during the pregnancy or difficulty in carrying a fetus full-term in the past. (Be sure to consult with a doctor as soon as possible.)

Many men are concerned about sexual activity during pregnancy hurting their partners or the fetus. For example, a common misconception is that it is no longer possible to have intercourse in the missionary position. This position is perfectly safe as long as it is comfortable for the pregnant woman. A side position is also good, as is the woman on top as long as she is sufficiently mobile. Another common concern is that deep penetration will harm the fetus. It is probably advisable to avoid very deep and vigorous penetration during the third trimester, but moderate penetration is quite sufficient and pleasurable. The basic principle is to communicate with each other and, as always, to alter behavior that your partner finds uncomfortable—you can rely on verbal cues ("Do you like this?") and nonverbal cues (is she moving away or toward you?).

After birth, most women are advised to wait at least six weeks after delivery before resuming intercourse, in order to minimize the possibility of vaginal and pelvic infection. Certainly, however, there are many alternative sexual behaviors that can pleasure both partners, either with or without orgasm for either person. One problem with sex after birth is the presence of the infant and the exhaustion or soreness of the mother. Or, the father may be responding to economic pressures and feel distracted and unaffectionate. Another difficulty is finding a suitable contraceptive. (IUDs don't fit properly for several weeks until the uterus shrinks to normal size; a diaphragm must be refitted; the rhythm method can't be used until a woman has re-established a cycle; and the pill may affect milk production.) The safest form of contraception appears to be the condom used with foam or jelly. This method will give you almost 100 percent protection until your body is ready for another method.

Another problem is that the demands of being a parent and a partner may seem overwhelming, even incompatible. Listen to Cindy, age 32, after her first baby: "I am utterly and totally exhausted. When I see my husband I want to crawl in his arms and sleep. Instead, as soon as he holds me he starts to nibble and pull, and it's upsetting. I don't want to hurt him, but I'm just not interested. I resent it, in fact. It shows he has little appreciation of what I'm going through."

Some might react, "Poor Cindy. She has a perfect right to feel that way. Her husband is a selfish man. He should use all that energy to help her, not rape her." Yet others may think, "How selfish of Cindy. She's a wife, too. You can't just forget about your man. He deserves attention, if not from her then from someone else." What does her husband say? "Cindy used to be a great woman, I mean, she would talk to me, and hold me, and support me. Now, I feel like a bit player in her life. I am trying to be helpful and sympathetic, but I need some loving, too."

One problem this couple was having was communication. What her husband really wanted was affection. Because he reacted sexually to her holding him, his wife pulled away. When they learned to tell each other that they both wanted affection, they were able to share their bed with little conflict. In fact, Cindy confessed, "Even though I don't feel like sex myself, I really enjoy pleasing him. It's very relaxing and loving for me. I'm sure it will also help me get back into the mood faster."

Some women report decreased libido (sexual interest) that persists well after pregnancy and seems physiologically based. One woman said, "Before my child I was always ready. Now it takes me longer to be ready. I don't lubricate even when I want to." (Petroleum or K-Y Jelly is a simple solution.) On the other hand, it is not uncommon for some nonorgasmic women to become orgasmic after the birth of their first child, perhaps as a result of hormonal changes or increased pelvic congestion.

Other sexual consequences may occur in response to changes in appearance as a result of childbirth (see the next section). Some men and women are very critical about their own or their lovers' bodies. A few extra pounds are sexual turn-offs. If either of you is like this, change your sexual approach, if possible. You will have difficulty aging, with or without children, unless you do!

PHYSICAL CONSEQUENCES OF CHILDBIRTH

One question many women have, but rarely ask, is how pregnancy and birth are likely to affect their overall physical condition. Now that women can choose to remain childfree or to limit the number of children they have, they are asking, "Well, if I have this child, what will be the consequences to my health and appearance?"

Nonmothers tend to have a higher incidence of endometriosis (a pelvic disorder where the uterine lining grows *outside* the uterus) and/or uterine, cervical, and breast cancer than women who are first-time mothers before they are 35 years old. However, other studies have indicated that women without or with the fewest number of children report being happier and have a lower incidence of neuroses (especially depression) and psychoses as compared to mothers or those with larger families. This finding is true even when social class and marriage variables are controlled, as in a recent study that looked at identical twins in which one of the pair was a mother and the other was not. While the authors conclude that these results may be a function of the physiological changes initiated by childbearing, there are also many lifestyle differences that may account for these data.

A number of women still die in childbirth every year. In fact, the United States ranks eleventh in the world in terms of infant and maternal mortality. In 1975, 12.8 out of every 1,000 birthing women died. While only 9.1 out of 1,000 white women die from childbirth complications, 29 out of 1,000 black women die. Most deaths occur as a result of shock, internal bleeding, lack of skilled help through birth, infection, and anesthesia complications. Many more women suffer long-term problems from the childbirth experience; common consequences are varicose veins, hemorrhoids, and lower back problems.

Pregnancy may also affect the status of genetically influenced health problems or propensities. Women suffering from endometriosis are often relieved, even cured, by pregnancy. Those with arthritis find the problem disappears during pregnancy, only to flare up again four to six weeks after delivery. Women with a high risk of diabetes (a family history of diabetes, obesity, hypertension, and so on) may find themselves becoming diabetic when pregnant. Therefore, if you are susceptible, you should consult with your physician before pregnancy (a special diet might be suggested), and you should be monitored carefully if and when you become pregnant. Dr. Henry Dolger, a professor at Mt. Sinai Medical School, has found that pregnancy-precipitated diabetes disappears after delivery and then reappears again after 20 to 30 years.

Another health problem that may flare up with pregnancy is high blood pressure, a disease common to 5 percent of all pregnancies, and a disease responsible for one-fifth of our maternal deaths and at least 25,000 stillbirths each year. Since black women and obese women with a hypertensive history are especially at risk, they should discuss this problem with their doctors and be carefully monitored, before and during pregnancy. Again, the high blood pressure may disappear after delivery and then reappear, usually about two years later.

The effects of pregnancy and birth are not limited to health considerations alone. Many women are concerned with vanity issues. Said Lynn, a childfree woman of 34, "I feel like a bitch saying this, but I'm proud of my body. I've never looked better, and I really am concerned about what a baby will do to my figure. I know it sounds selfish, but that's the way I feel." Lynn is just verbalizing what many women, and their partners, think. From birth, women learn to value their physical appearance. If they are attractive, they learn to use their good looks, to varying degrees, in securing the things and people they want and need. They may fear losing their own self-esteem, the attention of others, or the love and sexual desire of their partners. Are these fears realistic? Let us find out.

Weight Gain

Many women report that after birth their metabolism seems to change; some women experience an increase in rate, but most report a slowing. One recent mother described it as "feeling as though my period is coming all the time." Certainly, there are vast hormonal changes accompanying pregnancy and birth, but, theoretically, hormone levels are supposed to return to "normal" within a few days after delivery. It is reasonable to assume that many women's bodies do not respond perfectly.

Studies have found that women tend to retain 60 percent of the weight over 24 pounds they gain when pregnant. Medical opinions on the best weight gain during pregnancy have been inconsistent over the past few decades. Even now, some researchers think the 24-pound recommendation currently in vogue is too restrictive. SPUN (Society for the Protection of the Unborn through Nutrition) claims that babies have the lowest incidence of brain damage when the mothers gain 36 or more pounds.

New mothers report that losing weight is more difficult than before, and gaining seems considerably easier. Of course, there are lifestyle changes that may affect or accentuate weight gain—women are likely to be less athletic after birth, and they are more likely to spend greater amounts of time at home where they may be bored and tired. They may use getting fat as a way of avoiding sexual issues. At any rate, despite the many women who report difficulty in losing and a tendency to gain weight after birth, there are many thin and active mothers around. If you have trouble with your weight, you might want to consider ways in which you can establish good eating habits before, during, and after pregnancy and birth. A lot of women think, "I'll exercise after the baby's born," but if you have never taken care of yourself before, you are even less likely to do so when you have a child to care for. How much discipline and work you will need to get into prepregnancy shape will depend on your age, health and genetic makeup (look at your mother!).

Abdomen and Waistline

A thickening of the waist and a protrusion of the stomach often continue after birth. Again, the extent of these changes varies enormously from woman to woman. Some report that it is virtually impossible to lose this fat deposit; the majority claims it takes exercise, sound dieting and discipline. If you are overweight before or during pregnancy and/or have a tendency to put on weight in this area, it is likely that you will continue to have difficulty in controlling your waistline after birth.

Some women worry about stretch marks that frequently appear on the abdomen and often on the breasts. They are the result of the skin being stretched to accommodate the fetus and milk, and they can be minimized by exercise, weight control, and body lotions.

Often a cesarean section will leave a large scar on the abdomen that many women find unsightly. Recent medical advances have minimized scarring through the use of new equipment and procedures, so if you place a high premium on wearing bikinis and need a cesarean (or other sorts of surgery), you may want to ask your doctor to use what is called the "bikini cut"—an incision crosswise just above the vaginal hairline.

Vagina

Some stretching or tearing of the vagina always occurs if the baby is born vaginally. For women with episiotomies, there is considerable, but temporary, pain (see chapter 2, p. 77). The vagina usually heals and is ready for intercourse within three weeks and will be as tight, or tighter, than before. Some women claim that they were tightened either too much or not enough, and others develop infections or persistent soreness. With sound and prepared medical care, however, vaginal difficulties after episiotomies are infrequent.

For those who do not have episiotomies, considerable stretching may have occurred. This stretching can be minimized by performing vaginal exercises (see chapter 2, p. 78) regularly before birth and by having a nurse or midwife during birth carefully and knowledgeably massage and stretch the vagina and surrounding tissue. The vagina is very elastic and will readily resume its shape with minimal stretching if care is taken. However, if the baby is very large for the size of the vagina, or if this is your third or more child, you may wish to consider an episiotomy. An episiotomy should also be considered if this is your first child and you are over 35, since tissue elasticity seems to decrease as women age.

Breasts and Breast Feeding

Frequently stretching and subsequent sagging, even shrinking, of the breasts occur after birth (particularly if you breast-feed). Breasts usually swell considerably during pregnancy—"It's the only time in my life I ever had a cleavage!"—but, after lactation has stopped, the breasts shrink again and may not snap back into shape.

You can, in part, anticipate pregnancy–birth effects by examining your breasts. If they are high, conical, and firm, they are less likely to be affected than if they are low (and less surrounded by muscle), loose, and large. Of course, this issue forces us to consider just how much we, and others significant in our life, value our appearance. It is a fact that breasts will eventually sag—sooner with children (and to a greater degree) but also with aging alone.

You can minimize breast sagging by: (1) doing exercises to strengthen the muscles around the breast before, during, and after childbirth (isometrics are excellent); (2) wearing a good support bra as soon as your breasts begin to swell in order to minimize stretching of the muscles; and (3) breast feeding carefully with good support, exercise, and massage.

In 1971, only 24.7 percent of mothers breast-fed their babies. By 1978, 46.6 percent reported that they were breast feeding. Size and shape of the breasts have nothing to do with milk production, so over 90 percent of all women lactate sufficiently to breast-feed.

Breast feeding offers many advantages. Perhaps the most important is that breast milk carries antibodies for many diseases; thus, breast-fed babies are less susceptible to illness. Also, the breasts need not be sterilized (sterilization of bottles is hard work and is sometimes done incorrectly), and there are fewer problems with stomach gas and spitting up (which occurs frequently among bottle-fed babies). Another advantage is that human milk is considerably different from cow's milk or formula. It is much thinner, with a lower fat and protein content, which is important because some babies are allergic to cow's milk or formula. Furthermore, breast milk may establish later tastes and cholesterol levels. The infant's bowel movements are also fewer and less odoriferous, and the baby is less likely to overeat. (Few breast-fed babies are fat.) Yet another advantage is the closeness that can develop between the mother and child. After all, the breast is sensitive and the actual physical communication experienced in breast feeding can only be approximated via a bottle. Yet another advantage is that the frequency of breast cancer is significantly less among women who have breast-fed. These advantages have led the American Pediatric Society to strongly recommend breast feeding whenever possible.

A number of difficulties, however, are associated with breast feeding that warrant consideration. If the mother uses drugs or is exposed to chemicals or radiation, she will pass the harmful agents via her milk to the baby. Therefore, a mother who is a moderate to heavy drug user should not breast-feed. Another problem is that it is impossible to determine how much milk an infant is receiving via the breast, and sometimes supplementary formula is required. Further, very weak babies may not be able to suck hard enough to secure breast milk. A major strategical problem is that the mother must be present at a majority of the feedings. In days of yore, wet nurses were employed, but this is rarely done today. Instead, we have breast pumps that, by allowing breast milk to be stored, can provide some measure of freedom to the mother. Nonetheless, the frequent feedings infants require (every three hours for newborns, each feeding requiring 20 to 30 minutes) mean that working mothers have a problem.

A major interpersonal difficulty of breast feeding is that fathers cannot be the feeder most of the time, which can establish a script in which the father is an outsider. It can prohibit him from any attempt at long-term infant care, especially if weaning is late. This problem can be circumvented by the father feeding the infant from a bottle (either formula or breast milk) and by holding the baby often.

Some women find breast feeding embarrassing, and in public places retire to the privacy of a rest room. ("Ugh," said one mother, "how can you feed a baby in the toilet?") Bashful women can buy tops that permit very discreet feeding.

Breast feeding may pose a problem if you have other children that are jealous. Another problem is that it can encourage excessive dependence between mother and child, particularly if weaning does not occur until late. Most pediatricians believe that the optimum weaning age is six to eight months, although Europeans commonly wean at two to three months. By six months, the baby's digestive system is prepared for solid foods, and he or she is big enough to be cumbersome. (Recent studies are finding surprisingly high numbers of cavities among children who breast-feed past their sixth month, possibly because of the high sugar content of maternal milk.) Also, as baby teeth come in, infants often attack the nipple with painful ferocity. One explanation is that teething is painful and is relieved by chewing; another explanation is that the child is aggressing against the control of the breast. A bottle can be held and controlled more readily, and frequently children will reject breast feeding before the mother is ready. Despite the many theories about the emotional consequences of early or late weaning, there is little substantive data on the issue. Customs vary greatly from culture to culture and from decade to decade. The best advice appears to be to select the option most suitable to the family, including the infant, and to use your best judgment combined with the advice of your pediatrician.

We recommend contacting local LaLeche Leagues during the third trimester for information and advice on breast feeding. While they are somewhat zealous, they are an excellent source of help, comfort, and support. Said one nursing mother, "They were fantastic! They gave me wonderful assistance in increasing my milk production and in making breast feeding a very enjoyable and healthy experience."

One good way to deal with the physical consequences of childbirth is to consider the changes that accompanied previous births. While birthing itself gets easier, the physical changes that occur after birth tend to increase in degree with each child. If you are planning your first child, you may want to inquire about the experiences of your mother and/or sisters, which is an excellent way of learning more about yourself, birth, and your family. But do keep in mind that most models, dancers, even strippers, are also mothers. While it may require more work to stay in shape, it is certainly possible.

QUESTIONS TO ASK YOURSELVES
(About Having a Healthy Baby and Experience)

We have been discussing birth control, pregnancy, and birth itself as important components in pre-parenting. Other aspects of your life, past and present, also may affect your parenting experience. The following section contains questions to ask yourselves, and is followed by information pertaining to your answers. While much of the data is female-oriented, men ought to read this section also. You should be familiar with the information so that you can be active in alerting your partner to hazards and be committed to assisting in health changes. Additionally, recent evidence suggests that the father's health variables may play a significant role in a child's health, although we cannot yet say how much. Certainly, many predictable factors involved in having a healthy baby are genetic—and half of a baby's genes come from the father. This section ought to familiarize both of you with the experiences of others and help you predict the kind of experience you would be *likely* to have.

Health risks may also be an important part of your decision about whether or not to parent at this time. Of course, not even the physician who has examined you for years can, with assurance, predict your pregnancy and birth experience. In a recent English study, for example, high-risk mothers had no more birth complications than low-risk mothers. Our knowledge of the effects of various teratrogens (events that produce deformities in developing tissue) is seriously limited by the ethical restraints on experimenting with humans. Mostly we are limited to studies that try to correlate one event with another. In other words, these studies try to find out whether two events tend to occur together more than you would expect them to by chance alone. So, for example, we find that women who smoke cigarettes have 30 percent more stillbirths than women who don't smoke. We still don't know that smoking causes stillbirths, or that it is smoking itself that is related to stillbirths. For example, it may be that smokers have a tendency to drink alcohol, or eat less, or work harder than nonsmokers. Yet, with all its limitations, the information can still be useful in drawing a profile of what your experience is most apt to be. You are then better equipped to decide whether or not you wish to parent and to prepare accordingly.

How Old Are You?

The "best" time to have a baby is between the ages of 20 and 35. That is, when we look at the health of the majority of women and their babies, we see the least number of problems in this age range. Women are likely to be at peak strength, their life patterns regular, birth complications minimal, and the community supportive. While the data on fathers is more meager, the same optimum age range seems to apply. For one thing, the quality of sperm seems to decrease considerably as a man enters his forties.

If you are *under* 20, you should know that there are more problems with pregnancy and childbirth in this age range as compared to 20 to 35. For example, the younger you are, the more important nutrition is because your body needs calories and nutrients in order to develop. The fetus will compete for those nutrients, and your health and strength may suffer. Furthermore, you are less likely than older women to eat a nutritionally balanced, healthy diet. You may then have a more fatiguing and difficult labor with more complications, and you are likely to have a smaller and weaker than average baby. In fact, the mortality rate of babies born to mothers under 15 is more than twice as high as those born to mothers in their twenties. (Data show that 25 percent of all low-birth-weight babies born today are born to teenagers.)

Another problem with pregnancy and childbirth under 20 is that the younger you are, the more *unlikely* it is that you have adequate family and community support. Only 11 percent of mothers 13 to 15 go on to graduate from high school, and the rate of attempted suicides by school-age mothers is seven times the national percentage of girls the same age without children. Many teenagers do not know they are pregnant until their third, even fourth, month, and many wait even longer before they confide in a health professional. Their prenatal care is often poor—compounded by poor nutrition, lack of sleep, overexertion, anxiety, guilt, and, frequently, drugs. They have to cope with the social problems of being a teenage mother-to-be and a mother in a peer-oriented and age-segregated group.

A number of unwed mothers thought that pregnancy would endear them to their boyfriends. In fact, of those girls under 18, only 40 percent marry the fathers. Terry, 14, told how her boyfriend began "straying" and that she thought the baby would bring them closer together. Unfortunately, the opposite effect more often occurs. Teenagers who are married do not fare much better. It is estimated that 75 percent of all teenage marriages occur because of pregnancy (mistaken as well as actual).

Many married teenagers also believe that pregnancy will bring them closer together. While the divorce rate for adolescent marriages is astronomically high (over three times that of older couples), the divorce rate of teenage couples with children is even higher. The realities of childbirth and the expectations of family and peers that divorce will occur result in pressures that are difficult to withstand. Additionally, the high unemployment rates and low-paying jobs available to adolescents make self-sufficiency, especially with a child, most difficult.

In summary, the health statistics generally support the notion that pregnant women over 20 fare significantly better than teenage mothers, as do their babies. If you are under 20, pay particular attention to these statistics. Also, be sure to consult with your doctor as soon as you are seriously considering pregnancy or are already pregnant. You should be assured of your privacy when you take a pregnancy test. You may also receive contraceptives, or treatment for venereal disease, without parental consent. And, despite the odds, some teenagers do have an excellent birth–parenting experience, especially when they have planned a sound diet, moderate exercise, good prenatal care, and a supportive environment.

If you are *35 plus*, you should be aware of the increased risks and problems associated with pregnancy and childbirth, as well as the risks associated with *not* having had any children. Carole McCauley has written an excellent book entitled *Pregnancy After 35* that goes into more detail than is presented here and ought to be read. For unknown reasons, the risk of birth complications and congenital defects increases with age. The age of concern used to be 30, but recent advances in health research are raising the age to 35, even 40 and above. The age of motherhood appears to be rising as a consequence of economic, career, and romantic factors. From 1972 to 1975, first births among 30-year-old women jumped 21 percent; for 29-year-olds, they climbed 23 percent.

The older you are, however (particularly over 35), the greater the chances of having a Down's syndrome child (infants who are moderately to severely retarded and who comprise one out of every 1000 babies born); in fact, women over 40 have a 200 times greater risk than do those in their twenties. Other congenital difficulties also appear to be more likely when mothers are over 35, perhaps because of endocrine changes, cumulative environmental insult, and egg and/or sperm degeneration. Male sperm changes that occur when men enter their forties also contribute to increased birth defects, though how much is still being assessed. It is estimated that at least 24 percent of all babies born with Down's syndrome were conceived with faulty sperm (not egg).

Pregnancy may be more difficult for you if you are in poor physical condition, and a moderate exercise program (under a doctor's supervision) ought to be undertaken before conception even occurs. Many physicians tell their 35-plus mothers that pregnancy will be more fatiguing and the symptoms more pronounced than if they were younger, particularly if this is their first. However, there is a lot of variability in the pregnancy experience, and the difficulty experienced by so-called "older" women may be rooted in psychological rather than in physical causes.

Late pregnancy often raises special concerns about parenting. Sometimes, the late child is an "accident." There may be large family age gaps or many other children to contend with. You may be out of phase with many of your contemporaries—perhaps feeding a baby when other mothers are going back to college. However, many women in their twenties have reversed the patterns of their mothers and have gone to school, or developed a career *first*—then had their babies. While you're probably a more stable person now, you might find the demands of parenthood more disruptive and exhausting than when you were younger. "But," says one mother-to-be of 38, "I've never felt stronger and more together. I've never had the kind of desire to nurture that I have now."

For many women, crossing 30 is a biological two-minute warning. Barbara, age 31, stated: "My entire head changed when I hit 30. I never used to worry about tomorrow, or children, or money. I spent my time in school and in love. Now, like overnight, I know I'm getting old. And if I want kids, it's going to be soon." Mark, age 34 and childless, stated: "I keep waiting for us to get settled, ready for a baby. Forget it—we're never going to be ready—and I'm not about to go without kids." Linda, age 36, childfree: "I thought I had resolved this ten years ago. But it keeps coming up again, like a weed. You can't decide to be a nonparent—it's too negative." The pressure is felt by mothers, too. Karen, age 31: "I think of having a third child all the time, but I'm afraid to mention it. If I don't have it soon—you know, this is my last chance now."

Certainly, the decision to have a child is always difficult, but there is a particular intensity late in life surrounding the options. Women who do not experience their first pregnancy (not necessarily full term) by their early thirties have, for reasons unknown, greater risk of breast and cervical cancer and of endometriosis. But women who have their first child (later ones do not count) after 35, have a 20 percent greater risk of breast cancer than do childless women. Both groups ought to check their breasts monthly and have Pap smears and thorough gynecological exams at least once a year.

Fertility decreases with age (usually after 30), so there is also the knowledge that the longer you wait the harder it might get. As Eve told me, "What happens if I say yeah, let's—and we can't anymore?" The thirties are the real pressure years for those who went to school for long periods of time. "I just got out of school," said Jack, "and there I was, 32, in debt, with nothing. I want kids—but in about 20 years." His wife said, "In a way, I wish we had had kids sooner—but we really weren't ready for that." This hesitance is understandable since now being ready means considerably more than just biologically capable.

How Many Children Should You Have?

The greatest recorded number of children born to one woman is 69, to a Soviet mother. We assume you are not going to try to outdo her! In deciding how many children to have, keep in mind that first pregnancies and deliveries are usually more difficult and less predictable than later births. Firstborns also tend to be smaller than later babies. Thus, home births are not usually recommended with firstborns. After-birth depression is more likely after the third birth. By the fifth child, pregnancy and birth risks increase, so that the safest births (for mother and child) are the second, third, and fourth. An exception is when you and your partner have incompatible blood types (specifically, if one of you has Rh negative and the other Rh positive blood). Rarely is there difficulty in a first birth, but a second or third pregnancy may be extremely hazardous. You should be sure to check your Rh factors before conception, since precautions can be readily taken.

In addition to the consideration of the physical consequences of childbirth, other considerations should determine the number of children you plan on. Family size is very important to how happy and well one parents. Social and emotional factors relating to the number of children in a family will be discussed in chapter 5.

When Was Your Last Baby Born?

It appears as though it is physically better for mother and infant if childbearing is separated by at least 19 months. Children born less than 19 months after a sibling are smaller and more prone to infection and deformity. Also, the mother is more likely to have a difficult and wearing pregnancy and labor—and probably a difficult and wearing parenthood afterward.

Most women resume menstruating sooner when they are not breast-feeding. Therefore, one consequence of bottle-feeding babies is that women can become pregnant sooner than might be optimal for their bodies. Therefore, it's advisable to be careful about birth control after birth (see p. 41). If you do become pregnant soon after birth, you ought to arrange for especially good prenatal care and perhaps consider testing of the fetus as well.

What Were Your Own Birth Weights?

Birth weight is important because 5.5 pounds appears to be critical to an infant's survival. Babies under 5.5 pounds die more frequently than do those closer to the average 7.2 pounds. Also, if babies are very large (the record is 27 pounds!), vaginal delivery may be difficult, even impossible. Generally, birth weight (and relative health) increases for each child until the fifth-born, which tends to be more sickly than the others. Birth size of an infant is determined by several factors: by genetic influences (but a big adult was not necessarily a big baby and vice versa); by the space in utero; and by the nutrition available to the fetus.

You can estimate birth weight by averaging you and your partner's birth weights (partner's birth weight and yours, divided by two) and compensating for birth order by decreasing it for first and fifth or later-born. In addition, you would decrease size estimates if you smoked, drank, or used other sorts of drugs, or if you ate poorly. It's still only a guess, but it is a guideline in anticipating your experience. (For example, if you were both big babies, you would want to be sure to consider pelvic size and shape.)

What Were the Birth Experiences of Your Relatives?

Data indicate that breech births, cesareans, twins, danger of anoxia, allergies, length of labor, and pain tolerance tend to run in families. Check the heritage of you and your partner and tell your doctor about any common problems in your family. Have your pelvic size measured to see whether you are likely to have difficulty during delivery.

What Kind of Physical Condition Are You In?

If your answer is anything but excellent, carefully consider how your health might affect your pregnancy, birth, and baby. If you aren't sure, ask your physician. For example, if you are overweight, you are likely to have a more difficult pregnancy; therefore, it may be wise to go on a *nutritionally sound* diet before pregnancy. If your muscles are in poor shape, the baby's growth will stretch you considerably more than if your muscles are well toned. If you have high blood pressure, you will want to monitor it carefully, and if you are on any medication, you will want to know what effects it could have on the fetus.

It is essential to diagnose vaginal infections, for venereal diseases can be transmitted to the fetus with unfortunate consequences. For example, mothers pass syphilis to the fetus in about its eighteenth week of existence. It, like Mom, can be readily cured by penicillin. If, however, the problem is undetected, the baby will be born with congenital syphilis. Only barely noticeable symptoms are present until adolescence or later, when the disease may produce blindness, paralysis, and insanity. In fact, the behavioral changes associated with the last stages of syphilis may have sponsored beliefs as to the hereditability of madness. What was said to be lunacy might have often been the last stage of syphilis (which, by the way, may not show up for as long as 50 years!). Therefore, you should always be checked for venereal disease and infection *before* you decide to conceive and, if at all warranted, continue checking throughout pregnancy. (This check is routinely done by many hospitals and physicians.)

What Are Your Health Habits?

A number of factors appear to affect the health of a mother and infant. Again, these data are usually correlational and therefore apply to the *average* person, not a particular individual. Do you eat enough? Do you eat nutritionally balanced food? Regularly? It's a good idea to establish good eating habits before you actually become pregnant. That way, your body will be stronger, and the fetus will be less of a strain. Do you sleep well? If not, what are you doing about it? What is your blood pressure? Heart rate? Before you get pregnant, have a good physical exam and ask your doctor how you are likely to respond to pregnancy (see specific questions later in this chapter).

How anxious are you? Some studies have correlated high anxiety levels with birth complications and prolonged labor. This link is not surprising since women who report high anxiety levels frequently eat and sleep poorly, use drugs, and get poor medical care. Certainly, if you are a very anxious person, it would be worth trying to change your behavior before having a child. Almost everyone agrees that anxiety is, by definition, unpleasant, but there are a number of relaxation procedures you can learn, like yoga or meditation or deep muscle relaxation. Almost all schools of psychology agree that the reduction of anxiety is one of the primary goals of therapy. If either you or your partner is highly anxious, you should obtain some relief before you make major changes in your life, such as parenting.

Are you often depressed, or were you very depressed after the birth of your last child? Two-thirds of all women report at least some depression after birth, which is so common that it has been named "postpartum depression." It is particularly likely after the third or more child or if you have experienced it before. Depression is also very common among parents, especially mothers, of very young children. Even in studies of identical twins, the ones who had children were much more likely to suffer emotional problems (ranging from depression, anxiety, and drug addiction to psychoses). Medical explanations of postpartem depression tend to focus on the vast hormonal changes that occur in women after birth, which certainly may profoundly affect their moods. But, equally important, are the vast behavior changes that take place after birth. These changes affect men as well as women and are too frequently unexpected and unrecognized. In chapter 7 we detail some ways in which prospective parents can decrease the chances of having these sorts of problems. Certainly, if you are currently having emotional difficulties, or have a history of them, you ought to consult with your physician about ways of dealing with them before they become more pronounced and possibly prevent you from having a positive parenting experience.

What Drugs Do You Use?

Almost all drugs that enter a pregnant woman's body are passed on to the fetus. Furthermore, new studies are implicating male drug use (prior to pregnancy) as having an effect on the health of the fetus.

Drugs and the Fetus. The following factors determine how much a given drug will affect the fetus:

1. *The drug.* Some drugs (especially those that are of low molecular weight, lipid soluble, and readily absorbed) enter the fetus more rapidly and extensively than others.

2. *The amount of the drug.* Obviously, the larger and/or more frequent the drug intake, the more exposure the fetus will have.

3. *Other drugs in the body.* The more drugs, the greater the possibility of a wider variety of chemical interactions, some probably never extensively studied, even in a test tube.

4. *The age of a fetus.* A given drug will have different effects at different stages of fetal development. When certain structures are forming, they may be more susceptible to certain drugs than they are either at an earlier or later time. For example, German measles causes the most deformity in a fetus in the first trimester, but maternal smoking seems to slow growth the most in the last trimester.

5. *The particular fetus and mother.* There are large individual differences in the way people respond to drugs. There are also individual differences with regard to susceptibility to certain diseases, such as cancer or heart problems. (See genetic considerations, p. 66.) Certainly, you and the fetus's long-term reaction to a given drug may be affected by any propensities either of you have to disorders associated with the drug.

Most people immediately think of illegal drugs when discussing this issue; however, some of the most unfortunate health problems are linked to legal drugs. In addition to illegal drugs, prescription drugs, and over-the-counter drugs, other drug-related habits such as cigarettes, alcohol, and chemicals in general, must be considered when determining the health of a fetus. We will now discuss each category separately.

Cigarettes. There are data linking maternal smoking to a number of birth-related problems. Mothers who smoke (and 57 percent in one study did) have smaller babies, more stillbirths, and more difficult labors. By the fourth month of life, a fetus's heart rate increases significantly when the mother smokes. The more you smoke, the more likely it is that nicotine will affect your baby. The greatest effect on the fetus appears to occur from the sixth month on, as data indicate that fetuses of smoking mothers grow considerably less than those of nonsmokers. Of course, birth weight is a critical factor in infant health.

Alcohol. How much and how often do you drink? Over 85 percent of all pregnant women in the United States use alcohol during pregnancy. Very recently, evidence has been mounting that a cluster of symptoms exists called the Fetal-Alcohol Syndrome. This syndrome refers to certain deviations in infants that seem correlated with alcohol consumption of the mother during pregnancy. Some of these deviations are physical and mental retardation, limb deformities, cleft palates, small birth weights, and a tendency toward being diagnosed later in life as learning-disabled (some would infer that minimal brain damage may have occurred). This syndrome appears to be most frequently associated with heavy and frequent drinkers; however, three ounces of alcohol in a single dose appear to have been sufficient to produce the syndrome in some cases. A controversy over how the public should be informed about these dangers has resulted, with some suggesting that warning labels for pregnant women be placed on alcoholic beverages. Of significance to you as a pregnant woman is the knowledge that whatever alcohol you consume will also be consumed by the fetus.

Prescription Drugs. Surveys have indicated that 82 percent of a given sample of pregnant women were taking prescribed medication. The major drug categories included iron, analgesics, vitamins, barbiturates, diuretics, antiemetics, antibiotics, sulfonamides, cough medicines, antihistamines, hormones, tranquilizers, bronchodilators, hypnotics, and appetite suppressants. The sad fact is that we often do not know what effect a particular drug may have on a fetus (as in the case of Thalidomyde or DES). Many drugs have not been adequately tested, particularly for long-term effects on offspring (obviously, it takes a long time to collect this data).

Coffee, Tea, Cola, Cocoa. Do you drink these beverages? How much? Most people don't think about the health effects, but these substances contain caffeine, a drug whose effects may be quite powerful. Caffeine is a stimulant and, if you have ever overdosed on it, you know that it can produce insomnia, diarrhea, stomach cramps, and palpitations. Some people suggest that caffeine is an addictive drug that produces definite, if subtle, withdrawal symptoms. Some research has also tentatively linked the amount of coffee consumption with birth and infant complications (over five cups a day seemed to be a critical amount). Perhaps if you drink a lot of these beverages, you ought to cut back on your caffeine intake before you become pregnant. Cut back gradually—otherwise you may experience withdrawal symptoms, such as headaches and palpitations.

Over-the-Counter Drugs. Do you use them? Frequently? Americans spend billions of dollars a year on over-the-counter drugs, which are substances frequently advertised as health preparations that require no prescriptions. Examples are laxatives, vitamins, cough syrups, aspirin, nose sprays, sleeping aids, antacid tablets, and pain killers. Very few of these drugs have ever been tested or examined by any governmental agency, and the extent to which the manufacturer has safety-proofed the product is often unknown. Certainly, it is reasonable to think that these substances may also affect the fetus. In fact, recent evidence indicates that the use of aspirin for four or five consecutive days may cause a fetal heart defect that can possibly be fatal.

Chemicals Everywhere. Do you breathe? Do you eat? Do you drink? We are living in a world crammed with untested chemicals (a sort of chemistry set run amok). These chemicals are in our foods, in our hair dyes and nail polishes, in toothpaste, in spray cans, in water, in the air. We really do not know if these "natural" and man-made (though not necessarily unnatural!) substances are harmful—they may even be helpful. Not only don't we know the long-term effects of many chemicals, but we also don't know how these chemicals react with each other in different combinations. Therefore, if you live in a city, and like processed food, and spray different parts of yourself with different concoctions, you are most likely one large, experimental test tube. You cannot avoid this situation very easily, but you can minimize it, however slightly, by cutting down on your use of unnecessary concoctions.

Street Drugs. If you buy illicit drugs, you have two things you have to concern yourself with: the effects of the drug you supposedly have taken and the effects of the drug(s) you really have taken. Babies, of course, may be born addicted to heroin, amphetamines, barbiturates, alcohol, and a host of other substances. Few street drugs are pure—many have been tampered with extensively. Street dealers of drugs often open capsules and substitute less expensive substances, in part or completely. Marijuana is often steamed, soaked, sprayed, or baked with a variety of chemicals in order to increase its potency and/or weight.

Our own government has sprayed a highly toxic chemical (para-quat) over marijuana plants in Mexico. If the marijuana is eaten, the chemicals may produce vomiting, internal organ damage, and if enough has been eaten, even death. When smoked, paraquat may cause irreversible lung damage. Its effect on pregnant women is unknown. A number of people are outraged about this. (The response of one state's Department of Public Health was that people shouldn't be smoking marijuana anyway.) At any rate, while marijuana itself has not been demonstrated to cause birth defects, chemicals with which it is treated (perhaps by your own government) may be damaging. This same principle holds for most street drugs.

Dealing with Drug Use. We recommend dealing with drug use before you try to become pregnant for several reasons. It may take several months for our bodies to clean themselves of some drugs and their effects. Also, we may underestimate how difficult it will be to change our habits and how upsetting the change may be to ourselves and our relationships. There are frequently emotional and physical consequences to stopping drug use, often to our surprise and discomfort. Increased irritability and stress are common and can be handled more easily alone than when you are also trying to deal with pregnancy. Also, many of us fail in our resolutions about drug use ("Quitting is easy," the saying goes, "I've done it a hundred times").

What drugs might either of you have difficulty controlling? (If you have the slightest doubt, test yourself by going for a week without the drug.) Can you help each other? How might the change in drug use affect the way you relate to each other? ("Before the kid we used to have a good time together." "I'm not even a father yet and I have to give things up.") What will happen if only one of you eliminates the drug? If only one of you wants to stop the drug use? Often the power issue supersedes the health issue. Mike told us, "I won't let my wife smoke as soon as she's pregnant." His wife, surprised, snapped, "What? Since when do I need your permission?" Said Mike, apologetically, "I just meant for the health of the baby." His wife: "The baby? What about my health?" Mike, in trouble now, "Well, you're grown up and make your own decisions." Replied his wife, "But you make decisions for the baby, right?"

The advantage of coming to terms with these differences before you are pregnant is that the coming child will not be directly associated with these conflicts. Also, you will have a chance to consult with a therapist to help you decrease or eliminate your drug use if you have difficulty doing it on your own.

Are There Health Risks in Your Work Environment?*

What possible health risks are you exposed to? In some work environments, we are exposed to substances that may affect our health and that of a baby. Along with the dangerous substances we know about, like asbestos, are ones we only suspect. For example, preliminary research out of Johns Hopkins Medical School is correlating sperm deformities with frequent exposure to microwaves.

*For more details, see *Guidelines on Pregnancy and Work,* American College of Obstetricians and Gynecologists, 1977.

Fathers are most susceptible to causing deformities in the baby when they are producing or storing the sperm that leads to conception. Mothers, always susceptible because the eggs are already made and stored in the ovaries, are more at risk while pregnant, especially in the first trimester (before they may realize the pregnancy).

We strongly urge you to take full safety precautions if you work in a suspect environment, especially when you are trying for a pregnancy. We don't think a possibly pregnant woman ought to work around hazardous substances without medical approval. Many companies do not even permit it. Would they transfer you to a desk job? Provide a chair when you are pregnant? What special considerations would you have? Could you arrange to get some of them if and when you try to conceive (especially avoiding dangerous chemicals)?

Let's not forget the father, whose sperm quality may also be affected. We honestly don't know how, short of changing jobs or rotating positions, a man can avoid his customary work to father a child. He can, however, take *extra*-special precautions during this time.

GENETIC ROULETTE

The normal human being has 46 chromosomes, and each chromosome is comprised of about 20,000 genes. Genes determine a number of traits, including whether or not we are human, our sex, our physical constitution, whether we have or are susceptible to certain disorders, perhaps even important parts of our temperament or intelligence.

A child's sex is determined by the genetic information contained in the sperm. Men produce two kinds: an X, which makes females, and a Y, which makes males. (Henry VIII, who beheaded two wives for not producing a male heir, was beheading the incorrect source of his problem.) Most men produce varying amounts of both kinds, and whichever one gets to the egg determines the child's sex. The sperm differ in that the female X has a bigger head and a shorter tail and has less of a chance of getting to the egg first. Under natural conditions, about 160 males are conceived for every 100 females, but many more male embryos are spontaneously aborted, so that only 105 males are born for every 100 females. Can we change these odds and give an advantage to either the X or Y sperm?

The easiest, but least reliable, method of sex determination is recommended by Dr. Elizabeth Whelan. She claims her technique can increase chances of having a male from 55 percent to 68 percent, and for a girl up to 57 percent. To have a boy, have intercourse on the *fourth, fifth, and sixth* days before ovulation (that is, after menstruation but before mid-cycle). To have a girl, have intercourse on either *two days before or during ovulation.* She warns prospective parents to be wary of advice prior to 1975, since those theories (such as postulated by Dr. Landrum Shettles) have been proven incorrect.

A more sophisticated technique, with a 75 percent chance of producing a son, was devised by Dr. Ronald Ericsson, president of Gametrics, Ltd., in California (a firm dedicated to promoting his method). He and his colleagues can isolate the Y sperm and, through artificial insemination, increase your chances of having a boy. Unfortunately, the technique cannot help you conceive a daughter.

The third and most accurate way of predetermining sex is to wait until your fifteenth week of pregnancy, have a test called amniocentesis, and abort the wrong-sexed fetus. This decision is questionable, ethically and medically, and you should recognize that many medical personnel are unlikely to cooperate.

Many people have been concerned that there might be horrible consequences to being able to select an offspring's gender. People might have a very high proportion of males, feared some, and the population might become dangerously imbalanced. Recent surveys, however, suggest that Americans do not have that great a gender preference. According to a recent *Redbook* survey of over eighty thousand women, more than half said they had no gender preference. Other large studies (from Princeton University's Office of Population Research) came up with similar findings, but only among women. Males seemed to have more of a bias toward males, and both men and women prefer the firstborn to be a male. It does seem likely that in the near future, sex predetermination will be more reliable. We will all have to deal with the issue of choosing, or trying not to choose, the sex of our offspring. But perhaps we should remember that the parents of the first test-tube baby asked not to be told its sex!

There are a number of other traits, good and bad, that are passed on to offspring. Most of us have between three and ten genes that, if matched with the same type of gene from a member of the opposite sex, would produce undesirable traits. Some examples might be sickle-cell anemia for blacks or Tay-Sachs for European Jews. Some traits must be passed on by both parents, by matching genes, while others are passed on by only one parent. Sometimes the trait shows up in the offspring; sometimes it appears in grandchildren. Sometimes, as with Huntington's Chorea, the symptoms are not observable until middle age. In genetics, most outcomes are measured in terms of probabilities. You and your partner may have a 25 percent or 50 percent or 75 percent chance of having a baby with this or that. But these odds are derived from a very large number. Even if you have only a 25 percent chance of passing on a disorder, you could pass it on to every one of your children or to none of them.

It is possible for you and your partner to be genetically screened for certain kinds of problems. You could then know the likelihood of having a baby with a certain disorder and plan accordingly. The decision to consult a genetic counselor, or a screening clinic, is an important one and ought to precede a parenting decision. Counselors ask prospective parents about their family histories, screen their blood for certain disorders, analyze chromosomes for problems, and discuss the findings and alternatives. The following are some questions you should consider in evaluating whether or not to see a counselor or go to a clinic before conception.

1. *Do you or your partner have a genetically determined illness?* If so, ask your doctor about its hereditability.

2. *Do either of your families have incidences of genetically based diseases?* If so, speak to your doctor about it. Tell him or her exactly who had the disease and when. You should be particularly careful if the same illness appears in both families (which may also be a concern with nondisease factors, such as the number of twins born in your families).

3. *Is there a more than usual incidence of a certain kind of illness in your families* (for example, *cancer, heart disease, high blood pressure, diabetes, Down's syndrome*)? If so, you might want to discuss this incidence with your physician in terms of your own and the infant's health. For example, if your family has a high incidence of high blood pressure, senility, and coronary problems, you might want to monitor your (and your children's) cholesterol intake.

4. *Are you a member of a group that has a known propensity for certain illnesses?* If you are black, you can be checked for sickle-cell anemia in free clinics. If you are both European Jewish, you may wish to test yourselves for Tay-Sachs.

If you are at risk, it is important to consider whether amniocentesis can detect the disorder (see p. 30). If so, then you may decide to risk pregnancy. You may then test the fetus during the fifteenth week via amniocentesis and elect to abort at that time. If you do not believe in abortion, or if amniocentesis cannot screen for a disorder you are carrying, the issue becomes more difficult. You must evaluate the severity and probability of the disorder. While our society is becoming increasingly tolerant and supportive of special-needs children, parents still have the major caretaking responsibility. You must weigh the benefits and liabilities for yourselves, the future child, and society. This is best done in consultation with a genetic counselor and your physician.

QUESTIONS TO ASK YOUR PHYSICIAN
(Before Deciding Whether or Not to Have a Child)

Some people find it very difficult to ask doctors questions without feeling either pushy or foolish. It can be helpful to write down the questions in advance and to practice asking them while imagining you are with your doctor. In this way you can avoid being aggressive or timid. Both of you should be asking questions, although the potential mother has additional concerns. Let your doctor know at the start that you are thinking about having a baby and would like his or her assessment. Some of the following questions are suggested:

For the Man Considering Fathering

1. What is your blood type and Rh factor?
2. Do you have any disorder that may be genetic?
3. What problems tend to run in your family? Consider hypertension, heart problems, diabetes, twinning, and so on. Is genetic screening or counseling recommended?
4. If you are using any drugs or prescribed medications, be sure to mention them to your doctor. Ask about possible fertility or sperm-quality problems associated with their use.
5. Enumerate the unusual substances, if any, you are exposed to at work and ask about what hazards, if any, they might pose.
6. Are there any physical examinations pending that require X-rays or drugs? If so, can you have them several weeks before you attempt pregnancy? (For example, will you have to be certified as free of tuberculosis within a few months? Do you need a yearly dental X-ray? Shots in order to leave the country?)

For the Woman Considering Childbearing

Your first assurance ought to be that you are not already pregnant. If you are not, proceed with questions one through six above that applied to your partner. You should compare your answers. The more you share the same genetic risks, the more likely they are to occur. It may be especially wise to consider genetic counseling. If your Rh factors are different, be sure to discuss this in detail with your doctor. Although first pregnancies are rarely affected, precautions ought to be taken; later pregnancies may even be terminated if incompatibility of blood type was not known.

After discussing questions one through six, proceed with the following questions:

1. Do you have high or low blood pressure? If so, how will it be affected? Should you watch your diet?
2. Do you have a tendency toward diabetes? Should you be monitored?
3. Are you likely to have difficulty conceiving or carrying the pregnancy full term?
4. Are there any body "weaknesses" that you may discover during pregnancy (a weak back, varicose veins, hemorrhoids)?

5. How wide are you in the pelvic area? How likely is it that you might need a cesarean? (Be sure to ask the doctor to measure you).

6. If you are using drugs, be sure to discuss the possibility of terminating their use before conception and during pregnancy. If you can't, or don't want to, what effects do these drugs have on fetal development? Are there ways in which you can minimize any risks?

7. If you are going to stop taking the birth control pill, how long should you wait to let your body stabilize? What contraceptive can you use in the interim?

8. What can you do to increase your flexibility, stamina, and strength?

9. Should you be inoculated against German measles? Other diseases? How long should you wait afterward before getting pregnant?

10. Do you have any allergies?

Now that you have answered these and additional questions of your own, you have an accurate, individualized and useful understanding of the health factors to be considered when pre-parenting.

CONCLUSION

In this chapter we have considered various birth control methods and how you can select an appropriate one. We talked about why there are unplanned pregnancies and how you can avoid them. We also discussed pregnancy and how you find out whether you're pregnant. We described the pregnancy experience, for both men and women. We also talked about abortion options at various stages of pregnancy and how you felt about employing them. We examined the ways in which pregnancy and birth can affect your health and appearance, and presented personal questions to help you assess your chances of having a healthy experience and baby at this time in your lives. We also looked at ways in which you can influence the sex of a baby, and genetic factors that could be important to consider while pre-parenting. In addition, we listed some questions you might want to talk over with your physician.

In the next chapter we will look at childbirth. What we know and don't know and how we feel about birth may be influential components of our parenting decision.

ADDITIONAL READINGS

Boston Women's Health Book Collective. *Our Bodies, Ourselves.* New York: Simon and Schuster, Inc., 1971.

Fraiberg, Selam. *Every Child's Birthright: In Defense of Mothering.* New York: Basic Books, Inc., 1977.

Ingle, Dwight J. *Who Should Have Children?* New York: Bobbs-Merrill Co., 1973.

McCauley, Carole Spearin. *Pregnancy After 35.* New York: E. P. Dutton and Co., 1976.

Mumford, Stephen D. *Vasectomy: The Decision Making Process.* San Francisco, California: San Francisco Press, 1977.

Noble, Elizabeth. *Essential Exercises for the Childbearing Year.* Boston: Houghton Mifflin, 1976.

2

Birth Considerations

In this chapter, we describe the birth process and the feelings women and men have about the birth experience. We examine the various options prospective parents face when planning a birth. Would you want both of you to be present? A midwife? At home? With or without medication? We will help you select a compatible birth style, one which is likely to be emotionally positive and safe for all concerned. We will also list some questions you may want to discuss with an obstetrician if and when you decide to parent.

These sorts of considerations are worthwhile whether or not you elect to have a child in the near future. Birth is among the more powerful of human experiences. Our knowledge and feelings about it play an often important but unidentified role in our feelings about becoming a parent. For this reason, it is useful to consider objective information and your own subjective feelings about childbirth when pre-parenting.

COMING OUT: BIRTH

It is important to learn about birth when pre-parenting because fears and misconceptions may affect a decision about whether to have a child. It is reasonable, however, to fear what we don't know, and most of us, despite our common beginnings, know very little about birth. In fact, a recent survey of thousands of women found that seven out of ten admitted to having one or more irrational fears about pregnancy and birth—and the majority of these women were already mothers! Few women, and even fewer men, have actually seen a birth, especially before they themselves are expecting a child, and few of us know anyone intimately who can share the details and feelings of the experience.

Labor and Delivery

The feelings of birth usually begin with sporadic contractions of the uterus that last only a few seconds. The contractions occur in the third trimester, usually for weeks before they are strong enough to be felt. As delivery approaches, the contractions become stronger, longer, and more regular. About ten days before delivery, the fetus "locks" its head in the pelvic area (called engaging) which the mother can feel. It occurs only with firstborns. Labor is said to begin when the uterine contractions occur 15 to 20 minutes apart, each one lasting about a minute.

Labor is well named. Said one recent mother, "I've never worked so hard at anything in my life." Labor is commonly divided into three stages. During the first stage, the fetus "presents" itself for birth. During the second stage, the baby passes through the vagina or "birth canal." The final stage occurs after the baby is born and involves expulsion of the placenta or "afterbirth." When people know the stages of birth and what to expect, they are much less frightened throughout pregnancy, labor, and delivery.

The First Stage of Labor.   The first stage is the longest, lasting from 10 to 16 hours for the usual first birth, and 4 to 8 hours in subsequent births. An early sign is the expulsion of a slightly bloody mucus plug, called a show, that had previously been blocking the entrance (or exit!) of the uterus. This show may be followed by a rush of fluid from the vagina, often called "the breaking of water." This water is the amniotic sac that encloses and protects the fetus. A woman should immediately contact her physician so that she can take whatever precautions are advised, since after the rupture of the water, the fetus is much more susceptible to infection. Most women enter the hospital (if they are having a hospital birth) when contractions are five to ten minutes apart.

If there are complications, or if the physician and/or the couple wishes the birth to occur at a certain time, labor may be induced by administering drugs such as pitocin (frequently referred to as "pit") or by rupturing the amniotic membrane. Pitocin produces exceedingly strong contractions, and some researchers are now investigating whether there is a correlation between its use and the minimal brain dysfunction associated with learning-disabled children. Most physicians and couples now prefer to wait for natural labor whenever possible.

About 95 percent of fetuses approach birth with their heads first, the easiest position. In a breech birth the baby approaches either feetfirst or with its buttocks in the lower uterine segment. Sometimes babies will turn by themselves for a head-first presentation before the last month, but if this does not occur, the baby may not be able to fit through the birth canal. It is also possible for the baby to turn *out* of good position right before birth, and so it is always wise to be prepared for this occurrence.

When the baby is in poor birth position, cesarean section (so called because Caesar was so born) may be necessary. In this surgical procedure, an incision is made into the mother's abdomen, and the baby is removed without traveling down the birth canal. It is not true that once you have a cesarean section you must always have subsequent children that way also. This misunderstanding results from the fact that many women have cesareans not because of a baby's poor birth position, but because the width of the pelvis (through which the baby must pass) is too small. Some women, then, are too narrow to be able to birth children through the vagina, and these were some of the unfortunate women who, prior to cesarean sections, died in labor. The size of the baby is also a factor, since a woman might be large enough to accommodate a six- but not an eight-pound child. A physician can measure a woman's pelvis and inform her and her partner if there is likely to be a problem. This should be done prior to conception if possible.

Some women do not know whether or not they will need a cesarean until midlabor. Many factors determine the necessity of a cesarean section—size and shape of the pelvis, elasticity of the cartilage, size and position of the baby, and so on. Most obstetricians try to avoid cesareans if possible because of the physical trauma of the surgery and the increased risk of respiratory problems in the infant. But cesareans are much safer than a woman going through a very long and difficult labor, particularly when passing the baby is risky.

Recent advances in anesthesia have reduced the risks of cesareans for both mother and child. In fact, the death rate among C-sectioned mothers is less than one-tenth of what it was in the 1940s. Major complications, such as hemorrhages, infections, and blood clots, occur in about 6 percent of the cases. This is a deceptively low figure considering that cesareans are likely to be performed on women who are already in trouble. Approximately a third of cesarean mothers suffer some complications as a result of the surgery.

Some women are very disappointed about having needed a cesarean. Listen to Ann: "I feel like I missed something special—that I was cheated, that I didn't do the real thing." Not everyone agrees, however. Karen, a mother and nurse, had the following to say: "When you think about it rationally, a cesarean is the best way to have a baby. You can plan when you want to do it in advance. You don't get the ripping and vaginal tearing that hurts so many women. The whole procedure is clean, relatively safe, and predictable." Most women remain conscious throughout the cesarean, and now husbands are usually permitted to attend the birth as well. While the woman cannot see the surgery, she can hear everything going on and can hold her baby right after it is born.

The average hospital stay in uncomplicated cases is four to eight days. Full recovery to normal energy levels can take six weeks or longer. Since the percentage of cesareans has increased three times over the past decade (cesareans now comprise almost 15 percent of all births), the number of support groups has also increased to nearly 100 throughout the country.

The Second Stage of Labor.   During the second stage of labor the baby passes through the vagina. This stage lasts 45 minutes to 1 hour for an average first birth. It is often the most difficult and painful stage in which the woman must push the baby from her body. If anesthesia is used, it is usually administered prior to or during the second stage. The speed of delivery through this stage has much to do with the size and position of the baby, the condition of the woman's body, how alert the woman is during birth, her body position, and her anxiety levels. The baby is actually expelled from the vagina with considerable force. Sometimes if the baby is coming too slowly or if a problem is occurring, doctors may use forceps, a tong-shaped device that grips the baby's head and pulls him or her through the canal. Upon delivery, newborns are not held upside down, shaken, or spanked!

In vaginal births, the time when the baby's head first appears is called *crowning.* Many physicians then perform an *episiotomy,* an incision between the vagina and the anus (along the perineum) to reduce tearing and stretching of the vaginal skin and muscle. After birth, the incision is sewn up, and the stretching of the vagina is minimal. Episiotomy is not preferred by all women, some claiming that it is painful, disfiguring, and unnecessary (details will be discussed later in the chapter).

The Third Stage of Labor. The third stage of labor and birth occurs after the baby has been delivered. The uterine contractions expel the placenta (afterbirth), usually 15 minutes after the baby. In order to control bleeding, the umbilical cord is then tied and cut, hence the belly button. A suction tube dislodges any material in the lungs, mouth, and nose that might make breathing more difficult. A Vitamin K shot to speed up clotting is usually given, and, by law, silver nitrate or a similar sort of compound must be put in the baby's eyes (otherwise, if the mother had gonorrhea, blindness might result).

The newborn baby can be a startling sight to many unprepared parents who are expecting their infant to look like the "Gerber baby." Most pictures of "newborns" are really infants a month or even older. Some studies have found that pregnant women often fantasize their newborn looking three to four months old. As a baby comes out, it is frequently bluish before it has taken its first breath (after which it turns bright red!) One father, present at his son's birth, had not been prepared. "When I saw that blue head," he remembered, "I almost went down like an elephant! I thought for sure he was dead." Usually, the child's head is misshapen (molded), because it is soft and has been shaped by passage through the birth canal. This condition is only temporary and will straighten out naturally. Laughed a woman looking at her newborn, "When she was born she looked like her head had been through a pencil sharpener!"

At birth, the infant is covered with mucus, blood, and a white, cheesy paste called "vernix" that protects the infant's skin. Genitalia are very large (it is normal!). The child is mostly head (it's one third of the body!) and often thin, even scrawny, in appearance. Many have hair on their heads, some even on their bodies, but it usually falls off in the first few days (the color is not necessarily the same as the hair that will come in later). Black babies are relatively light-skinned (they will darken gradually) and, like Caucasian and Oriental infants, have blue eyes that will darken over the first six months of life. For the first hour after birth newborns are especially alert and responsive. Parents who are able to share this time with the infant often find it to be a powerful experience.

The Pain of Childbirth

How painful is childbirth? Is it so excruciating as to be fit punishment for Eve's greatest of all sins? It seems that there are many differences, individually and culturally, in how both women and men respond to childbirth. One woman told us that it was the most painful experience of her life and hoped she would never have to go through it again. Another said, "It was fantastic, like a great orgasm. I can't wait to have another." Women who have menstrual problems (irregularity, light blood flow, cramping) are more likely to report pain during birth, but this is a very general finding. Cultural differences are as profound as individual ones. While Victorian ladies spent months recovering after birth, slaves in the fields kept right on working. It appears that active women, even those who continue their activity through labor, have easier births than do more sedentary women.

The father's experiences during childbirth are also variable. Margaret Mead describes the Arapesh people's birth customs: In a separate hut, the father-to-be goes through the motions of an excruciating, vicarious childbirth, while the laboring mother has the baby quietly and with minimum discomfort. In other cultures fathers behave in a disinterested manner, are frequently absent from the event, and treat the whole process with the disdain accorded "woman matters." Obviously, we will all respond differently, often unpredictably, depending on hundreds of factors related to both our present and past experiences.

Of comfort to expectant parents should be the fact that never before has birth been safer for mother and child, and never before have prospective parents had so much choice and control over the birth experience.

BIRTH OPTIONS

If and when you are ready to select a birth style, you will have to consider at least seven factors: (1) the procedures to be used, (2) the kinds and amounts of drugs to be employed, (3) the nondrug pain-control techniques practiced, (4) inclusion of the father and/or significant others during the delivery, (5) home birth versus hospital delivery, (6) the use of midwives, and (7) the treatment of the family following the birth.

Procedures Used

Three routine procedures are debated by many women and doctors: enemas, shaving of the pubic hair, and episiotomies. An enema and shaving have traditionally been employed prior to delivery in order to reduce the risk of infection, but many women claim that the procedures are humiliating, uncomfortable, and unnecessary. Many obstetricians now recommend a mini-prep (or "poodle cut") that involves trimming only the longer pubic hairs.

The episiotomy procedure is more controversial. An incision between the vagina and the anus (along the perineum) is made to reduce tearing of the vaginal skin and muscle when the baby passes through. After birth, the incision is sewn up, and the vaginal stretching is minimized. Sometimes the vagina can be, inadvertently or purposely, tightened. One mother confessed afterward, "I felt like a virgin again!" (Her husband agreed wholeheartedly.) Yet many people oppose the routine use of episiotomies. For one thing, the healing of the incision is slow and often more painful than birth recovery itself. One mother who did not have one told me, "Here I am, walking around, feeling great. Look at them," she said, pointing to two women who were walking slowly, with great pain on their faces. "Episiotomies! They're worse than anything natural!" Other women claim episiotomies are "men operations" and see them as disfiguring and humiliating. "Our bodies were meant to have babies," said one feminist. "It is a male hangup if they don't like a little stretching. If doctors took more time during birth, vaginal tearing wouldn't happen so often, anyway." If midwives are present during delivery, they sometimes massage and manually stretch the vagina to minimize tearing and possibly avoid an episiotomy.

Many doctors and midwives recommend muscle-tightening exercises that keep the vaginal muscles strong, elastic, and quickly reconditionable after birth. (They also are great during intercourse!) One such exercise involves tightening the vaginal muscles, holding them for a second, and then letting them go. Start by doing several a day (anytime—they are invisible to others) and increase gradually. To test whether you are using the right muscles, spread your legs apart while you are urinating and stop the flow. These are the muscles you are strengthening.

People who want nonmedicated births ought to be assured that if an anesthetic is employed for an episiotomy, the birth is still considered natural. Usually, the physician injects a local anesthetic into the perineum, and this may be done for women who use no other medications. Since this sort of anesthetic is simple, effective, and virtually free of maternal or fetal complications, there is little reason to endure the pain of a nonanesthetized episiotomy.

Obstetrical Drugs

Obstetrical drugs have been in routine use since the mid-1800s (Queen Victoria modeled this approach with the birth of Prince Leopold). It has been estimated that women are given medications in 95 percent of all labors and deliveries in the United States. In recent years, however, the medical community has opted for the minimum amount of drugs necessary for the relief of pain and anxiety. Recent studies are suggesting that obstetric medication may have long-term effects on children's behavior.

The Effects of Obstetrical Drugs. A large-scale study by Dr. Yvonne Brackbill and Sarah Broman of the National Institute of Neurological and Communicative Disorders and Stroke is examining data on over 3000 healthy full-term babies born in the 1950s. They selected only the healthiest women and least complicated pregnancies and births. Still, they found that obstetric medication affected the children's behavior through at least seven years of age, and the degree of impairment was related directly to the size of the drug dosages and strength of the drugs employed during labor. The impairments were most marked in gross motor ability (the children were delayed in sitting, standing, and walking) and intellectual functioning (they cried more persistently, did not stop responding to repetitive stimuli, and were delayed in language development).

We should mention that this study is now under considerable attack by many notable researchers for having been released prematurely and mishandled statistically (the statistician for the project, John Bartko of N.I.M.H., has disassociated himself from the study because his advice was not followed). The major substantive criticism is that the analysis did not ensure that it was the same children who were retarded in their development over the seven-year period. It could be that different children had problems at different times, most or all of which were temporary. If so, it would scarcely support there being long-term effects attributable to the use of obstetric medications.

The amount and use of drugs is one of the most major parent–child conflicts experienced for some prospective parents. The frightened, pain-sensitive mother must compromise between her needs and those of the infant. As throughout, we emphasize the need for compromise. While minimal drug use is advisable, so is maternal relief. Each of us has a different tolerance level for pain, and each experiences different amounts of birth discomfort depending on hundreds of factors, many of which cannot be predicted beforehand. Women who wish to forgo medication should not make their suffering a test of their womanhood. Drug use should remain an available option, and because of the variability in types and dosages, the use of medication should not be viewed as an "all or nothing" decision. There are many degrees in between. The best compromise is to use as little medication as you and your doctor feel necessary and to discuss the different kinds of drugs available beforehand so you can use the ones most suitable for you. What is essential is a clear understanding with your obstetrician on who controls when and if you get drugs and under what conditions.

Types of Drugs. To clearly understand the drug options prior to birthing, it is wise to be knowledgeable about the types of drugs used to relieve obstetrical pain. The following drugs represent some of the more common types of obstetric medications; let's find out when they are used and what they do for you:

Sedatives and Narcotics. During the start of labor, mothers are sometimes given barbiturates, even tranquilizers, if they are frightened or very anxious. Because these drugs may affect the fetus and make the mother feel "out of it," they are used carefully and in low dosages.

Narcotics, like Demerol, are sometimes used but usually not until labor is quite active since they may slow the progress of labor. While they decrease a mother's fear and anxiety by reducing discomfort and encouraging relaxation, they have a peak effect on the infant about two hours after administration. Thus, they are given well before delivery so as not to affect the baby during its stressful transition to the outside world.

Paracervical and Epidural Blocks. For complete relief of pain (not partial as by sedatives and narcotics) paracervical and epidural blocks are used. They may have pronounced effects on infant development. They permit the mother to be awake, but will eliminate the urge to "bear down" during the second stage of labor. They also require skill and experience to administer properly. Be sure to discuss your doctor's preference with him or her.

For a paracervical block the drug is injected in the lower part of the uterus so as to relieve pain during the first part of labor but not during the second and third stage. Another procedure is used later on for delivery, which blocks pain very well, within three to five minutes after injection and lasts one to two hours. While maternal complications are rare with the paracervical block (it may stop labor if given too early), there is a 10 percent incidence of the fetal heart rate becoming arrhythmic (called *bradycardia*).

An epidural block is not administered until active labor begins (it will slow labor if given too soon); it is considered the "ultimate" in pain relief. The drug is injected in the lower back and provides relief within three to five minutes. There may be a drop in maternal blood pressure, so it is carefully monitored. (If you have low blood pressure, be sure to tell your doctor.) Epidurals in no way interfere with body mobility or awareness—just with pain.

Spinal Blocks.   During delivery spinal blocks are the most common anesthetic procedures used and are more powerful than the procedures listed previously. The low spinal block (saddle block) is very short-acting (half hour to 45 minutes) and low dosage. The mother can still wiggle her toes; it is called a saddle block because it numbs only the lower portion of the pelvic area (like a saddle). However, it often produces a headache later on, so mothers are advised not to elevate their heads for six to eight hours after delivery. This procedure is used almost exclusively for obstetrics, so that anesthesiologists associated with obstetrical units are likely to have the most experience and skill in administering appropriate dosages.

The surgical block is much longer lasting (four hours) and is a higher dosage than the saddle block. It affects considerably more of the body. One of its main advantages is that the mother can remain conscious during a cesarean section.

The pudendal block numbs the perineum (the line between the vagina and the anus) so that there is no pain in this area during delivery and episiotomy (if performed). It is not used very frequently because while it eliminates the urge to bear down, it does not eliminate the pain of labor contractions. It is also tricky to give and has a higher rate of inadequate anesthesia than the other methods mentioned.

General Anesthetics. The use of inhaled, general anesthesia in obstetrics is increasingly rare because it usually results in reduction of awareness and participation, infant depression, long postpartum recovery, and nausea and vomiting (it is one of the foremost causes of maternal death). It may still be employed when necessitated by certain serious obstetrical problems.

Nondrug Pain-Reducing Techniques

These techniques can be used alone or in conjunction with the drugs previously described. As with medications, it is not "all or nothing"—some women find the techniques more effective than others. Data indicate that prepared parents usually require less medication than others and that they are less likely to feel out of control during labor. These techniques are taught in hospitals and through various societies throughout the world. A good coach–supporter is very helpful—it can be your partner, mother, best friend, nurse, midwife, or anyone who is reliable, dependable, and to whom you can turn, with confidence, for support.

The Dick-Read Method. In 1932, an Englishman, Grantly Dick-Read, developed procedures aimed at reducing tension and anxiety that interfere with labor. One of his procedures was a set of physical exercises (including squatting, pelvic rocking, and sitting) designed to improve circulation and flexibility in the lower body. Another procedure was alteration of breathing patterns. There were four patterns designed to be timed with different phases of labor. The first stage of labor required deep breaths for relaxation, and then more rapid breathing during contractions (25 breaths per minute). When pushing, breath-holding was recommended and, during delivery, panting (40 breaths per minute). (We know now that panting can produce severe hyperventilation that can be unpleasant for mother and fetus, so care is taken not to overdo it.) If you have seen a cat or dog birth, you know that panting is precisely what these animals do in labor.

Dick-Read also advocated deep muscle relaxation training (contracting and relaxing each part of the body separately). He also advocated "the three P's" (patience, peacefulness, and personal interest) and "the three C's" (confidence, concentration, and cheerfulness).

The Lamaze Method (Psychoprophylaxis). Dr. Fernand Lamaze, a French obstetrician, believed that the best way to reduce discomfort was to learn to do something else other than responding to the sensation as painful. The techniques are taught by members of the American Society for Psychoprophylaxis in Obstetrics (ASPO).

Like the Dick-Read procedures, Lamaze methods emphasize breathing patterns as an alternative response to feeling pain. Shallow, fast breathing is to be done during contractions and is practiced during the last weeks of pregnancy. During the first part of labor, slow breathing is recommended, then expansion of the abdomen during active labor. Mothers learn to place pressure on their spines to reduce abdominal and back pain during the stronger contractions. The mother is also taught to relax her muscles by half-sitting, with her knees over a pillow.

Combined Techniques. Many organizations such as the International Childbirth Education Association use a combination of the above-mentioned techniques. They sponsor group instruction and education throughout the world.

Hypnosis. Hypnosis may shorten the first stage of labor by two to three hours and may be a very effective technique for some women. About 40 to 50 percent of women prepared prior to labor can be successfully hypnotized. It is a good idea to test your responsiveness to hypnosis before or during the early stages of pregnancy to see how effective it is for you. If you wish to employ it, you will need your hypnotist present during the actual delivery and a relatively nondistracting environment. Be sure to discuss this option with your doctor and see if she or he and the staff would be supportive.

Acupuncture.   Used by the Chinese for centuries, acupuncture was quite a rage in the late 1960s but has fallen into disfavor because it did not perform the miracles attributed to it. Nevertheless, it can be very effective in reducing, even eliminating, pain. Dr. Louis Chertoff attended three operations in Canton, China—a gallbladder removal, a delivery, and brain surgery—and witnessed the patients talking and moving throughout the procedures. No one is quite sure how acupuncture works, nor why postoperative pain is more pronounced and lasts longer than when anesthesia is used. If you are interested in exploring this option, talk with your physician and get reputable names of people in your area who will work with you and your obstetrician. You may wish to consider this option before or immediately after getting pregnant since many physicians may not be cooperative, and since many patients do not respond well to acupuncture.

The Presence of Others during the Birth

Until recently, fathers were excluded from the birth process. Listen to Phil, age 33, father of two children, ages 12 and 8:

> I remember it so clearly that I still get furious thinking about it. When we got to the hospital, a nurse came out and said, "She's ready," and off she went, with my wife, through a white wall that turned into a door. I started to follow, but the nurse came back, snatched the bag with my wife's things out of my hands and said, "You're not allowed past this door," and out she went. Well, I stood there, confused and scared, waiting for someone to tell me what to do. No one came. After an hour or so, I wandered around until I finally asked someone what I was supposed to do. "Go home," she said, so I did—and waited and waited. Finally I got drunk and read *Playboy* and that's what I was doing when my baby was born.

In October of 1964, the California Board of Health adopted a rule permitting fathers to be present at the birth. Illinois followed in 1967, but state regulations still vary considerably. (Be sure to check yours by calling your state attorney general's office, the state medical society, or asking your doctor.) It wasn't until 1974 that the American College of Obstetricians and Gynecologists supported the husband's remaining with the woman in labor (given agreement by the attending physician).

Why the reluctance? First, there was concern of infection. But in more than 45,000 husband-attended births surveyed by the International Childbirth Education Association, not one infection or malpractice suit was attributed to paternal presence. Second, medical staff was concerned that a nonessential person would get in the way of the experienced staff, especially if he became overwrought. However, studies have found that although fathers are nonessential to the birth, they are useful in reducing fear and promoting an easier labor and delivery.

Third, there was and is concern for the emotional reactions men may experience during labor and delivery. But most studies have found that participating fathers rate their experience as a father more positively than those who did not participate in the birth. However, participation may be a result, not a cause, of these feelings. We do not think fathers ought to be pressured to attend. Some may feel helpless and guilty, watching a loved one undergo the strong feelings of birth. One man told us, "My wife was fine, but I was crying like a child. I couldn't stand to see her go through that!" The birth can evoke the ambivalence associated with having impregnated the wife and elicit conflict between the feelings of not going through birth directly—"I'm sure glad that's not me," and "It's not fair I can never experience that."

Home Birth versus Hospital Delivery

Planned home births comprise about 19 percent of all births in the United States. Proponents argue that 94 percent of all births are normal and need minimal medical care. They say an ambulance, or specially prepared car, can be standing by in case of an emergency. They claim that hospitals are for sickness and that birth is not a disease. Furthermore, they point out that those countries with the lowest birth mortality rates (the Scandinavian countries) almost always have home births or special birth clinics with midwives in attendance. However, the Scandinavian countries are set up for home births and have years of experience. They have extensive, government-subsidized prenatal care and are better able to predict and prepare for possible difficulties.

On the other side are those who claim that now couples can pretty much design their own birth in a hospital, with the benefit of modern technology as nature's backup. Opponents say that birth complications may arise very suddenly and require emergency action within a few minutes. An ambulance is not fast or reliable enough in many cases, such as when the fetus becomes entangled in the umbilical cord, cutting off oxygen. One experienced nurse told me, "Frankly, a hospital is the last place in the world I'd want to be sick in, but it's the only place in which I'd have a baby."

The American College of Obstetricians and Gynecologists warns that having a home birth is two to five times riskier to an infant's life than is a hospital birth. This data has been collected from 11 state health departments. The major risk of home delivery is still-birth, *especially when attendants are untrained.* (This is an important qualification, since no professional is likely to recommend a home birth without trained attendants present.)

In some states planned home births are illegal. While some people feel this is an infringement of their freedom to select a compatible birth style, others feel it is a restriction necessary to ensure or increase the chances for a healthy baby. Most people are cautious about giving birth at home, particularly when it is the first child (labor is usually prolonged and complications less predictable), or when there is a family history of birthing problems. Certainly, home births require careful planning, preparation, and backup services in case of problems. Special care must also be given to your partner's feelings, since home births can produce considerable anxiety, require additional behaviors, and if something should go awry, result in enormous guilt feelings.

Many hospitals are now providing special services for birth, such as alternative birth rooms, that are furnished in an apartmentlike fashion suited to a family's needs. Some allow your other children (depending upon age) to attend. Others offer special 24-hour services that allow the mother and child to go home almost immediately after birth (barring complications, of course). You should check the maternity resources and rules of the hospitals with which your doctor is affiliated. A good idea is to make sure they do a lot of deliveries (so their equipment and staff are adequate), have a neonate intensive care unit (in case of problems), and have an attending neonatologist or pediatrician who checks the infant immediately after birth.

The Use of Midwives

Another consideration is whether you wish to employ a midwife. Many couples lack a community to help them through the birth experience. All too frequently they view their doctors as too busy to be supportive and to answer questions that may seem silly or ignorant. Most people (not just pregnant women) find it very difficult to be assertive with their physicians. Even the most argumentative among us may be cowed into silence by a doctor's directives. "After all," as one doctor said, "I spent 10 years studying medicine and another 15 practicing it. You can't expect me to teach every one of my patients what I know." Also, many of us don't want to think when our health is in jeopardy. We don't want to entertain the idea that doctors are human and may not be absolutely certain of their decisions. We often insist that they assume the Marcus Welby role so that they can minimize our own fears. Listen to Tara, a psychologist: "Ordinarily, I am assertive, even difficult. But when I was sick last year, suddenly I was like a child. 'Yes, doctor,' I said meekly to everything. I never questioned his judgment or asked for a second opinion. If he had doubts, I didn't want to hear about them. I just turned myself over to him and in effect said, 'Take care of me.'"

The consumer–patient is a relatively new concept in the United States. The fact that couples have birth-style options forces them into a difficult situation for which there are few models. Most physicians have their biases, as do we all. At what point is the doctor being prejudiced and at what point is she or he delivering informed and competent medical advice? Who is in a position to tell the difference? While some people approach birth as meekly as Tara approached illness, others have become overly aggressive. One physician told us the following story:

This woman came to see me last week. She was six months pregnant. She knew exactly what she wanted me to do and when. It was all written down. She had read everything, she said. She didn't want an episiotomy, she didn't want an enema, she didn't want bright lights—she went on and on. I asked her if I could get some information about her so I could decide what procedures ought to be followed. She said I was a consultant—*she* made the decisions. I had to justify every procedure at length. Finally I said maybe she would be happier going to medical school than having a baby.

One of the functions served by a midwife is that of an intermediary between the couple and the physician. She helps them communicate their desires and preferences to the doctor and is their advocate through labor. She protects the parents' interests and supplies the kind of support for which many doctors do not have the time. You ought to seriously consider a midwife if any of the following situations are applicable to you:

You have difficulty telling your doctor what you are feeling.

You are embarrassed to ask your doctor questions.

You often leave a doctor's office confused and depressed.

You rarely understand what the doctor is talking about and can't get him or her to clarify what she or he is saying.

You often worry about something after you've left the office but can't bring yourself to call and bother the doctor about it.

You are suspicious of doctors in general. Even two opinions do not ease your feelings of distrust.

You believe doctors are trained so as to make it impossible for them to deal with you as an intelligent and responsible person.

You make doctors uneasy by the number of difficult questions you ask.

You want more information on medical decisions than doctors are willing to give you.

You want a lot of support and reassurance.

Of course, if you find it very difficult to communicate with a particular physician, why are you using him or her? This personality conflict in no way reflects a physician's competence, just a style of interacting with you, for what works well for one couple can be disastrous for another. We recommend selecting and meeting with an obstetrician *before* you are pregnant. If you don't communicate well, or share viewpoints, shop around before you are under time pressure. Pregnancy and birth are much more assuring when you have a knowledgeable, sympathetic professional with you throughout.

Many people believe midwives are far more capable than the role of intermediary permits. Some midwives are certified by the American College of Nurse Midwives. They are permitted to deliver babies without being under the direct supervision of a physician, but the obstetrician must be within summoning distance. In some states, midwives are lobbying extensively for the right to provide full birthing care. Some physicians, however, are very hostile to the notion. Said one, "This is absurd. Who in her right mind would want someone other than a physician?" On the other hand, a midwife told me, "We are highly skilled. I am a nurse and I hate to tell you how many babies I've delivered myself in hospitals. We can give women support and help. We haven't been trained to monopolize the experience, but to guide it. The use of doctors in normal deliveries is a waste of training for the doctor and of nature for the woman. Midwives and doctors can work together for the benefit of everyone."

How You Are Treated after the Birth

The selection of a birth style extends into the period following birth, which is sometimes called the fourth stage of labor. There are a variety of ways of handling a newborn, depending on the health of the infant and the parents and how the parents feel about the postbirth experience. Further, many theorists believe that the basic source of human sorrow is birth trauma—that is, the horror and confusion we experience when we are thrust from the womb. The garden of Eden could be a symbolic uterus. Many people love warm water and sleep on their sides, their legs drawn up. Some kill themselves by climbing in a tub and slitting their wrists.

A French doctor, named Frederick LeBoyer, observed that the transition from the womb to the outside world could be made less abrupt and frightening. He suggested a "nonviolent birth" in which the baby should be placed in warm water and on the mother's belly, that the cord be cut after it has naturally withered—in short, that the whole procedure be reverent and soothing to mother and child.

This method sounds very reasonable, but some doctors protest. The lights are bright, they explain, because it is important for doctors to see what's going on; no one is purposely torturing a newborn. The traditional routine has been designed for maximum safety, and a minimum amount of discomfort is a small price to pay. Others disagree. They claim that birth trauma *is* important, not a mere discomfort. They believe the kind of birth we have influences the kind of person we become.

Data are being gathered now to see whether babies born nonviolently grow up to be less aggressive than babies born in the usual way. (The problem, of course, is that nonviolent people would tend to want LeBoyer's method, but the research can be controlled by matching a control group on some sort of violence measure.) Preliminary data from France indicate that LeBoyer babies do seem to be more gentle, and data also point to the surprising findings that many LeBoyer babies are developmentally advanced and ambidextrous.

We do know that infants at birth are far more responsive to their environment than previously believed. All their senses are working (though hearing may be muffled by mucus clogging the ear passages), and researchers have demonstrated that newborns can learn relatively complex tasks within a few hours after birth. For example, newborns can learn to turn their head to the right when a buzzer is sounded. Even more remarkable, they can learn to turn to the right at the sound of a buzzer and to the left when a clicking noise is made. And more remarkable yet, within ten trials (or times) after they have learned this, they can learn to reverse it and turn left to the buzzer and right to the clicker!

Additionally, evidence is mounting to support the amazing fact that newborns prefer to look at a human face when given a choice between a series of similar facelike shapes. (Researchers infer "preference" by measuring the relative amounts of time babies look at paticular forms.) We used to think babies looked at human faces only because their visual systems were particularly sensitive to contrast and complexity. However, newborns prefer ordinary human faces to those with scrambled features as well as to those similar shapes with more contrast and more complex details. No one yet knows why and how babies do this.

Some researchers are looking into how and when the bond between the baby and the parents is formed. They want to know if there is a certain very sensitive time after birth during which the strength of the parent–infant attachment is at its greatest. Obviously, if there is a certain time limit, we would not want to separate the family past this point, unless it were necessary for survival. Proponents of natural childbirth techniques believe that the mother's being alert during labor enables her to touch and see her baby immediately, thus strengthening the bond. Others go even further and suggest bonding may be increased by having the baby and parents stay together for some time after birth (as opposed to having the baby immediately removed to a crib or nursery).

There are problems with the bonding theory. For example, it is very difficult to define this "bond" in some observable or measurable way, so that you can see who has how much of it. And, even if you could define it well, you would have to control for many factors that influence the ways mothers feel about their babies, so you could look only at the effects of the amount of time mother and child were separated after birth.

It may have also occurred to you that we haven't yet talked about father–child attachments. This bond has been studied even less. The tendency of men to engage in eye contact with newborns has been called "paternal engrossment" rather than attachment (attachment for some unknown reason, seems to be reserved for mothers only!). Some data from Sweden indicated that fathers who spent thirty minutes with their newborns played more with them when they were three months old than fathers who did not—but, of course, there are many other plausible explanations for this difference.

Another assumption has been that the response of a parent to a newborn is somehow different from the response of other humans (perhaps even children). Again, this may or may not be so. All of these problems do not mean that the whole question of infant attachment is unanswerable—only that no one has yet answered it.

Certainly, regardless of theory, many parents enjoy and cherish time with their baby right after birth. It seems reasonable to want to enjoy this first opportunity to communicate with your child. The father (or significant other) can hold the child with the mother, helping her catch her breath. Studies have also found that when parents are left alone with the baby, the mother stays awake and alert after birth longer than when the baby is removed.

The handling and interaction of baby and parents, and parents with each other and the baby, can be facilitated by having support around during the first few days. In hospitals where doctors and administrators cooperate with parents having access to their newborns, parents seem happier and less anxious when they go home. On the other hand, a 1970 hospital survey reported that only 30 percent of U.S. hospitals allowed mothers into the nurseries, and only 40 percent of these allowed mothers to touch their infants other than at feedings. Our advice is that you investigate the hospital policies in your area before you commit yourselves to a birthing procedure you may resent.

SELECTING A BIRTH STYLE

We can look at the birth experience as a blueprint, behaviorally, for the kind of interaction between family members that is likely to follow. It establishes a pattern that may continue for years to come, particularly if the parents are not aware of what they are feeling and why. When we try to avoid dealing with certain problems, we tend to develop elaborate strategies for continuing to avoid dealing with them, and the longer the problems go on, the more convoluted our reactions may become. By considering the style of birth you and your partner think you want before you are pregnant, you can learn a lot about how you both really feel about yourselves and a baby, and you can anticipate problems before they arise. You may want to reconsider parenting when you picture a more realistic, less fantasized or fearful, birth scene. You might wish to try the following exercise. We suggest that you take the time to write the questions and your answers so that you might more easily review changes and differences in attitudes.

Some Questions about the Ideal Birth Experience

What, for you as a mother, would be the ideal birth experience? Describe it in as much detail as you can. Where are you, who is with you, how are you reacting, and how is each person with you reacting? How long is the experience lasting? Is your partner present? What is he doing and saying? How does the baby react after birth? What do you feel? How are the people present treating you afterward? As a father, describe in equal detail what the ideal birth experience would be for you. Where are you, and what role are you playing? How involved are you in the birth? How do you see yourself responding both to yourself and to the others present before and after the birth?

The purpose of all this fantasizing is to find out exactly what and how compatible both of your birth scripts are. Scripting is a term that refers to the pattern of responses we desire or expect in certain circumstances. Birthing is a major event in our culture (and in many others!), and both men and women may bring powerful and elaborate scripts with them. As a consequence, we can disappoint each other and ourselves by not knowing each other's, and our own, expectations. We can play a script that is shared by both of us but may be destructive to the baby, or we may blindly act out a half-understood scenario that cheats us from experiencing the reality of the situation.

This is not to say that scripts ought to be eliminated. They are very useful in that they may help fill a "behavior vacuum." In new and emotionally powerful situations, scripts provide us with structure, with goals—in short, with behaviors that are acceptable to us and hopefully others. Manners, for example, are social scripts that grease (so to speak) social intercourse. We believe that the success of the relaxation and pain-reducing techniques we described (in childbirth and out) is in part due to their supplying us with something well rehearsed and acceptable instead of leaving us overwhelmed by the power of the moment. Therefore, the aim is to have a script that is useful to you—that is, not impossible or foreign to how you have behaved in the past—and one that will provide you with structure, purpose, and achievement.

Keeping this discussion in mind, as a woman think about the following questions:

1. *Will you behave during birth according to your ideal experience?* Is it realistic, given either your previous experiences or the information you have read in this book? At the end of labor, do you picture yourself looking as lovely as a movie star? Is your behavior consonant with you, or have you portrayed yourself as someone else? For example, do you see yourself as stoic and considerate—a modern Melanie from *Gone With the Wind,* lying in agony and saying to your husband, "Are you all right, dear?"—when you are, in fact, timid and more likely to want assurance than to give it? What are your pain thresholds, and is your ideal experience in keeping with how you have behaved in the past?

How do you respond to pain in your genital and pelvic area? Does it hurt to have a Pap smear or a regular gynecological exam? If you have had an abortion, or a D & C, or an IUD inserted or removed, was it more painful than you imagined it would be? How calm and controlled are you in situations in which you are in pain? Do you, like many, tend to attack others when you are hurting? (A man bangs his head and kicks the cat, or a woman gets a headache and screams at her children.)

If you tend to push people away when you are hurting and to become irritable and testy, it may not be wise for you and others to expect you to be totally different. This is not to say you should expect, and permit, yourself to be a screaming shrew in labor, but rather that you can prepare for behaving differently by practicing alternative scripts that are acceptable *and* attainable by you.

You may be a different sort of person—one who tends to require support and concern when you are in pain. You may need to be held and comforted. In the dentist's office you squeeze the nurse's hand or ask your partner to come in with you. If you tend to behave this way, is it fair to expect yourself to be independent and self-reliant during birth? Are you trying to prove something that doesn't need proving?

Now read over your idealized birth experience in terms of your past behavior. Given what we have discussed, is your idealized experience a useful script? If not, càn you rewrite it so that it is still an ideal, but one you can at least approximate? How would you feel if the experience does not go as you want it to? It may help you to remind yourself that the primary goals of birth are good health for you and the baby. Everything else is secondary.

2. *Will your partner behave during birth according to your ideal experience?* Are you being fair and realistic to him? Or is your script unlikely to occur? One woman told me, "Until I did this, I never realized how romantic I thought birth should be. I would hate to go into labor expecting my husband to behave the way I would like. He hasn't been romantic in ten years—why should he start now?" Just as you should not expect yourself to behave in ways foreign to you, neither should you expect your partner to behave in ways foreign to him.

Now, as a man, ask these same questions:

1. *Will you behave during birth according to your ideal experience?* Is it realistic? One father told us that his experience was a nightmare. He cried for 12 hours and, after the birth, looked as though he had been the one birthing. He said later, "I should have known this would happen. I saw my sister die in a car accident years ago, and since then any sort of sickness in people terrifies me. We had talked about it, and both of us felt that birth wasn't a disease. I was looking forward to the experience and so was my wife, and yet when it happened, I was out of control."

The point to this story is that reason has its limits. It was one thing for the man to see films of birth, or imagine the birth abstractly, or to talk about birth as a healthy and natural process. It was, for him, another thing to be present while he watched his wife behave in ways reminiscent of his dying sister. We know that the responses of strong emotions and sensations are difficult to label. A woman in birth looks as though she is in pain (whether or not she labels her feelings as pain). Are you calm in these sorts of situations? Are you supportive, and positive, or does it "hurt me more than it hurts you"?

2. *Will your partner behave during birth according to your ideal experiences?* Is your script one in which she could not get the part? Can you revise it so that your ideals are more in line with her?

Comparing Scripts

Now both of you ought to look at your scripts together. Are they compatible? If not, how can you compromise your expectations so that both of you can look forward to a harmonious experience? Sometimes it takes a bit of doing. Randy and Susan were married for three years. Susan decided to have a home birth with a midwife. Randy didn't like the idea because he is suspicious of nontraditional approaches to anything. But he acknowledged his ignorance in the matter of birth and felt it was Susan's experience and decision. (If it had been up to him, she would be in a hospital, and he would be home getting drunk!) Instead, he participated in the home birth, which went beautifully. Mother and child were healthy and happy. However, afterward, Randy found himself resentful and angry. He himself was not sure why until, in therapy, we asked him about the birth of his daughter.

Randy: It was great watching her being born, catching her as she came out.

Therapist: You enjoyed the experience.

Randy: Well, not exactly. I mean, enjoy is a little strong. You don't enjoy seeing someone go through that.

Therapist: Through what?

Randy: You know—birth.

Therapist: Didn't you go through it too?

Randy: Me? I didn't—I mean it was her experience, not mine. I didn't feel anything. It was nice to watch.

Therapist: You were numb, just watching.

Randy: Yeah, I was. I was an actor, you know. I did what I was supposed to do.

Therapist: Who said what you were supposed to do?

Randy: They did, the biddies! The wife and the nurse bitch had it all worked out.

Therapist: And you were numb? You don't sound numb to me.

Randy: No, I was mad. But I was more scared than mad. I mean, they knew more. What could I say? The bitch!

Therapist: Who?

Randy: Both of them! They used me. I didn't have a chance. They took over!

Randy was actually surprised that he had been, and still was, angry about the birth. He had tried to play a script that wasn't right for him. While the helpful, supportive partner role is wonderful for many men, for Randy, it was a disaster because it emphasized his isolation and ignorance. However, he was so compliant that his wife misread him (and it was easy to!). She was delighted in thinking that his script and hers fit so well and was puzzled by his subsequent coolness.

How else could this have been handled? Had they done these exercises even before pregnancy, both would have seen that Randy very much wanted to either be passive or very actively involved in birth. He could have happily adapted to either style, but felt cheated and used by being active but directed. This communication exercise may have helped him articulate what he ended up saying in therapy, which was, "I really could have enjoyed it too, damn it! It could have been an experience for me, too, but Susan hogged it. There was enough to share!"

What does your approach to birth say about your feelings about becoming a parent? About your partner as a parent? In the previous example, Susan had set up a script for parenting that she was not aware of—"*I* will make the decisions, and you will do what I think best. And you'll like it, too!" What do your scripts say?

QUESTIONS TO ASK AN OBSTETRICIAN

The following are some suggested questions for both of you to ask an obstetrician on the first visit. Explain that you are planning to have a child and want to go through the entire pregnancy with someone you know. How well the obstetrician handles your concerns and how much he or she includes both of you is helpful in predicting how well he or she is likely to interact with you later on.

1. Is the doctor a member of the leading professional organizations (certified by the American Board of Obstetrics and Gynecology and/or a Fellow in the American College of Obstetricians and Gynecologists)? If you don't see plaques on the walls, ask.
2. What are the doctor's customary delivery and birth procedures?
3. How does the doctor feel about prepared birth? What anesthetics does he or she prefer? Does he or she routinely use

enemas and pubic shaving or does he or she prefer mini-preps? When does he or she recommend episiotomies?

4. Does the doctor have any objections to family presence during delivery? How does he or she feel about the LeBoyer method of treating the newborn?
5. Does the doctor work with midwives or assist at home births?
6. With what hospitals is the doctor affiliated? What differences are there between them? For example, do they have the same policies? Special alternative birth facilities? Intensive care nurseries? Staff pediatricians?
7. Does the hospital permit the parents to be with the baby immediately after birth? If so, for how long?
8. Can the father sleep in?
9. Can the parents have the infant with them for long periods of time while in the hospital?
10. Is there a tour of the hospital obstetrical facilities and, if not, can one be arranged? (You might want to look at more than one hospital.)
11. Under what conditions might labor be induced or amniocentesis recommended?
12. Under what conditions might one of the doctor's colleagues deliver the baby?
13. Is there provision for 24-hour a day coverage and emergency care?
14. If this is very definitely your last child, you may want to discuss the possibility of sterilization after the birth. How does the doctor proceed if this is the case? How would this affect your birth style and after-birth recovery?

SOME CONCLUDING THOUGHTS

It is important to re-emphasize that childbirth should not be seen as falling into one of two extremes: one in which you are "out cold" and the other in which you are "au naturel." In fact, very few women are now rendered unconscious during birth, and a so-called "natural" birth is not at all natural. Natural childbirth means birth with minimal or no medication, but it entails systematically learning new, positive responses, few of which are likely to occur naturally.

Birth styles actually fall on a continuum, and the choices available include where to have the baby, who will be with you, what kind and how much medication will be employed, what nondrug pain-control techniques will be used, and how you will be treated afterward. Regardless of your choice, the common, contemporary approach to childbirth is best summed up as "awake and prepared," which means that the woman is not so heavily drugged that she is unaware of what is happening or unable to participate. Childbirth preparation is very important because many women fear losing control over what is happening to them. High levels of anxiety sponsored by fear, ignorance, pain, and lack of support slow labor and are correlated with increased problems.

Some people (the exact number unknown) are so scared of birth that they avoid having children. If you have such feelings, perhaps you should do some additional reading, watch some childbirth films in your local hospital, and talk to others before you make a parenting decision. If you are still frightened, consider entering behavior therapy. Behavior therapists have been employing very successful fear-reducing techniques in many areas of human behavior, from fear of flying, dentists, and heights, to fears of sex, examinations, and animals. Most of the time, this sort of therapy is relatively quick and effective, and the bill will be paid for by most insurance companies if you go to a state-licensed psychologist (call your state psychological association or the Association for the Advancement of Behavior Therapy for reputable behavior therapists).

While some people avoid having children because they fear birth, others fear being childfree not because they want children but because they don't want to miss pregnancy and birth. The experience is seen as a way of connecting with some natural, biologically ordained cosmic order. "I was in love with being pregnant and giving birth," confessed one recent mother. "I just never thought about anything past that time. Having to care for a baby was a shock." A professional childfree woman mused, "I keep asking how I can deny myself this basic, female experience. Am I denying my womanhood, trying to be a man? Will I regret not having experienced this supposedly indescribable event?" There is no easy answer to this question. Men, of course, manage full lives, even though they don't bear children. So too, do women who are anesthetized or who don't have full vaginal births. And there are others who experience birth but who are not necessarily fulfilled by it afterward. Many women even prefer not experiencing it. A client once said, "Men like to mystify pregnancy and birth because it helps keep us in our place. I love babies, and birth may be necessary, but no one can convince me that it's pleasurable."

One illusion some people have about childbirth is that if a couple shares the experience, they will be much closer. The birth is seen as some sort of interpersonal glue that pastes together a real family out of what had been an unstable couple. Unfortunately, a good relationship through pregnancy and birth is more often a result than a cause of sharing and togetherness. Sometimes these events can and do seriously disrupt relationships.

One reason that partners may not experience togetherness during pregnancy and birth is that men are biologically excluded from the physical experience. There are ways around this obstacle, however. For example, men can take an active, not passive, role in the decision to parent. In addition, both partners can attend office visits and birth training and share reading material. The woman can describe the covert experiences of pregnancy as much as possible. The man can provide enormous amounts of support when the physiological effects become wearing and depressing. Helping with housework or a romantic cuddle can be very important. Both can participate in the decision making, and both can help each other over the predictable after-birth letdown. (For more details on postbirth depression, see chapter 7.)

Sometimes, women hoard the birth experience and are unwilling to allow the partner full participation. "It's my body," proclaimed one woman, to which her husband replied, "It may be, but it's *our* child!" Men who fail to be as assertive during this stage may "get even" at a later date. We have seen fathers systematically pit their children against the mother—and we have found that these fathers often report anger about being excluded from a major participative role during the early years.

Sometimes men do not want to be involved in pregnancy, birth, or even infancy. They view this role as "women's work" and are either disinterested or believe it unfitting for men. It is best to discuss this attitude before pregnancy because, if nonnegotiable, it can very profoundly affect the parenting experience.

Regardless of your approach to birth as an experience, it is not nearly as important as your approach to the end result—the baby. Even nine months of a novel experience—the quality of which, as we have seen, is variable—cannot compensate for the creation of a human being who is not wanted or inadequately cared for. Birth will not in and of itself provide meaning to your life. It is sometimes tempting to seek easy and biologically programmed answers to difficult questions, but these answers are rarely sufficient.

ADDITIONAL READINGS

Arms, Suzanne, *The Immaculate Deception.* Boston: Houghton Mifflin, 1975.

Elkinds, Valmai Howe, *The Rights of the Pregnant Parent.* Canada: Waxwing Productions, 1976.

Macfarlane, Aidan, "What a Baby Knows." *Human Nature* 1, no. 2 (Feb. 1978).

Phillips, Celeste R. and Joseph T. Anzalone, *Fathering: Participation in Labor and Birth.* St. Louis, Mo.: C. V. Mosby Co., 1978.

Smith, Manuel J., *Kicking the Fear Habit.* New York: Bantam Books, 1977.

3

Economic Considerations

In this chapter we examine the costs of parenting. In the first section we look at the conditions under which the costs vary and your role in determining these variations. We then summarize some of the expenses involved in prenatal and birth care, postbirth to public school, from age six to completion of high school, and from postsecondary education on. In the last section, we discuss what changes in your priorities and goals should be considered if you decide to parent. Throughout the chapter, we address both the direct and indirect costs involved so that you can better assess the impact of the economics of parenting upon your lifestyle and goals.

IMPORTANT PRINCIPLES TO BEAR IN MIND

The Industrial Revolution changed the economic relationship between parents and their children in some very significant ways. It heralded the transformation of children from economic investments to liabilities. The restrictions on child labor, the passing of the mandatory education act, and the erosion of family-determined occupations have increased the length of time children are dependent upon their families.

The decline in extended families has increased the time and energy demands of parenting while reducing the extent to which grown children contribute to the economic welfare of their parents. In short, children are costly and are becoming more so. It seems mercenary to think of children in economic terms, but as one mother sarcastically commented, "My husband sees me nursing a dollar sign, not a baby." Even those who do not wish to consider the worth of the parenting experience in dollars and cents should have a clear perception of what their children will economically require from them, and what they will have to do or forgo to fulfill these requirements.

The impact of many child-rearing costs can be attenuated with good fiscal planning and a realistic appraisal of your resources and priorities. And, equally important, you can consider the portion of your time and energy you want to allocate to economic gain and the portion you wish to dedicate to your family. This division of time and energy is a major source of conflict in many households. Working parents can find themselves so pulled between job, home, child, and spouse that there is nothing substantial to give to anyone!

Many parents find the expenses of child rearing unexpected and, as a result, are frequently unprepared and resentful. Also, couples sometimes fail to have realistic economic expectations of each other. If you come from different socioeconomic classes, dormant conflicts can arise in the presence of the increased economic demands of parenting.

In the following sections we will detail some of the minimum costs you can anticipate as the child develops. But before we begin, there are a number of important principles to bear in mind:

1. *Every cost entailed in parenting is variable.* While it is true that children require food, clothing, and shelter, there are enormous ranges in the kinds of food, clothing, and shelter provided. The style in which you elect to parent is one of the most important factors in the expense entailed. Jean Pennock, in a talk at the 47th Annual Agricultural Outlook Conference, put it this way: "What does it cost to raise a child? The answer to this question is another question —how much can you afford to spend?"

Because of the variability in costs, parenting expenses are best estimated by taking a percentage of your income. We have found that the more money parents have, the more (and greater percent!) they spend on their children. This percentage averages per child between 15 to 25 percent of most parents' income, excluding higher education costs.

There are more specific figures to consider. Carolyn Edwards, family economist, and Bruce Gray, mathematical statistician, have compiled for the Department of Agriculture some estimates on the cost of raising a farm child in 1977. Please keep in mind that farm-child costs are the lowest in the country. Furthermore, location is important—the same lifestyle can cost you 30 percent more on the East or West Coast than in the Midwest. And these costs are based on stable currency. Given our current inflation rates, the costs may actually double, even triple, over 18 years! And they do not include birth, special needs, or private education. Estimates of the cost of raising a farm child from birth to age 18 in 1977 dollars are:

$27,000—Thrifty Level
$38,700—Low Level
$58,700—Moderate Level
$88,500—Liberal Level

2. *Many "hidden costs" are involved in parenting.* Living in a neighborhood with a good school system can increase your monthly payments 25 to 50 percent. If your electric, heat, and hot water bills cost you $200 a month now, a child will raise the cost to around $250. There are missed opportunity costs that are more difficult to quantify—the refused relocation, the procrastinated investment, the risk untaken, the burden of a second job. These "hidden costs" may generate more resentment than any actual cost outlay.

3. *Each subsequent child costs more, but the percentage increment gets progressively smaller.* In fact, costs per child in five-child families average 20 to 24 percent below costs in two-child families; standards may be lower and many fixed expenses (car, home, insurance) are·shared. These fixed costs mean that a childfree couple can live as well as a typical family of four by earning, not one-half, but two-thirds as much. Table 3-1 lists the costs associated with different family types in an urban setting.

4. *What parents "give up" economically for their children varies not only with income, but also with priorities and preferences.* One mother of six told us, "I have to honestly say that our kids never stopped us from doing anything. If we wanted to travel, we piled them in the car and off we went." Contrast this with the mother of five who said, "The only kind of vacation we could afford was camp-

TABLE 3-1 ANNUAL CONSUMPTION BUDGETS FOR FAMILY TYPES, URBAN UNITED STATES; 1977 (IN DOLLARS)

FAMILY SIZE, TYPE, AND AGE	LOWER LEVEL	INTERMEDIATE LEVEL	HIGHER LEVEL
Single person, under 35 years:	$3,030	$4,560	$6,280
Husband and wife under 35 years:			
No children	4,240	6,390	8,790
1 child under 6	5,370	8,080	11,130
2 children, both under 6	6,230	9,390	12,920
Husband and wife 35–54 years:			
1 child, 6–15 years	7,100	10,690	14,720
2 children, older 6–15 years	8,657	13,039	17,948
3 children, oldest 6–15 years	10,040	15,130	20,820
Husband and wife, 65 years and over:	4,410	6,650	9,150
Single person, 65 years and over:	2,420	3,650	5,030

Source: U.S. Department of Labor, Bureau of Labor Statistics, 1977.

ing. Some vacation! I washed dishes in a lake instead of a sink. I never really got to vacation at all."

5. *The child itself is a determining factor in how much he or she will cost.* If the child has special needs, bad teeth, a talent that deserves extensive private lessons, costs will increase. Additionally, parents play a very critical role in shaping a child's economic behavior, often without realizing the consequences. The child who has never worked for money is chastized because "he has no appreciation of the worth of a dollar," the child whose broken toys are replaced "thinks money grows on trees," and so on. Parents can, and often do, attempt to raise their children to a higher socioeconomic class—but they then may have difficulty accepting the economic differences that result.

6. *The costs of raising a child increase as the child grows older because of his or her increased needs.* Keeping the same value to our dollars, costs in the eighteenth year are about 30 to 45 percent higher than in the first year. Boys (because of dating and transportation needs) are more expensive than girls. If you also include inflation over the 18 years, costs can more than double—and we are still excluding higher education expenses.

7. *Many couples' lifestyles are based on both partners working outside the home.* As a result, some difficult questions about the economics of child care are raised. Being a working mother has many

advantages, but most of them apply only to professional women. For the majority, the economic picture is quite different. Women still earn just 58.9 percent of the median male salary. A college-educated woman makes about the same amount of money as a man with a ninth-grade education. Mothers are often exhausted by the sheer volume of work required both on the job and at home, and they frequently perform below their best ability at both roles. They are also discriminated against in promotions. Said one executive, "We're not supposed to consider this, but, listen, I know when I hire a mother of four that when one of them gets sick, *she's* the one who's going to miss work."

In 1977, the median yearly income for families with a working wife was $22,128—only $3061 more than families with only a male wage earner! Subtract from that extra taxes, child-care expenses, the cost of more expensive convenience foods and eating out more often, and the cost of utilizing more services (laundry, housework, gardening). Subtract also the cost of better clothes and transportation and the money lost because neither parent has the time for comparative shopping. After all that you have very little monetary gain for a great deal of work. In fact, Colien Hefferan at Pennsylvania State University estimated that a typical working wife actually nets only 10 to 30 percent of what she earns!

Why then, do so many mothers (over 50 percent now) work outside the home? Giving up your job means you have to deal with some major personal changes in self-esteem and independence. It is true that the American homemaker, if salaried, is worth $7500 a year; however, most don't get a dime that is considered payment for services rendered. There is little job security, no pension or disability fund, no cost of living increases, no promotions, and little recognition. And if you want to count lost salary as part of child-care costs, then count the average female salary of $8618 (plus about $2500 in benefits) as a loss of $11,118 *per year*! Listen to Carol: "I like being a full-time mother. But I can't get used to not earning my own money, even though I work so hard. John never questions me or anything, but I'm still beholden. If I want or need more, I have to get it from him. And the longer I'm out of work, the less say I seem to have in economic decisions." Some women love their work (7–10 percent), and others do not think they are well suited for primary parenting. But most work because they have to meet present expenses, and they usually don't have the freedom to make a choice.

It takes careful planning for most of us to be able to choose whether or not to work. As you read through the next section, consider whether you want to make economic estimates based on your both working, or whether you want to entertain the possibility of one of you staying home. It is one of the most difficult parenting decisions—but if you don't consider it before you become a parent, you may not even have the luxury of deciding. Said one father, "If only we had thought this through before! We never would have bought this house! My wife has to work now—and she is so exhausted and we're both so testy that it may cost us our marriage!" We think it is very difficult to combine full-time work and parenting—and it is even more so if you must do it because of economic necessity.

8. *Don't necessarily assume your income will stay fixed.* Ask your parents what their financial situation was when they had you! As one father put it, "If you wait until you can afford kids, you'll never have them!" On the other hand, don't necessarily assume your income will blossom as did that of your parents. We baby boom children have had to compete with each other before—and in all likelihood we will continue to vie over limited and increasingly expensive resources.

PRECONCEPTION INVENTORY

Before you decide whether or not to conceive a child, you may want to evaluate some of the immediate costs and changes that will affect your economic picture.

1. *Evaluate your life insurance and disability coverages.* Some life insurance policies are more costly than others, and some have special considerations for children. Disability insurance is especially important when you have a dependent, since the cost of replacing either of your services might be prohibitive. You should consider covering both of you, if economically feasible. What is the cost?

2. *Carefully assess your health coverage.* If you both have different plans, compare and consider joining under one. Do you have the most complete pregnancy coverage possible? Exactly what is

and is not covered? (If you can't decipher the booklet, ask your representative. It's your right to have it explained to you in lay terms!) You should consider this reassessment *before you are pregnant,* since many policies cannot be changed retroactively—that is, once you are pregnant, your benefits are fixed.

Be sure to find out whether limits are placed on the entire pregnancy cost (and what services are included, as policies differ!). Find out if the policy pays a fixed cost (called a customary and usual fee) or a percentage of the bills and whether you are financially responsible for the remainder of the fees not covered by insurance. A normal hospital delivery in 1978 cost about $1500 to $2000 for a private patient. Cheaper alternatives (called house patients) run about $800, but you have to accept whatever hospital staff is available. (In a good hospital, you may prefer this arrangement.)

A law, effective as of April 29, 1979, requires that health benefits cover pregnancy-related disabilities and that medical expenses associated with pregnancy and birth be reimbursed as fully as other medical expenses. In the past, medical plans that paid 80 percent of all procedures would pay a fixed, much smaller percentage of childbirth costs. In addition, numerous pregnancy-related expenses were exempted. Under the new law, insurance companies must pay the same percentage of childbirth costs that they pay for other medical procedures, and they must reimburse you for the same sorts of procedures (X-rays, first visits, and so on) covered for other medical procedures.

Check your insurance policy and be sure it's up to date, since many companies have just finished their new benefits brochures. See how the costs of appendicitis or a broken arm are covered; childbirth costs should be treated in the same way. If not, the company is violating the law. If it refuses to comply, you can take legal action. You may also want to check whether your insurance policy covers:

Prenatal visits with a gynecologist and obstetrician (about $35 per visit)? With or without complications? Does it include first visits? (Many policies did not cover this in the past; check the new procedures and compare them with those of other medical problems.)

Diagnostic tests? Any cost limit? Any conditions?

Amniocentesis (costs around $500)? Under what conditions?

Consultations? Any limit?

Medication and special equipment?

Ultrasound? Blood workups? Laboratory fees?

Midwife?

Private obstetrician? Pediatrician?

Ambulance?

Blood transfusions?

Miscarriage expenses? (If you require uterine scraping, the costs may run as high as $1,000.)

Anesthesia? Anesthesiologist?

Surgery and operating expenses?

Private, semiprivate, or ward hospital rooms? Alternative birth rooms? For how many days and under what conditions? (Some hospitals now have quickie 24-hour packages, but they apply only when there are no complications.)

Postnatal checkups? How many? Consultations?

Incubator or special surgery costs for the baby? Intensive care nursery costs? Until what age is the infant covered? (Some policies cover only the day of birth instead of up through 14 days. This coverage makes a big difference because some defects don't show up immediately.)

Home-care assistance? Before or after birth? Under what conditions?

After answering and analyzing these questions, determine how much it will cost you to obtain good pregnancy coverage.

3. *What will it cost to join a family health plan if you are not already on one?* This coverage can be a major additional expense if you are both presently covered individually. For example, Doug and Jan had to take out a family health policy in order to cover their child. While each of their employers paid the entire premium for an individual's policy, neither employer paid more than half of the family plan. Thus, they had to spend an additional $70 per month. Compare your policies to get the best coverage for the best money. Shop around! See if one of your employers would be willing to give you the money it had been paying for your individual plan so you could use it for part of the extra family plan costs.

4. *Also check your insurance policies for special pregnancy*

compensation. For example, Alice had one insurance policy paid for her by her company, and David had another, half of which was paid by his company. They discovered that Alice's policy had a $500 maternity/paternity award, but only if you had the family plan for a minimum of three months prior to pregnancy. Therefore, David cancelled his policy and joined Alice's (the extra fee for the family plan came to only $1.20 more than he had been paying before). Thus, when they had a baby, they already had family coverage, and for an extra $1.20 for eleven months, or $13.20, a bonus of $500! (These awards are likely to become rare, given the new law. If your insurance policy has one, check to see if it is up-to-date.)

5. *Working women, check your employer's policies about pregnant workers.* New legislation (part of the new pregnancy law we discussed earlier) makes it illegal for an employer to refuse to hire a woman because she is or might become pregnant, or to force her to take an extended pregnancy leave if she prefers to work. This means that you can plan on working until your doctor says to stop, or you feel uncomfortable. Furthermore, if you have a strenuous job, or one that requires you to stand much of the time (which can be painful in the last trimester for some women), check how your company handles men with temporary disabilities. If they are laid off, then you might be also. But if they are assigned less strenuous jobs while disabled (and at the same pay), then as a pregnant woman you have the same privilege.

The same principle applies to company sick leave and paid disability leaves. If the company pays only two or three weeks for other conditions, that is all you will get for pregnancy. But if there is a 26-week disability plan, it also applies to pregnancy and childbirth. However, the leave only covers the time you are actually disabled, which is about six weeks for a normal pregnancy and delivery.

6. *Consider the timing of the birth.* Joked one father, "We made it on December 31, just in time for a tax deduction." It may seem silly, but it saved them a silly $750 deduction!

Check your company's policies and benefits. Do you have to have been employed for a certain length of time to be eligible for certain benefits? Fathers may want to check if their companies have paternity leaves. If not, can you take some sick days or vacation time? Women might also consider whether they have vacation time coming that they could use if they want more time from work that wouldn't

be covered by a disability leave. By careful planning you can maximize your benefits. Of course, babies don't always arrive when
planned, but it doesn't hurt to try.

7. *Check your housing needs.* Do you have enough living space
and, if so, for how long? Is the space well designed for a baby? Is it
safe? Can you make it safe with gates or additional doors? If you
have expensive furniture, how can you child-proof it? (One mother
regretted not doing this after her two-year-old crayoned on her
oriental rugs.) Do you have safe and accessible play areas inside and
out? If not, can you redecorate or redesign your living space to
provide them? And if so, at what cost?

If you do not have sufficient space, can you move now? Housing
costs have not come down—there's every reason to believe that
moving later will be more expensive than now. If you rent, you can
plan on paying an extra $60 to $150 per month for another room
(minus furnishings, of course). If you own a home, you may consider
adding a room or converting the attic or basement. It can be considerably less expensive than buying a new home.

If you want to buy a first home (or another), plan what you can
afford carefully. Being house-poor can be devastating to a child. Listen
to Robert: "We always lived in neighborhoods a notch above what
we could afford. I was always the worst dressed and couldn't go out
to the movies with the other kids." You may also find yourselves
forced to work very hard for a home and family you have little time
or energy to enjoy. Be sure to compute the PIT (principal, interest,
and taxes) on a home. Figure the taxes will go up several times and
that running the house (heat, hot water, electricity, gas, repairs,
gardening, and so forth) will cost you 50 to 75 percent of your
monthly PIT. Many couples are seduced by "well, it's only $400 a
month," and then are left gasping by the unexpected expenses.

8. *Assess your neighborhood.* What are the children like? The
schools? Parks? Community resources? Do you want a child who is
similar to those in your neighborhood? If the school system is not
very good, what private schools are nearby that appeal to you? What
do they cost? Too many people wait until their children are 5 or 6
before deciding they want to move—and then find they can't afford
to.

Many suburban parents are reconsidering their lifestyles. What is
ideal for a couple may not be adequate for a family. Listen to

Theresa: "We live in a lovely house, all private and quiet. Who needs it! I'm tired of shipping kids around all day. We're all so isolated. There are no parks. Everyone stays on their own property. It stinks!" Others have moved closer to the cities for more community support and resources (you can sit in a playground with others, and older children can travel independently on public transportation.) What resources does the community you live in now have?

9. *Check your appliance needs.* Is your hot water tank sufficient? How are your heating costs? Is your home insulated? (Babies need more warmth than you do, and your heating costs will rise accordingly.) Check your dishwasher, refrigerator, osterizer (for baby foods), and so on—are they dying and, if so, prepare to replace them. A baby adds considerable amounts of strain on appliances, and it can be inconvenient and expensive if they are constantly breaking down.

10. *Assess your transportation costs.* Along with housing and insurance, transportation is a major expense. Will you require two cars because of where you work, live, and shop? If you have a small, two-seater car, should you replace it? At what cost?

COSTS OF CHILD REARING

Prenatal to Birth

Once pregnant, several expenses (not including the ones previously referred to—that is, housing, medical, and transportation costs) are often encountered up to and immediately following the birth. Increased food intake and diet supplements for mother cost an estimated 25 percent over the food costs prior to pregnancy, perhaps more if you switch to natural foods and fresh produce. In addition, you will probably purchase maternity clothes at an estimated cost of $325.

Decorating a room for the baby and accumulating baby clothes and equipment can cost upward to $1100. This estimate can vary considerably depending on whether you are a do-it-yourself type, whether you have many of these supplies from a previous child, and whether you receive several items as gifts. Understandably, some new parents report lesser costs. Do plan on providing a bassinet, crib, high chair, playpen, infant carrier, stroller, car seat, car bed, clothes, blankets, diapers, hamper or diaper pail, toys, and assorted paraphernalia, such as baby powder, oil, soap, and diaper pins.

Income Loss during Pregnancy. Many women miss several days of work during pregnancy because of morning sickness, doctors' visits, and general fatigue, which can be costly if you are paid on a daily basis. Piecework productivity often decreases. Again, check to ensure that you are treated identically as a male co-worker with a temporary medical problem. If you are a homemaker and if your pregnancy is difficult, you may require household help, especially if you have other young children. As a father, you may be called away from work several times, especially if you want to be very involved in the pregnancy. The costs will vary depending upon your job or employer.

Postpartum to First Year in Public School

Assuming you have had a healthy baby and birth, you will face the following expenses during the early years:

Diapers. An average of fourteen per day from birth to about the age of two-and-a-half (usual toilet-training age). You can get by with two to four dozen cloth diapers if you launder them yourself. (The estimated cost of diaper service is $30 per month; the cost of paper diapers, $25 to $35 per month.)

Clothing. Since this is the period of most rapid growth for children, clothes must be replaced continuously, usually every six months. You should start off with at least three to six undershirts (size six months), some cotton gowns, several one-piece stretch suits, and two to three plastic pants (a size that fits!). In considering expenses, you should keep three important issues in mind: (1) Children's clothes are proportionately more expensive than you would expect. A $100-adult parka will cost $60 in a child's size. We recommend a browse through the children's department the next time you shop. (2) The style in which you dress your child may comprise an important variable in future, as well as present, expenses. As one mother said about her teenager's extravagant tastes, "It is my fault! I always dressed him in silk, in cashmere, in the very best. It is no wonder that he treats himself the same way." (3) The fewer the number of outfits and diapers, the more frequently laundry will have to be done. If you don't wash every day, you will need at least ten outfits.

Toys. This is another very variable expense, depending on your preferences and the generosity of friends and family. Most families spend a conservative $100 to $150 per year per child for toys.

Food. Expenses, barring special diet considerations, are minimal. Breast feeding, including Vitamin D supplements, costs $3.50 to $5.50 per week, according to the U.S. Department of Agriculture, whereas formula costs between $5 and $19.68 (ready-to-use and disposable). Homemade formula would cost about $3 per week. Through the first year or two, children can eat baby food (two to three jars per day at about $.30 per jar), but many parents now process adult food in a blender.

Entertainment and Travel. Expenses are moderate since infants and young children are often free (as in motels, where they can cramp your romance more than your wallet) or half-price (as in air travel, movies, restaurants, and so on).

Missed Work. The mother should plan on taking a minimum of six weeks off work after childbirth. The father should consider using paternity leave or vacation days. The cost will depend on your job benefits. The help of others during this period is critical—especially from family and friends. If you do not have such resources, consider hiring an experienced child-care worker (approximately $90 to $150 per week).

Child-Care Costs during the Early Years. In 1972, 70 to 80 percent of child-care arrangements for working mothers were not paid for by cash, but instead were received from relatives, neighbors, and so on. How about your parents or in-laws? In some communities, it is almost expected that grandparents will do some, even much, of the rearing. This arrangement can work very well for all concerned if the grandparents are willing and in good health. Studies have found considerable hostility for the elderly among children who have not been exposed to them. This animosity is not in anyone's best interest, especially given the rising crime rate against the elderly. When older people have been employed in day-care centers, camps, or pediatric hospital wards, both they and the children seemed much happier. However, one should not presume upon your relatives without consulting them! Ask. How often would they be willing to babysit? For how long? If you go on vacation? Weekends? How much notice do they want and need? Will you feel dependent on them? If so, is your relationship with them fundamentally a good one?

While many grandparents used to live with their children (and thus were able to provide a lot of child care), this arrangement is decreasing. In Massachusetts, only 49 percent of the families have an adult nonparent living with them. Often, parents and their children live miles, even states, apart. Some prospective parents are reconsidering this lifestyle. "We're trying to talk my parents into buying a two-family house" said Sheila. "It'll be the best of both worlds." But close living arrangements require that everyone gets along relatively well. If this is not the case, perhaps you should explore other resources, such as the adoptive grandparents program, in which you can arrange for an elderly couple to assume a grandparenting role. It is unlikely, however, that you will get free, even cheap, child care out of such an arrangement, although you may get many noneconomic benefits. Don't forget to also consider aunts, uncles, nephews, cousins, and so on. Would they help happily? Reluctantly? If paid? Never?

Other children in the family can help enormously. They are not nearly as helpless as many of us think they are (and perhaps encourage them to be). Children love younger children and can care for them very well. In fact, large families operate this way, and there is no reason why smaller families can't also. How old will your other children be before you would consider leaving them to care for their younger siblings? (Of course, each child is different, but most parents wait until the child is in early or middle teens.) To be competent, the child should be able to phone for help, react intelligently in case of emergency, be able to get himself and others out a planned escape route, and evaluate situations in terms of possible consequences. Many tragedies have resulted when parents have left young children unattended, or attended by too young a child (even for just a few minutes!). One recent case of child abuse involved a 12-year-old who was systematically torturing her 8-year-old sister for whom she was responsible.

If children can't babysit, they can help around the house. Some schools have instituted programs to teach 8- and 10-year-olds how to dust, vacuum, shop, and so on. It is important not to overuse a child, of course. According to Diane, "I never dated or anything because as soon as school let out, I had to come home and babysit. On weekends, I had laundry, housework, and stuff. I never even got to go to a football game." Or according to Phil, "I would be out in the ice-covered yard, chipping the laundry off the clothesline. The clothes were frozen stiff, because while Mom had a drier, it was cheaper for me to hang out the wash than to use it!"

But children are part of the family, and they should be expected to contribute according to their abilities. The opposite extreme was experienced by Renée: "My parents did everything. Be a child, my parents believed. But now I'm an adult, and I can't get used to having to deal with everything." What can your other children do? Can you work out with them acceptable chores and number of hours in advance? Be sure to have certain things, like an allowance, contingent on them completing *responsible and agreed upon tasks.* (Children often do not follow through on commitments unless helped—just like adults!)

Many friends, neighbors, and co-workers trade children and exchange babysitting time. Mothers' cooperatives are becoming increasingly popular (check your area). If all parties give each other acceptable notice and balance the time distribution, this can work very nicely. Sometimes they get together to parent, which can be very enjoyable for housebound parents. If you don't know your neighbors (and many childfree couples tend not to), get to know them *before* you have a baby. See what services you could exchange and if this would be appropriate. What works for the other parents around you? You can learn a great deal as an objective observer. You may not want to exchange sitting with people if they seem irresponsible or if their children are overly aggressive. However, if you are continually finding other parents inadequate, perhaps you should reevaluate your criteria.

Paid child-care provisions include babysitters, organized events, day care, preschool, and home-care workers. Costs will vary depending upon your needs. It is best to have reliable, responsible sitters at your disposal. You can find out from your neighbors who the best ones are. If this is not possible, call your community center. Be sure to get references. Most sitters now get transportation, $1.50 an hour, food and drink, and usually a 20 percent tip. Thus, a night out can cost an additional $10. You must pay the minimum wage to any babysitter you hire for more than 20 hours a week. There are also professional services listed in the telephone directory. You must provide transportation, and they tend to be expensive ($3 to $4 per hour), but each sitter has been trained for reliability and responsibility. They are also available on very short notice.

There are day camps, sleep camps, and a wide variety of organized children's activities in most communities, some of whose costs are minimal. Call your community center and get a list of the activities available for children of different ages. When it's supervised, you will be able to drop off the child and do your own thing, at least for a little while.

Costs of day care vary considerably depending on the state you live in, the style and quality of care, and the amount of time you use it. Most centers will not take children below the age of two. Those that do usually charge more, have to be specially licensed, and may require months of waiting—so put yourself on the waiting list at least six months in advance! That may mean before you give birth, which is why we will be discussing the different types of available child-care arrangements.

Day Care Centers. Full-time costs range between $30 and $60 per week; more with transportation. Some quality centers will cost as much as $115 per week! There is usually only a slight discount for a second child. Some centers take children part time, usually for mornings or afternoons at a cost of $20 to $30 per week, again with considerable variability. Centers are usually open from 7:00 AM to 7:00 PM to accommodate working parents. Check to ensure that the center is licensed, that the personnel are well trained, and that there are males on the staff. How long does the average staff member stay (many centers have a very high turnover, which can be difficult for children)? What schedule do the children follow, and is it flexible? Is the adult–child ratio acceptable? Examine the adequacy and safety of the play areas and equipment. The bathroom facilities should be sufficient and clean. Check the lunch and snack menu and the cleanliness of the kitchen facilities. If there is transportation, check the safety features, length of travel routes, and standards for drivers. Ask if the center has part-time provisions and what holidays are observed. Observe the center in operation. How mixed, by sex, race, and age, are the children?

In *communal* centers parents participate in the operation. There is often a shared philosophy, but you must contribute a number of hours (usually five to fifteen) per month, and costs vary.

In *family day care,* people take children into their homes. The advantages are that these settings are usually more personable, less hectic, and less expensive. However, the facilities are likely to be less extensive. Inspect the home for safety. Make sure it is licensed. Check references carefully. Ask what the greatest number of children in the home could be. What are the children like? What daily activities are scheduled? What equipment (indoor and outdoor) is provided? What about food? What holidays are observed, and what is done in case of illness?

Preschools. Preschools are usually privately owned or affiliated with colleges or universities. Unlike day care centers, their primary role is educational. They are likely to be open shorter hours (sometimes 9 to 3), and often conform to public school holidays. The staff should be comprised of teachers with degrees in early childhood education, and there is likely to be a well-defined school philosophy. Apply the same checks as mentioned for the day care center.

Preschool is not necessarily beneficial nor harmful to a child. Despite all the arguments as to when a child ought to start school, no one really knows. All we can say is that it doesn't really seem to matter. Disadvantaged, problem children do better when they go to preschool programs, but their social and intellectual gains disappear rapidly. Children who learn to read early do not necessarily read any better than those who start later. This is not to say that children should not go to a preschool—especially if the home environment is not stimulating or the parents are preoccupied—only that preschool is not necessarily beneficial in the long run. We Americans have a peculiar bias toward associating speed of development with quality of development—an early talker does not necessarily become a better talker. Baby animals are a lot smarter and more functional than infants—but not for long.

Visiting Nannies. Some parents prefer to give individual attention to their child by hiring a person to come to the home while they are away. The cost is usually $50 to $80 per week, plus food and transportation. This environment is particularly beneficial if the child is very young or shy with others. Of course, play facilities and social interaction are more limited. We interviewed a number of parents who were delighted with this kind of an arrangement. They suggested the following criteria for selecting the right person:

1. Ask the applicant for references and check them out! (Be particularly careful about alcohol use. It is not an unusual problem.)
2. Ensure the applicant's sense of responsibility. (Is she or he "dizzy," or prompt, considerate, and proud of her or his accomplishments?)
3. Look for a sense of humor. (This ranked very high on their lists. "People who laugh tend to be open and warm" believed one mother.)
4. Confirm that the candidate has experience in child care.
5. Ensure that the applicant is affectionate and warm, especially toward your child.
6. Ensure that the applicant is well organized and clean but not compulsive.
7. Determine that reliable transportation arrangements can be worked out.

8. Confirm that the person is likely to stay with you at least a year. Consider health, family demands, and so on.

You can find the right person by asking around your neighborhood or by reading or placing ads in "Situation-Wanted" columns; also, check church and market bulletin boards. But be sure to demand references!

Live-In Help. It was very common in years past for upper-class families to employ persons to care for their children. They were the primary caretakers, although they were expected to enforce the rules and standards established by the parents. Some parents are returning to this system.

Foreign people who wish to improve their English can teach your child another language and provide individual attention. A local college student is another option. The cost of such help can range from about $50 to $100 per week, including room and board. Sometimes some light housekeeping as well as babysitting at night is included. Live-in nannies (older women with experience and sometimes training) are more expensive. Consider whether you have separate enough quarters to comfortably house a nonfamily member. Otherwise, considerable strain can develop if you are not very compatible or value privacy but have limited space. Special consideration should be given to bathroom and kitchen facilities, as well as to transportation needs.

Before starting a live-in arrangement, be sure to put the rules of your house (if the person is young, the parents' rules as well) in writing. What duties are (and are not) expected? What conditions regarding persons of the opposite sex are to be met? Who buys the food and what if preferences differ? What are the vacation and holiday arrangements? We emphasize putting all of these conditions in writing, because rules can be easily misinterpreted, especially if a foreign language is involved, and matters can then become quite sticky. Another important consideration is interpersonal. An unrelated, young person can set the occasion for sexual jealousy and unpleasant game playing. Consider yourselves and the person you select, if any, most carefully.

You can locate live-in help through a local college, or you can contact a foreign embassy and request the names of reputable agents who handle domestics and au pair girls, or you can place an ad. Check references carefully.

All these child-care costs are tax deductible, but only under certain conditions. You can deduct only those costs necessary to your employment, and then only if you make under a certain amount of money. Since the tax laws change so frequently, it's a good idea to check the most recent provisions with your accountant or the IRS at the time you are considering utilizing any of these resources.

Throughout this chapter, we have assumed a healthy and normal child. If, however, your child has special needs that require special facilities, many costs must be met by your town under new federal laws. Children are covered from the age of 3 to 21, or graduation from high school, whichever comes first. How broadly these special needs will be defined is yet to be determined. They are usually defined as any deviation from the norm, but they now specifically exclude the gifted and talented. Other special needs may be excluded in the future.

The Public School Years (Ages 6–18)

The following are some of the major customary expenses associated with the school-aged child.

Dental. Most health insurance policies do not cover dental costs. Most children should see a dentist twice a year from the age of two on. Fluoride treatments, checkups, and fillings (the most cavity-prone years are between 8 and 15) can average about $500—and this figure does not include orthodontic work, which may run up to $2000. If both you and your partner have bad teeth and/or needed orthodontic work, there is a good possibility that your children might, too. Don't be taken by surprise.

Clothing. Between 6 to 11, clothing costs are not very great, since the rapid body growth of early childhood has slowed considerably. Of course, children will continue to outgrow clothing and shoes, but not as rapidly as before. During the early teen years, costs escalate because of another growth spurt (about age 11 for girls and 13 for boys) and because of an increased concern with being fashionably dressed according to the peer style. Some parents defray these costs by limiting spending or by requiring that the child contribute in some way to the purchase price. Grooming costs (cosmetics, hair cuts, and so on) also increase.

Food. Naturally, the older a child gets, the more he or she approximates the cost of feeding another adult. Teenagers frequently eat a great deal, especially preceding the growth spurt. Teenage boys may increase their caloric intake by as much as 90 percent.

Entertainment and Travel. Most childhood price benefits disappear after the child is 12 years old, so he will add a full third to the costs in which he is included. Teenagers spend considerable money on music, cosmetics, and clothes. As with clothes, some parents expect their children to contribute in some way for these "extras."

Transportation. Transportation needs for school-aged children vary depending on where you live and your schedule. Will a child be able to get around? Will he need to be driven everywhere? If so, are there likely to be car pools in the area? Where do the school buses stop, if there are any? Is there public transportation to the school, library, playing fields? Are there parks, candy stores, recreational facilities within walking distance?

Lessons. Most middle-class children take at least one lesson, frequently more, on an instrument or sport instruction. Amateur ski, tennis, and musical players often have had small fortunes spent on them by their families. We strongly believe that talents deserve to be nurtured; unfortunately, our government does little to support all but our most talented, so parents have to put up the money. Private lessons can cost about $6 to $30 per hour, depending on the teacher and whether taken individually or in a group. Instrument or equipment costs can vary from $12 (a recorder), to $300 (ski equipment), to $3000 (a piano), as does access to facilities ($12 per hour for tennis courts and so on). One father of a budding tennis pro told me the following, "I can't tell you what my wife and I have given up so that she could have tennis lessons. Not that she isn't worth it, mind you. But every cent we could save we've spent on developing her talent." Without at least some of this kind of dedication, we would all be poorer, but it is wiser to anticipate such an expenditure than to be surprised and unable to provide for a talent worthy of development. And do keep in mind that many cities and towns sponsor low-cost recreational activities and lessons; you may want to consider these when selecting a community.

Summer Camps. Luxury, sleep-away summer camps can cost $150 to $200 per week and even more for specialized facilities. Agency and boy scout camps are less costly or between $40 to $100 per week.

Evaluating a School System. Some people feel that considering school systems before having a child is premature. But we don't think so. School is one of the most important variables in the child and parents' life. School can spark, or extinguish, love of learning. It can promote the values you hold dear or undermine them. Often parents find themselves economically and strategically trapped in a community that doesn't fit their child's needs. Because they had not considered the problem soon enough, they are not able to extricate themselves. Before you have a child, decide carefully where to live. Evaluate the school and become familiar with alternative schools in the area. Decide whether you want the little $50,000 house in the good school district or the big $50,000 house elsewhere.

Evaluating a town's school system is a very tricky business. You should consider the following questions:

1. *How much per student does the town spend?* This figure is an important reflection of the emphasis the town places on education—but the higher figure does not necessarily mean a better learning environment. Of course, money is important, even necessary, in a modern school system. Obviously, children can't learn about audio-visuals or computers or music unless they have access to such equipment. But new textbooks and elaborate architecture are not synonymous with learning. Neither is money.

2. What is the school and community's philosophy of education? How does it fit with yours? The schools generally reflect the values of the community they service. Most parents wish their children to be exposed to values and goals similar to their own. If you live in a wealthy, conservative, Republican town, the schools are likely to reflect those priorities. You might chat with the president of the PTA, or even the superintendent of schools, to find out some of the basic philosophies of the school system:

What percentage of high school graduates go on to college? This figure will tell you about how college oriented the academic and counseling programs are likely to be.

Are there controversial courses offered, such as sex education, religion, comparative culture, and so on? If so, how conservative are the programs?

How much freedom of choice is offered to the elementary, junior, and senior high students? Do first graders sit in rows? Does the school emphasize basics, or self-exploration?

What are the school's rules, regulations, and punishments? Some schools still permit corporal punishment—and that tells you something!

How active are student organizations? Parent organizations?

In what direction is the school moving? Five years from now, what changes would you predict in its philosophy? In the town's population?

3. What kinds of programs does the school system offer? According to the new federal law, communities are responsible for the education of *all* their children. What kinds of classes, if any, does the school offer for gifted and talented children? For children with learning disabilities or speech problems? For "regular" kids? Under the new federal law, a parent or teacher can request that a child be evaluated both educationally and physically and that a specialized educational program be drawn up and executed if necessary. A child is eligible for these benefits from the age of 3 to high school graduation or the age of 21. The larger the school system, the greater the number of services offered and the fewer the number of private services covered. The extent to which communities will share their resources is yet to be determined.

4. *How large are the schools?* Smaller schools are not necessarily better, but they are easier. Large schools are competitive and socially difficult, but students can learn a great deal about leadership and politics in a large system. So, while one can learn more in a larger organization, fewer students rise to leadership positions, fewer are involved in extracurricular activities, and fewer are given special attention. There is no clear evidence that children in large classes learn any less than those in small classes. An assertive, active, sociable, and ambitious child can do very well in a large context. If you tend to be shy and somewhat retiring, your child might be similar and might do better in a smaller, more personalized system.

5. *What is the teacher-student ratio?* Ask your school board or town hall for student-teacher ratios for those schools in your district. You may also want to speak to neighborhood parents and children about their school experiences.

6. *What are the teachers like?* Teachers play a very significant role in children's lives. A recent study found that students of a certain first-grade teacher tended to do better throughout their schooling in comparison to other, similar children.* Certainly, we all had teachers who changed our lives for the better—and worse. How dedicated are the teachers? How much individual attention do they pay to the children? Are there field trips? Interest clubs? Of course, teachers differ. You can find dedicated staff among duds and vice versa. But teachers reflect, as well as share, the quality of the school system and its students. If many teachers are enthusiastic and hard-working, they are likely to have a supportive administration and a responsive student body.

7. *What are the students like?* Ask the counseling center for data on how well the town scored on national standardized tests. You may not consider these scores as the major measurement of education, but they are reflections of how well students are functioning in terms of basic skills. If basic skills are not the end goal of education, they are certainly prerequisites. What are the children like? Are they nice, happy, clean? One family would scout a town by spending an hour at the local McDonald's and watching the children!

*Pedersen, Eigil; Faucher, Therese Annette; with Eaton, William W., "A New Prospective on the Effects of First Grade Teachers on Children's Subsequent Adult Status," *Harvard Educational Review* 48, no. 1 (Feb. 1978):1-5.

"If many of the kids act like I wouldn't want my kids to act, we don't live there!"

8. *How mixed is the student population?* Are there different social classes in the town? Ethnic groups? Racial groups? Parents have very different ideas as to whether they want their children to interact with other sorts of people. It would be unfair to send a child to a very mixed school and insist he socialize only with students who are like himself, especially if he is a member of a minority group. However, for all our attempts at integration, most research indicates that children usually form homogeneous groups by the time they are six or seven. People generally group with people who are like them. Schools that are well mixed are frequently stratified— the mixing is only statistical. However, the opportunity for mixing is there, and the lack of interaction may often be a reflection of parental desires rather than an unalterable preference on the part of the children.

Listen to Sherry: "I grew up in such a cocoon! I never had a chance to see anyone but people like me—white, middle class, WASPy. It's a real hindrance—my perspective is so narrow. And I'm very uncomfortable with blacks, Jews—anyone else. I regret not having been exposed to the richness and variability of other cultures and values. It's hard for me to make up those kinds of experiences." Now, hear Paul, a black high school student in an integrated school: "It's a sham, integration. Yeah, it was integrated in first grade, but the older you get, the bigger the gap. You can't look at a white girl without being threatened by someone. We blacks sit in the cafeteria together. We have our own dances and clubs. At the end of school, we climb into the bus and go into our own neighborhoods."

9. *What transportation is available for school children?* This last question is a "minor" question that often becomes "major" after five years of hauling children around. You may also want to check the quality and safety of bus service. What provisions are there to ensure a safe walk between home and school? Are there crosswalk guards, traffic police, and so on?

Some parents want more control over the school system than is afforded in many communities. Small private schools flourish because they cater to a particular philosophy, socioeconomic class, or ethnic group. Over one million students are now in nonsectarian schools.

The costs can vary between $2,000 and $4,500 a year, and some have scholarships for the needy or gifted. Some people have advocated using a voucher system, in which your school tax monies could be allocated to the private institution of your choice, but this has not as yet been a very successful movement. Check the private schools in the area for quality and cost. In this way you will know your options.

Boarding schools cost considerably more: between $4,000 to $5,000 yearly. While more common in Europe and high-income brackets, boarding schools afford independence from the family, a good education, and exposure to similar sorts of peers. Because of their unusualness in American culture, some children feel rejected by their parents when they are enrolled (some probably *are* rejected!).

The Working Child. The majority of American school children work outside the home for money. Below the age of 14 children are permitted to do farmwork, perform odd jobs, sell newspapers, caddy at golf clubs, and so on. Between 14 and 16, teenagers may work in supermarkets, factories, and other businesses, but their hours and working conditions are regulated by the state. The advantages of children working are that they learn money management and how to assume responsibility and that they take pride in contributing to their own upbringing. The disadvantages are that children are often exploited by those who hire them and that they may learn to become cynical and equally exploitive. How do you both feel about a child working? Would you exercise control over any earnings? In days of yore, it was expected that working children would contribute significantly to the family's income—many homes felt the pinch of hunger when the child labor laws were enforced! Today, we don't tend to think of children as self-sufficient, let alone "bringing home the bacon."

Post-Secondary Education and Beyond

Most parents rank this age range as the least satisfying—it is also the most expensive. It is the most ambivalent stage because the "child" is no longer really a child, but his or her economic dependence does not permit the independence of adulthood. Money is often the focal point of the struggle.

While college seems a long, long way off, you can't plan too soon considering the costs of higher education. A private college now costs approximately $4,000 a year, without room and board. At this writing, the customary residence college experience of four years costs $30,000, including books and moderate dress (excluding transportation costs for home visits). Every indication is that these costs will escalate.

At present, a college degree is necessary to enter, or stay in, the middle class. (In fact, according to one professor, the maintenance of the middle class is the prime function of higher education!) At this writing, college-educated males earn $25,071, while those with high school diplomas earn $17,592. A recent Gallup poll reported that 75 percent of U.S. teenagers plan to go to college!

How you and your partner feel about providing a college education for your children is very important in your fiscal planning. How do you feel about sending a C student to college? Is it important to you that your child be able to choose any college, or are you willing to afford only the least costly, like state schools? (If so, consider the state you live in. Some have excellent, inexpensive colleges that are likely to remain so.) How do you both feel about a child contributing to the funds for his education? About working while in school and how much? (While a part-time job is fine, it is unreasonable to expect that a person can work full time and attend school full time. Very few people can do both, which is one reason why married students have the highest attrition rates.)

Graduate schools have also become necessary for many occupations. Certain competitive fields such as law and medicine have minimal scholarships. Even those that do provide support provide little other than tuition. Thus, the proud "my son/daughter, the doctor" may cost you up to $300,000.

Inflation, recession, and postponed occupations have been responsible for prolonged dependence. A relatively recent redevelopment has been young working adults staying at home. Said one 25-year-old woman, "I can't afford anything but a roach-infested apartment on my salary, and I would have to live with roommates. My last few have been very unpleasant. There's really nothing like home." And how do her parents feel? "Frankly," said her father, "we're ambivalent. Sure, we'd rather have her here than living in a slum—and we love our daughter. But we were looking forward to being alone. I'm getting ready to retire—and it's difficult to have an adult child at home. We can't help worrying about her late nights. She's still a kid to us—and it's hard not to exercise control when she's still dependent." Of course, it has only been since World War II that young people could afford to live independently before marriage. This trend may have been an aberration based on a short-lived economic boom—perhaps we are now returning to a more usual family style. Nonetheless, an adjustment is necessary—and somewhat difficult. Do you believe that there is a time when a child should be economically self-sufficient? Under what conditions?

When your children are grown and presumably independent, what economic benefits will accrue? According to the most recent Census Report, more than 80 percent of elderly widowed people are living alone, as compared with 72 percent in 1968. Those who do live with their adult children often do housework or babysitting. However, no one really knows how many adults give how much to their parents. But from what we have seen, many children give their aging parents little or nothing: some adult children are neglectful; some don't have help to give; some are indifferent; some are even hateful. "Parent abuse goes on a lot," said one emergency room nurse. "We see a lot of old people who have been neglected, beaten, even enslaved, by their sons and daughters. Even the parents don't want us to know what happened." It is not uncommon for adults to treat their old parents as they believe they were treated (which may or may not agree with their parents' version). Yet many people do give their parents money, take them shopping, handle difficult matters— in short, parent for them when necessary. The rewards (and not only economic ones) you receive as an aging parent are determined by the relationship you establish with your children—and their marriage partners. (Only-children seem to care for aging parents the most reliably.) Careful provisions ought to be made for old age. For example, seeking out a trusted executor and safely investing your money will help to preserve one's dignity in later years, with or without children.

ESTABLISHING YOUR PRIORITIES

As you saw in the previous pages, the cost of parenting is very variable, given your standards and priorities. We think that many people of childbearing age are experiencing downward mobility—that is, they are earning a significantly lower standard of living than their parents. Yet, when and if they have children, they often expect to raise them as they were raised. Too late, they discover that it is impossible, and they must either sacrifice their own goals (resentment!) and/or give less to their children (guilt!). One way of avoiding this occurrence is to do a fiscal evaluation before you decide whether or not to parent.

Naturally, attempting to predict your economic future in a changing world is difficult. But you can make some useful, if cautious, assessments. The following questions are applicable to anyone who works outside the home and who will continue to do so while parenting.

Are you hardworking and ambitious? Realistically, given your past job behavior, are you likely to move up?

If you did move up, what would your income be? What is the lifestyle of people in that bracket?

If you have little room for advancement, have you thought about changing fields? If so, consider at least getting started before you become a parent. (Not that you can't do it afterward—it's just more difficult.)

Will your job commitments permit you the time and energy you want to devote to parenting?

One father put it this way, "When I come home and there's my daughter wanting to play, I could scream. I really want to read the paper and sip a martini or talk to my wife. But then I think I wanted kids and now I have to attend to them."

Sometimes, parents give up their ambitions for a more positive parenting experience. Allen, 33, was a businessman who quit his well-paying administrative job and became a mailman. "Yeah, I lost a lot of prestige, and salary, and the opportunity for advancement. But I gained security and peace of mind. I like going to work now, and I come home clear, with energy, and without all those worries and pressures that made me snap at the kids." To do that, Allen changed his goals—and his priorities. His wife told us, "We sold our second car and got a used VW. We dropped out of the tennis club. We buy old furniture and cheap clothes. They're really little sacrifices for the enormous benefits we've experienced."

But not all people feel the same way. Listen to Terry, 45: "My husband once had an opportunity for a large promotion, but it would have meant a very long workday. He refused because he said his family came first. I have had to work much harder because he didn't earn very much. I've given up a lot of nice things. But he has been a devoted father. I really don't know how I feel about the decision, even now—years later."

Many fathers we interviewed felt as though their wives were giving them double messages. On the one hand, they were encouraged to make more money, but on the other hand, they were resented for not spending more time with the family. We hope that by answering the following questions you will be able to form more realistic and open expectations of yourselves and each other, even before you reach a parenting decision.

What are your economic priorities? What would you like to spend more on? Less on?

necessities
transportation
housing
clothes
travel
entertainment and hobbies
savings and investment

In what style (thrifty, low, moderate, liberal) would you like to parent? Your partner?

> In what type of store would you want to buy your children's clothes: bargain, medium, quality?
>
> Do you want household help?
>
> How often do you and your partner want to go out during the week?
>
> How many vacations do you want to take each year and for how long?
>
> In what style do you want to vacation? What would you do with the child?
>
> Do you want to send your child to private schools?
>
> What kind of living space do you want for your child? His own room?
>
> What kinds of opportunities do you want to be able to provide? College, graduate school? A car? Do you want your child to have to work?

Be sure to discuss these options and their ramifications with your partner.

Some couples find their parenting styles clash, especially when they come from different backgrounds. As Christine explained: "My family was well-off. If my folks wanted to travel, they did. If they wanted to eat out, we ate out. That's how I see it. But Fred's family stayed home, ate linguine, and blamed it on the kids. He's got this thing that we can't spend money on frivolous things like eating out now that we're a family." This conflict happens more often than you might imagine.

Can you comfortably afford your preferred parenting style? If not, will you be able to in the future? If you can't, how are you willing to compromise? Go back and look over your present economic priorities. What personal expenses are you willing to reduce? A less expensive car, a smaller home, fewer vacations, cheaper clothes, less eating out? If that is not enough, what parenting preferences are you willing to modify? Can you settle for your child going to a state college? Having a paper route? Sharing a room?

The balance parents strike between satisfying their own economic needs and those of their children is critical to the happiness of the family—but not all people are happy with the same balance. One extreme is Linda, age 32. She and her husband travel extensively and spend most of whatever they earn. When we asked her how they were going to finance their son's education, she replied, "I'm going to give you a straight answer, even if it sounds brutal. We'll help him get a loan and lend him what we can—but it's not much. He'll have to work his own way through. And why not? Listen, my husband and I were put through college and we learned nothing. We love our kid—but we couldn't see giving up everything to send him to school. I think he understands." Now consider Judy, who worked for 20 years to put her three sons through medical school: "We never had anything," she told us. "Everything for the boys. I don't know if it was right or wrong. I just look at them now, so successful and all, and I'm very proud. You can't live just for yourself. You have to think of your children first." Perhaps a more reasonable approach would be to balance your priorities with the needs of the child, rather than indulging either one.

Many parents are able to work out compromises that require minor sacrifices relative to the noneconomic benefits of parenting. Said one father: "My child is more than worth eating hamburgers instead of steak!" Because this chapter has focused exclusively on the costs of parenting, we have neglected to discuss the noneconomic rewards for which most people parent. In strictly economic terms, having children doesn't pay, but then neither does getting married, making love, or playing tennis. Most of us get money so that we can do these sorts of things; we don't do these things in order to get money.

This chapter is important precisely because prospective parents don't view having a child as a financial decision. While the economics of parenting are unlikely to determine whether or not you parent, they will profoundly affect your experience. It is not so much the direct costs of a child that impact upon parents, as much as the costs of overcoming the lifestyle limitations of being a parent. Most of us can afford to feed and clothe a child, but we may not be able to afford to go back to school, take a vacation, or even attend a show.

Prospective parents benefit from having a realistic picture of what they may have to give up in order to parent. But they also need to have a clear idea of what their sacrifices would be *for*—and that can't be described in economic terms. Some of you may be unwilling to make this sort of exchange. Others of you may be able to plan ahead and lessen the impact of costs that catch others by surprise. When we choose to parent and acknowledge the costs entailed, we are more likely to focus on other aspects of the relationship and less likely to resent the predictable privations. While you cannot place a cost value on children, you can, and should, appreciate what the values you place on children will cost.

ADDITIONAL READINGS

Benning, Lee E. *How to Bring Up A Child Without Spending a Fortune.* New York: Dolphin Editions, 1976

Edwards, Carolyn S., and Gray, Bruce. *The Cost of Raising Farm Children.* U.S. Department of Agriculture, November 15, 1978.

The Family Economic Review. A publication by the United States Department of Agriculture.

Interview with Colien Hefferan. "Pros and Cons of Whether Wives Should Work." *U.S. News and World Report,* November 25, 1978.

Kagan, Jerome. "All About Day Care." *Parents Magazine,* April 1977.

Norton, Arthur J., and Glick, Paul C. "Changes in American Family Life." *Children Today,* May/June 1976.

Pennock, Jean L., "Costs of Raising a Child." Talk on February 18, 1970, U.S. Department of Agriculture, Agricultural Research Service.

Simpson, Peggy. "Pregnant Workers Have a Tough Ally." *Parade Magazine, The Boston Sunday Globe,* May 20, 1979.

4

Lifestyle Considerations

In this chapter, we will address four major changes that would occur in your lifestyle if you were to raise a child now.

1. *A day in the life of parents.* We'll talk about how children's needs change as they get older, and we'll present typical days in the lives of four parents. We'll also examine exactly what parents do and give you exercises to help you assess whether you and your partner enjoy doing these sorts of things.

2. *Resourceful parenting.* We'll present some of the main child-care resources available and discuss whether or not their use is harmful to a child's development. We then ask you to discuss your attitudes about how much nonparental care is acceptable to you.

3. *Sharing the caring.* We talk about why so many men spend so little time parenting and ask questions to help you determine how much you would like to share with each other. How well are you likely to do this?

4. *Parenting mostly by yourself.* If one of you is going to take a more active role, or if there is no partner, what are some of the issues you need to anticipate?

The entire chapter has been designed to help you evaluate the strategic part of parenting so that when making your decision you will be able to estimate and appreciate the extent of the commitments and changes involved.

A DAY IN THE LIFE OF PARENTS

Parenting is something you do, not something you become. The more your present lifestyle differs from that which you adopt when parenting, the more difficult the adjustment is likely to be. One major consideration to deliberate is how much time and energy parenting actually entails. Of course, these time demands vary considerably depending on the parents' approach to childcare. Some parents devote every waking moment to their child, to the point of smothering initiative and prohibiting independence. Other children are emotionally neglected because their parents are too busy with other aspects of their lives. Most parents find that it takes planning to be able to divide time and energy between parenting and other endeavors.

As a society, parents are spending less and less time parenting. Families are smaller, both in terms of adults and children. Work is now located outside the home, in childfree areas. In 1900, only 79 percent of children between 14 and 18 went to school—now 94 percent do. We are becoming increasingly age-segregated. In a recent study,* 766 twelve-year-olds reported spending twice as much of their weekend time with their peers than they spent with their parents! The average television viewing time for children between 6 and 12 is 22 hours per week. The numbers of children in day care centers have risen dramatically over the last decade. Yet, parents are busier than ever. It is not that they are choosing to minimize parenting time, but rather that the fabric of our culture now makes parenting an *additional,* rather than an integrated, undertaking. As a result, parenting is more of a strain than in previous generations, even though we may actually be parenting less. And, even though many of us have less time for parenting, our standards and expectations for ourselves and our children have never been higher.

In the following pages, we will consider only that parenting time necessary to the child's health and safety, assuming, of course, that the child does not have special needs. Time and energy demands vary

*Bronfenbrenner, U., "Another World of Children," *New Society Magazine* (Feb. 1972).

with your style of parenting, the age of the child, and the resources available to you. We recommend taking a course in child development or reading a book on the subject (some are referenced at this chapter's end) so you can better envision your experience. You will read that during the first five years of life, children require considerable care for which parents are responsible (either by providing it themselves or via substitutes).

The most time- and energy-consuming period is the first three months. We asked Nancy to estimate how much time she had spent on her three-month-old son thus far. She laughed for five minutes and then replied that her working day was about seventeen hours long, and sixteen of those hours were devoted to her child. While this statement may seem extreme to some, infants do need considerable care. If a woman breast-feeds (and more are doing so), she must be prepared to meet these demands in person, or to somehow prepare a schedule in which supplementary help can be provided.

One interesting exercise was designed by a professor at the University of California. Students were required to carry with them a wetting doll for one week; during this week, they had to feed the doll every two to three hours (as one would a live baby), to change the diapers when wet, to change clothes and clean the baby at least six times a day, and to provide 24-hour supervision (their explanations to babysitters must have been interesting). *All* were overwhelmed by the experience. Of course, dolls are not very interesting, while babies are; furthermore, this period of parenting is a relatively short one, and care must be taken to keep such demands in perspective. Nevertheless, for those who have never parented, it is an excellent introduction to parenting's first experiences.

By the age of six months, infants are on a more regular and extended schedule, and they are beginning to eat solid foods. They still require almost constant attention—they must be cleaned, dressed, fed, and then cleaned, dressed, and fed again. They are often cranky while teething. They usually are beginning to crawl and must be watched carefully. Between the ages of 8 and 12 months, they often become very frightened of strangers and upset when their parents leave the room. This behavior is quite normal and usually passes.

Many parents report the first year to be the most demanding and the least rewarding. This feeling can be problematic unless you realize that this experience is temporary—and that qualitative changes are to follow.

Between the ages of 18 months and 4 years, children are learning language rapidly (in fact it is the most significant period for language development in which children's vocabularly expands from a few words to an average of 2,000!). They are also learning to be independent, physically and intellectually. Most are toilet trained by age two and a half. They are often negativistic—"no!" answers the child requested to eat or to stop pulling kitty's ears or whatever—and temper tantrums are common. They are called toddlers and are old enough to get into trouble that they are too young to appreciate. During a mother's momentary daydream, a child can be running into the middle of the street or tasting the contents of the bathroom cabinet.

Toddlers are constantly active and display fatigue by becoming even more restless and irritable. The attention span is very short. If you're the sort of person who is frequently drifting into inner spaces, parenting may be a constant chore unless you organize a child-safe environment. This is also the "why is the sky blue?" period, in which children often love to ask questions. (Children rarely want to hear the answers parents give them, according to researcher Jean Piaget.* They don't want to hear about light refraction and so on; they want functional answers like "the sky is blue so the clouds stand out!") While child-care demands are great during the preschool years, many parents find them to be the most rewarding.

After about the age of five, the time necessary for adequate care is assumed, in part, by the child who can now wash, eat, and go to the toilet fairly independently. School becomes important and assumes some of the parental responsibilities. But many schools ignore the fact that a majority of parents now work outside the home; they often schedule conferences and meetings during the school day or have extended vacations or holidays without child-

---

*Piaget, J. and B. Inhelder, *The Psychology of the Child.* New York: Basic Books, 1969.

care provision. Some schools schedule double or triple sessions (parents may have one child in each session!) or have hours that make it difficult for parents to hold jobs. Children still require constant supervision and cannot be left unattended for long, especially at night. Most children prefer that someone be home when they return from school; this can be problematic. There are also group activities to be handled—den meetings, pajama parties, lessons, and appointments. There are demands to join the PTA, be classroom mothers, coach sporting teams, and to attend meeting after meeting, night after night.

As a child enters the teen years, time demands for caretaking may decrease considerably. However, time demands for interacting and sharing may increase. The larger portion of a child's life now occurs outside the family context. Unless communication lines are open, parents may find themselves across the table from a stranger. Moreover, teenagers are consumers and are independent enough to get into trouble they can't get out of. There are often impositions and problems, a lack of funds, and car troubles. There are late nights when parents can't sleep and discover bottles of alcohol in drawers. Many parents report that the teen years are the least satisfying and emotionally the most trying. And the amount of time the offspring is dependent is increasing as more preparation for adulthood becomes necessary. However, there are proud times, too, perhaps when your child has the lead in the school play, or makes the honor roll, or receives an award.

The failure of some people to realize that parenting is time consuming can result in poor decisions and inadequate planning, even unrealistic regrets. Deborah, age 22, was enrolled in a doctoral program and living off a small scholarship when she had an abortion. Now, childfree at 35, she told us, "Sometimes I so regret what I did (the abortion). It was so weak of me. I could have taken a semester's leave and then returned to finish my degree. I could be doing what I'm doing now, but also have a ten-year-old child to enjoy." It is unlikely that this would have happened had she had the baby. This is not to say that she wouldn't have been happier as a parent, or that she wouldn't have benefited professionally even more by delaying her career. Certainly, however, things would have been far from "the same."

Parent Interviews

In order to better portray the parenting experience, we will now present interviews with four parents (of a 4-month-old, a 4-year-old, an 8-year-old, and a 14-year-old) on how they spend their days. We hope you find the portraits interesting and informative. While you're reading, ask yourself how similar your behavior would be and whether these days sound as though you would enjoy them.

Kristine and Rob. Kristine, 33 years old and the mother of a 4-month-old son, is an attractive woman with short blonde hair. Before having her baby she worked in her own shop as a goldsmith. Her husband, Rob, is owner of a sizable factory. She and her husband agreed that their son required her attention full time for a few years.
Kristine tells us:

> Rob and I get up at a quarter to six in the morning. That gives me time to make some coffee and toast. Rob and I get a few minutes to talk. We really treasure them. Then, oh, about six or so, the baby starts to cry, and I go in to take care of him. Rob takes a shower and gets ready for work. He usually leaves around seven o'clock, having had little opportunity to interact with the baby.
>
> Let's see. I go in and kiss Clark and change his diaper. I have to wash his bottom and all that—it takes about 10 minutes. Sometimes he doesn't like it and he screams, and I wish I were back in bed. But other times he's very cooperative and delightful to be with. Then I feed Clark. It takes about 15 minutes and another 15 to burp him and clean him up after he spits. Then I put Clark to bed and he usually sleeps about an hour or two. He's a real good baby.
>
> While he's sleeping, I sterilize any of the bottles or nipples from yesterday, and I do housework and laundry. I try to get the heavy stuff done before he wakes up. I also think a lot while I work, about designs I'm going to create when I start work again.
>
> Clark gets up around eight thirty, and I play with him a little. I have a little chair he likes to sit in in the living room. I move him around a lot with me, and he seems to like that. At about ten, I weigh him (and then worry!), and after that, he usually takes a full bath. I wash his hair and everything—every day. He likes the water, though I know some kids don't. But he's heavy now, and it's very tiring to hold him still while I do all that. Then I diaper him.
>
> Now it's about eleven thirty or so, and I give him his biggest meal—usually pureed carrots. Then he usually sleeps until two o'clock or so. I usually finish up the house-

work, if I can, and have a light lunch. The time goes by so fast! I wish I had more time to visit with neighbors—but most of the women work anyway.

Around two the baby wakes up, and I play with him a little, clean him up. Then I feed him again—just milk this time. After this feeding, he's usually restless. He plays, but he cries more now than at any other time. There's little I can do about it, though. I hate the sound of it, you know, but I think about other things. He falls alseep about five. And then I start dinner.

Rob comes home around six, and we have dinner. Sometimes Clark wakes up while we're eating, and we get annoyed. You know, we shouldn't, but we're both tired, and he distracts from our talk. After I clean up dinner, I feed the baby. Rob does some paperwork or reads the paper. Then I change the baby, and clean him up. He's usually asleep by seven thirty or so. And we're lucky because he sleeps through the night most of the time.

It doesn't sound as much as it feels. By night I'm really tired. And the routine gets to me sometimes—day after day, you know. But it's not bad. I look forward to getting back to work, but it's going to be a problem. We don't like to hire people to care for Clark. So I guess we don't get out as much as we could, but we're too tired anyway.

According to Rob:

My work keeps me from having much to do with the baby or helping Kristine during the week. If she's not feeling well, I will tend to the baby at night. But, to be honest, this doesn't happen very often. On weekends, however, I enjoy being with both Kristine and Clark. I especially like the sense of family when I'm with them. While Clark isn't much to interact with yet, I look forward to spending more time with him as he gets older.

Vicki and Ted. Vicki and Ted are parents of a 4-year-old. Ted is a professor at a small college, and Vicki works part time, at home, as a typist. We interviewed them at home, with their daughter, Barbara, nearby.

Vicki tells us:

We get up around eight or so, with Barbara. One of us, whoever is least rushed, washes her hair, brushes her teeth, and supervises her at the toilet. Sometimes we still have to wipe her. [Note: At this point, Barbara interrupted by whispering, "Tell them not to put anything about my rear end in the book."]

We have breakfast together, with me cutting up her food if necessary. She doesn't eat much—cereal, toast, eggs sometimes. Ted leaves for the university around ten and drops her off at the preschool. I do some housework and laundry. Around noon I get to work—typing and editing. I get pretty intense, and I always regret it when I have to stop. Most days I pick Barbara up around three or so, but if I'm really busy, Ted picks her up on his way home, around five. When she gets home, she tells me all the news about school. I love to hear the stories! Then she plays with some puzzles or coloring books while I make dinner. If Ted is home, they often play together.

If we have to go shopping, we either all go, or just one of us. I hate it, so Ted does most of it. Oh, and Barbara watches Sesame Street every day—but except for specials, that's all we let her see on television. It's getting harder now—the other kids at the school are always talking about television.

Then Barbara eats dinner with us. She eats just what we do. I don't make anything special for her. After dinner, she and Ted help me clean—we make it a game. We send her to bed around seven. I bathe her—help her now. Then she goes through her "how to delay going to bed" routine. She has the longest prayers you ever heard—she blesses everything she can think of. But by eight she's usually asleep for the night.

Later, after Barbara is out of the room, Vicki tells us:

I think we really miss sleeping late and cuddling. Barbara keeps you up and around, and I think she's made me a little jingly, kind of wound up. Most of all, I don't like all the concentration she takes. We spend so much time talking about how to handle this or that. She's always doing something, and we have to decide the best way to handle it. A lot of parents never think about what to do—they just do it—but we're not that way. Like for a while, she was going to the bathroom under the dining room table, or tantruming at school.

Ted adds:

Barbara is a wonderful child and we love her dearly, but once we became parents, things changed. You have a worry, a person who always depends on you—without even thinking about it—and you can never put that away again.

John and Norma. John, 37 and a father to an 8-year-old, is a businessman who usually has to travel at least once a month. He earns a good living and is pleased with his career. His wife Norma is a homemaker by choice. She has a small, close circle of friends and is active in a number of civic organizations.

John tells us:

I don't do that much parenting during the week. I get up with Mike and Norma about seven and we share breakfast. It's usually pretty hectic. Sometimes, if Norma has a busy day, we discuss who's going to take Mike here or there, but generally she manages these things.

I come home around seven or eight. Frankly, when I come home I'd like to unwind, but Mike is all wound up. I often would rather be relaxing than playing with him, but Norma would be furious—and I see her point. Then we have dinner, and Mike tells me about his day. There always seems to be decisions that need to be made about Mike's activities. And getting him to bed is a chore. The weekends are better. We sometimes play ball, or he helps me around the house.

He's a little bratty now, shouting, breaking things, trying to get out of doing chores, but he's really a good kid. I wish I had more patience with him. But the older he gets, the more we like each other, and the better we get along. I think we'll get even closer as the years go by.

Norma says:

I think our weekdays are rather ordinary, much like that of other families. We all get up around seven. I make breakfast with occasional interruptions to help find this or that for Michael or John. After they've gone, I relax with a cup of coffee and then talk with a friend.

My mornings and afternoons are spent shopping, doing housework, or going to the club with the girls. Michael is old enough to take care of himself and is pretty independent now. I usually spend time with him talking about his day while preparing dinner. We all talk during dinner—it's one of my favorite times. Then while I clean up afterwards, Michael reads or watches TV. By eight I'm on my own time again.

Ann and Frank.   Ann, 43, is the mother of a teenage girl, 14, and a son, 11. She has some grey in her hair and a keen, eager face. She is a social worker, and her husband, Frank, is an insurance salesman. According to Ann:

Cindy is wonderful. She reminds me a lot of my older sister—very pretty and bubbly. But she's getting harder for me to know. Kids don't want to talk any more with their parents; it's too childish. She just likes to sit in her room and listen to music. If I so much as go in, forget it! She's real sloppy now, when before she was always very clean, very neat. Well, it'll pass.

I get up around five—no, I don't mind—and jog for almost an hour. It's my time! Then we have breakfast. There's always some emergency in the morning—guaranteed! When everyone is out, I clean the dishes and leave for work.

I work until two most days. It's a hard job, very competitive. The office keeps increasing its caseload so that you can't function very well, and that upsets me.

I usually shop on the way home for food or drugstore items. I go home and meet the kids when they come home from school. They're always hungry and have things to tell me. But sometimes we have appointments, or meetings, or shopping, or lessons, and I'm driving them around like a chauffeur. Nobody but me coordinates anything. I crisscross Boston like Moses in the desert.

From four to five is my rest time, if I can get it. I've had to scream about it because the children resent my withdrawing, but I have to, really, and they're good most of the time. From five to six, I make dinner. Cindy used to help me very willingly—it was nice. Now she's not as willing. Dinner is often squabble time, especially over what to watch on television—important things! After dinner, everyone tries to get out of helping me clean up. Then it's television or homework time.

Frank agrees and then adds:

> By eight or nine, I'm pretty tired. We go to bed and talk over any problems with the kids or the budget. We're beginning to worry about saving for college. Cindy is only a C student, and we've had some disagreements about her education. But we think she ought to have a choice of schools. College is more than an academic experience now.
>
> I get very depressed sometimes because being a parent is so one-way. I don't think it's just us, either. You get so tired. But most of the time, I'm happy. As soon as my youngest gets older, I'd like to change careers. But he's going to need money for school, too, so I don't know.
>
> My days are very busy—but I'm that kind of person. We're starting to have to deal with teenage problems now—you know, we find cigarettes and even some liquor. Sex is going to be an issue, and we're trying to get ready for it. And the house needs work. I guess it's the petty things that get to me. I'd like to come home and just be able to relax with my family. But we don't. We're all into different things. We cross, sometimes for good, other times not. We're all consumed by the demands outside the family.

As you can see, each parent's experience is different. Each is happy and sad about the day-to-day demands of parenting. What about your reactions?

In order to help you assess the amount of time and energy you would spend parenting, it might help to do the following exercises. We realize that some of these are time consuming and require some thought and discussion. However, each of us has a different lifestyle and a different parenting style. It is only by looking at our unique, individual experiences that we can come up with useful approximations. Even those of you who have parented before have changed—as has your memory of your past experiences at parenting.

Exercise

If you have had other children, review your pictures and baby books. Try to remember the time spent at various ages. Talk to parents of children older than those you already have so you can anticipate future time demands.

Exercise

Ask a parent whose parenting style seems similar to your own (or what you would like yours to be) to record his or her parenting time and activities for 24 hours. Get estimates from different ages—an infant, preschooler, school-aged child, adolescent, and young adult. Even better, spend a day with them!

Exercise

Where are you going to get the time to parent? When Alice, 32, had her baby, she told us: "I didn't anticipate the changes. I never realized that I was already so busy that I couldn't just add parenting to what I was doing. I had to give up something but I had no idea what!" What makes up a typical day for you and your partner? Weekend? Vacation?

Morning_____

Afternoon_____

Night_____

Now show how you would arrange 24-hour daily child care and supervision into your schedule. What activities would you rearrange? Give up?

Exercise

1. What percentage of your life so far have you spent on:

   Travel_____

   Romantic and/or sexual love_____

   Work for money, career advancement, and so forth_____

   Home and family_____

   Leisure activities_____

2. What percentage of your future would you like to spend on each of these activities? Is this realistic?

3. Now imagine you had a child. How would this change your life?
4. Answer these questions for your partner.

Exercise

Some couples find that a child is a joy in their lives. Others claim that a child ruined what had previously been a good relationship. To help you assess your reaction, list the five activities you and your partner prefer to do together:

1. _____
2. _____
3. _____
4. _____
5. _____

How compatible are these activities with child rearing? For example, if you and your partner enjoy working around the house, a child would not require a major change. However, if you like to sleep late, make love in the morning, and snack on potato chips, a child might herald considerable change.

Parenting Activities

As you can see, when people parent, they do more parent-type activities and much less of other kinds of things. Therefore, the happiness of parents may in part be determined by how well they like the trade, *independent of the child*. What kinds of things do parents do, and how well do you like doing these sorts of things? Parents do a lot of things, of course. But here is a list of some of their major undertakings.

Teach.   Parents model, instruct, and answer questions. They demonstrate self-care, putting things together, catching a ball, playing games. They introduce new experiences and outline standards for appropriate behaviors. Happy parents are often good teachers—interested, helpful, and patient. Unhappy parents are intolerant of error, impatient, and disinterested. They often end up snapping, "Here, let me do it!"

Doctor. Parents wipe noses and bottoms, apply medication, treat bruises, and give hugs and kisses. They serve food and clean up—often. They mend clothes, treat rashes. The happiest parents are ones who are efficient and clean, but not compulsive. Frustrated parents get upset by dirt or messes, or are so careless that health problems develop.

Observe. Parents watch, supervise, and set up environments. Happy parents enjoy watching the energy, curiosity, and investigations of children. Impatient parents prefer to have children "sit still and be quiet."

Play. Parents play. They build snowmen and sand castles, dance, sing, and play baseball. One parent put a slide and small sandbox in her living room! Unhappy parents find the playfulness of kids impractical and distracting. They find that they can't get things accomplished when the children are around.

Exercise

List the activities you would enjoy doing with a child of different ages.

0–2 _____

2–5 _____

6–12 _____

13–18 _____

18+ _____

Would your partner enjoy participating? Do you do these things now? If so, what will a child add to the experience? If not, why not?

One woman complained about having to take her kids to "stupid children's movies," while another childfree woman goes by herself because "I love the cartoons and hearing the kids in the audience laugh."

Judge. Parents set rules, enforce consequences, settle disputes, establish limits (which children love to test!). They lecture, interpret, and intervene in disputes. A great deal of parenting time is spent when the child is not there—many couples spend hours on strategy, so that they can act in accord and intelligently. Happy parents explain and model their decisions and enjoy strategy sessions, while unhappy parents often cite rules and authority or resent planning time. Said Jim, "Sure, I love my kid. But I miss the late night talks we had about our dreams and each other. Now we talk about the kid instead!" How well do you set limits? Stick to what you say? How well do you and your partner talk things over and agree to solutions that suit both of you?

Purchase. Parents buy and resist buying. They purchase clothes, often during the child's most rapid development (birth to 6, and again, 11 to 18). They buy special foods and toys and teach children to resist advertising and to buy wisely. Shopping is a major strategic problem for most parents because it requires either child care or being accompanied by a child.

Interact. Parents communicate; they listen to stories and swap experiences. Happy parents, like people, are open-minded and appreciate differences, but unhappy parents don't enjoy hearing "children" stories, pass judgments on what they hear, and find it difficult to relate honestly to their children. They often prefer things to relationships.

Exercise

If I became a parent today, I would probably do more (list five behaviors you would engage in more frequently):

1. _____

2. _____

3. _____

4. _____

5. _____

I would therefore do less (list five behaviors you would have to cut back or give up):

1. _____

2. _____

3. _____

4. _____

5. _____

Do you resent the trade? Does your partner?

Exercise

One of the major lifestyle changes that occurs when you parent is that you are likely to become more home-centered. To help assess your feelings about this sort of change, consider, for example, how many hours a day are you at home during the day? Weekends? Evenings? Your partner? Obviously, if you go out a great deal, parenting will change your style unless you employ extensive child-care resources. Even if you do, there will be many a missed evening out because of babysitter complications, expenses, and illness.

Also ask yourselves if, when you do go out, you engage in activities that can be adjusted to include children. You can go to a children's museum if you are a museum goer; you can ice-skate, sled, cross-country ski, camp, fish, hike, and so on. Less adjustable activities are downhill skiing, mountaineering, night-clubbing, and so on. The more your present leisure activities exclude the possibility of children being included, the more changes you will have to make.

Laura and Jim were rarely home before the baby. Now Laura tells us the following:

> We don't have the money for a sitter all the time, and sometimes they don't show. And Jim gets so restless, especially when the baby cries. So now he just says, "I'm going out," and out he goes! Even if we could find a sitter, Jim doesn't recognize that we're a family now. He works and then wants to play. I feel trapped and deserted. [We asked her if this really was a change in him or rather if she had just expected that he would change when the baby arrived. Thoughtfully, Laura replied:] No, now that you mention it, he hasn't changed at all. He has always been restless at home. He has always wanted other people around all the time. I don't know why I thought he would just—change.

What you do at home also changes. Most primary parents indicate that there are four major changes in the way they behave when home:

1. *"Sitting-on-your-butt time" decreases.* Most parents have little time to sit down and just read, or daydream, or listen to music—at least during the early years. "Heaven," sighed one mother, "is being able to read a short story from start to finish without interruption."

2. *Private time decreases.* Most parents complain that they no longer have time to themselves. "I can't even go to the bathroom by myself," said one parent. Obviously, there are considerable differences in how we respond to this.

3. *Food-related activities increase.* Eating out, the mainstay of many working couples, decreases until the child is old enough to behave appropriately. Much more energy is spent on shopping, cooking, planning and serving meals, snacks, and so on. Said one mother, "I just can't believe how much more time I spend in the kitchen. I don't use convenience foods that much because they're too expensive and artificial. As a couple, we would grab a quick breakfast, skip lunch, and eat out. As a family I make nutritious breakfasts, lunches, dinners, desserts, snacks, juices, you name it. And while my husband eats everything, my son eats nothing—at least not two days in a row!"

4. *Cleaning activities increase.* Joked one parent, "If you've noticed my swollen right arm, it's from tossing clothes into the washing machine." Another commented, "I never believed one little person could triple my washload." Cleanliness standards must also change, at least through the toddler stage. A dirty floor is not all that impor-

tant—unless you have a two-year-old crawling on it. Leaving out a stack of papers is harmless enough—until your three-year-old wants to see if papers can fly. Even older children may be socially outcast by their peers if you keep your home in a state of disarray that was acceptable to you as a couple. If you both tend to be sloppy, it will be difficult to have neat children. Unless your tolerance for disorder is very high, you would probably end up working to set a fair example so that the children would cooperate. On the other hand, those of you who enjoy the spotlessness of "Home Beautiful" also would have to adjust to the disorder that accompanies an active, playful child.

Since most of us have limited supplies of energy, parenting can exhaust us, physically and emotionally. It's hard to be enthusiastic about anything, or anyone, when you're exhausted.

Exercise

On a scale of 0 (as energetic as a snail during a heat wave) to 10 (you have so much energy you can't sit still), rate yourself and then your partner. Also, do you intend to combine parenting with another activity you are presently doing? If so, how much energy do you have to spare now? When you come home from work, what do you do? How do you feel about coming home to play and care for a child? How much of the time and energy that parenting involves would you and your partner be willing to relegate to others?

RESOURCEFUL PARENTING

As more and more parents are entering the labor force, more and more resources are being developed for child care. The costs and details of these resources have been outlined in chapter 3 on economics, as has a discussion on the pros and cons of both parents working outside the home. These available resources include nannies, live-in-help, babysitters, day sitters, family day care, day care centers (community and private), preschools, nursery schools, family, friends and neighbors, and mothers' cooperatives (a relatively new resource, often locatable only through word of mouth).

Most parents do not use these resources as best they can because they are ambivalent, even guilty, about relying on them. We come from a culture that supports the ideal of a stay-at-home parent whose main purpose is the raising of children. Parents, especially mothers, who do not, or cannot, play this role often feel guilty. But those who do stay at home feel guilty also, especially as costs rise and more women enter the labor market. One childfree woman asked us, "Does parenting have to be an all-or-nothing commitment for me? Do I have to give up everything else in order to be a good mother?" Obviously, this question is of great importance for those deciding whether or not to parent.

What's Good for Children?

Opinions differ as to whether or not children require a constant one-to-one relationship with a parent. We do not believe they do. The isolated, small, nuclear family is a rather recent invention and quite unlike child rearing in many cultures and times. While children do benefit from love, attention, and care, it is not only parental love, attention, and care that will suffice. In the seventeenth century, for example, it was very common for well-to-do children to be completely separated from adult quarters; they often visited their parents only before dinner or on special occasions. Yet, they grew up relatively well-balanced and with behaviors appropriate to their station (not those of their nannies who raised them!).

Many parents fear that a hired helper may not be a "perfect" role model (such as themselves). But you cannot shield a child from other models, even if you think it would be desirable to do so. Besides, by far the most significant influence on a child is not television, or school, or peers, or teachers, or nannies—although they all play a part. The best predictors of a child's interests, personality, and success are his parents—whether or not the child is cared for by a nanny, a day care center, or a parent! Of course, parents should select warm and responsible caretakers. No one would defend leaving a child with a neglectful, abusive, or seriously troubled person—parent or not!

Some theorists have postulated that children should not be separated from their mothers until they reach a certain age. But there is little agreement on whether or not this statement is true, let alone on what this age might be. Actually, infants adapt very readily to warm, substitute caretakers. And while children do experience a short period (usually around 8 to 12 months of age) in which they evidence "stranger anxiety" and "fears of maternal separation," they do so whether or not they have been reared solely by the mother. In one study, researchers found that fully one-third of the infants had fears of separation about *more* than one person. Furthermore, these separation and stranger fears pass whether or not the child stays at home. The adaptability of infants is often painful for parents to accept. The ones who say "oh, my child throws tantrums and is so terrified whenever I leave him" have spent a lot of time shaping up this behavior. We all crave being irreplaceable, but this may not be in the best interest of our children or ourselves.

Other parents fear that their child will feel rejected if they employ child-care resources, especially if they do so voluntarily. There is no evidence that this is so, except when the parents really do reject the child (in this case, an alternative caretaker is probably the *best* option!). Children of working parents have no more problems or insecurities than home-reared children. Regardless of how fashionable it is for some people to trace our problems to our lack of early maternal love, the data in support of this notion is scanty. For example, we assume that the unloved child becomes unlovable—and not the other way around.

If full-time parent care is not necessary, is a one-to-one, full-time relationship with an adult necessary? Again, we believe the answer to be no. In other cultures and times, the rearing of children was only one of many tasks performed by parents. Adults had neither the time nor inclination to hover about children and do little more than parent. Additionally, families were bigger—there were more adults and more children. This exposure to many different people is a facet of development curtailed by our small, isolated family.

Studies support the notion that a ratio of one adult per three children is more than sufficient for optimal learning. In fact, one adult can adequately handle six children over the age of three and ten over the age of four. Furthermore, modern theorists have a way of underestimating the learning that children achieve with other children. Even newborns smile and vocalize more when they are with other babies! Although children don't engage in cooperative play until about the age of three, they definitely interact with each other. We remember a group of two-year-olds who were very depressed because one of their playmates was ill that day! In fact, children who attend day care centers at early ages have marked social acceleration in the early grades at school. This difference disappears by third grade, but such children evidence no deficiencies when compared with home-reared children.

Of course, children, like adults, differ in how well they respond to different environments. Some children thrive in busy centers, with lots of children and adults. Others prefer quieter surroundings with fewer people. And all children change as they develop, so that they outgrow some settings and grow into others. It is important that parents tune in to the most appropriate settings for each child at various stages of the child's development.

Additionally, it is important for the child to relate to a relatively stable group of people. Data support the theory that changing, short-term caretakers interfere with learning subtle, but important, communication skills. Therefore, it is very important that parents make sure that children have relatively permanent caretakers (there can be many!) and that these caretakers be warm and attentive. But there is virtually no convincing evidence demonstrating that 24-hour-a-day parenting is necessary, or even optimal, for a child.

What's Good for Parents?

If children do not require constant parenting, do parents? Do they need to experience that close, intimate, daily contact with their child? Asked Sarah, "Will I regret going off to work and missing the development of my baby?" For some of us, the answer is yes. Some people really do enjoy full-time parenting and are very good at it. If you are one of these people, we hope you have the opportunity to do what you enjoy. However, some people would argue with this kind of "choice," and suggest that.it is far from a free one. Rather, they would argue that this choice is made almost exclusively by women who are playing a script they have been raised to play. Listen to Dr. Barbara Hagaman, cultural anthropologist and feminist:

> Women are told child rearing is the most important task one can perform. We have economically independent women abandoning their paid services to the larger community. They tell me that being a mother is more important than teaching, medicine or business. But I don't see anyone encouraging our top men to drop out of medical school, or resign from corporations to become fathers. And I don't see where teachers and child-care workers are paid any more than waitresses or assembly-line workers. If you want to wade through the bullshit, look at how the society distributes its resources.

Many parents, especially mothers, feel guilty if they even suspect that parenting will not transport them into the realm of ecstasy. The truth is that many (even most?) parents do not enjoy constant, daily, primary parenting. For one thing, they are granted little credit or respect from other adults. "Oh, I'm just a housewife and mother," mutters a woman, abashedly. Fathers come home and ask, "What the hell have you been doing all day?" Nonprofessional full-time mothers are dismissed as not being able to do anything else, anyway, and professional full-time mothers are considered cop-outs. Said Christine, "As soon as I graduated law school, I got pregnant. I have never practiced my profession. I am one of those statistics that help chauvinists discriminate against women. I have heard them, right to my face, say how they should limit the number of women in professions because they just stay home and have babies." While this statement is not true (women professionals work as many years as do their equally paid male counterparts), Christine is hardly in a position to argue the point.

Additionally, parenting is hard work that leaves the parent economically dependent and segregated from the resources of others. One consequence, according to Dr. Hagaman, is "we think we own our children. That's what happens when you ask a full-grown person to abandon paid labor and not to measure benefits the way everyone else in society does." Other emotional consequences of full-time parenting have been found in many cultures. Women who have the heaviest child-care loads are less consistent in expressing warmth to a child. They are also more likely to have hostilities *not* related to the child's behavior. Furthermore, studies of 45 different cultures have found that isolated families, in which a one-to-one child-rearing model was common, evidenced parents who were much more likely to slap, punish, or in other ways inflict pain on their children. This may well be true in our society as well. A number of abusive parents might better handle their tempers if they could have some time away from their children on a regular basis.

It may be, then, that our idealized parent–child relationship may not be all that ideal for many parents, or their children. Most research has found that the quality of the parent–child relationship is far more important than the quantity. They may even be inversely related unless you are one of a rare sort of people. Most of us can relate very positively, warmly, and enthusiastically with children when we have additional sources of stimulation and reinforcement.

Some people believe very strongly that at least one parent ought to be with the children full time. Many couples have had intense arguments because they differ on the use of alternative child-care resources. Certainly, a couple who is open and compatible in its approach to this issue will be more flexible than one deeply committed to home rearing. Listen to Sheryl: "I can't believe the fights Jack and I have had. I want to work but all of a sudden, Jack gets on this 'you're the mother of my child' bit. It's unbelievable!" And Bill: "We agreed to have a child and that Betty would work as soon as she was able. Now she wants to stay home! I don't want my wife to be a babysitter, and, frankly, we need the money. But whenever I bring it up, she acts as though I want to send our kid to a vivisectionist!"

Exercise

How does each of you feel about the following questions after having read the previous section? An open discussion now, before another person is actually involved, may allow for more honesty and compromise.

1. Should a parent be with the child whenever possible?
2. How old should a child be before the primary parent works outside the home? Full time? Part time? (Age is being used here as an approximation of a certain level of development. Of course, children vary, and it is inappropriate to set predetermined age limits.)
3. Should a parent of a young child take a full-time job outside the home? Under what conditions:

   Any conditions the parent chooses? (It is her or his decision.)
   For some extra money for vacations, travel, or for savings for college funds?
   Because of economic necessity? (Without another income, you can't pay for your current obligations.)
4. At what age do you approve of children entering part-time day care setting? Full-time?
5. Is it necessary for a parent to be at home when children return from school? Until what age?

After having discussed your willingness to use outside resources and the extent to which you would use them, you can better discuss how you and your partner would share parenting. This is a major concern of most couples and can have profound effects on the kind of experience you will have as parents.

SHARING THE CARING

For some people, sharing is critical to the decision of becoming a parent. Listen to Charlotte: "I want a third child very much. But I feel as though I raised the first two by myself. I want another only if it's going to be different, you know, *shared.*" And Barbara: "If we want kids, then *we* raise kids. It's that simple."

But it isn't that simple. Many women have earned money for the family, a service once provided primarily by males among the middle and upper class. Said Ellen, "Of course I expect my husband and I to share parenting. He expects me to earn money, I expect him to help around the house." Yet, when asked who did the majority of housework, Ellen replied, sheepishly, "Me." Is her partner likely to assume what she considers to be his fair share of child-rearing responsibilities? "Yes," she insisted, "we've talked it over and agreed. After all, it's only right. We want a child together." What happened? By the time her son was six months old, Ellen had left her job, and her husband had been promoted to a more lucrative and time-consuming position. This sequence is not uncommon. Moreover, it should also be quite predictable. The majority of parenting is still done by women.

Why Fathering Isn't Mothering

There are many reasons why men often play a relatively small part in parenting. The division of labor portrayed by traditional marriages allowed for very efficient and supporting functions. For example, it takes hours to earn the money for a new appliance, and it also takes hours to shop for the best one at the best price. The division of labor into the producer and consumer is most efficient (although some believe it is also exploitive). Any full-time working couple can tell you how infuriating it is to spend all day Saturday on house chores that couldn't be done during the week. A friend provided this example: "It was 9:30 p.m., and Pat and I were exhausted after a hard, long working day. We fell into our kitchen chairs. The dogs were jumping, we were starving and in need of someone to listen to us bitch. We looked at each other and simultaneously said, 'I wish I had a wife.'" Thus, many men and women "revert" to very traditional sex-typed roles when they become parents because the sheer volume of work pressures them into the most efficient division of labor they know. The man who washes dishes for two may not wash dishes for three. The wife who didn't mind doing all the housework now minds considerably as she experiences increased demands.

When financial pressures are felt, the father frequently increases his career investment and simultaneously decreases his time at home. Sometimes this exchange is a way of avoiding parenting, especially during infancy and early childhood when the demands are greatest. When Michael told us his child was beginning to enter the "terrible twos," he laughingly said, "Well, I'd better work overtime a little more." And he did! For some, there is little choice. The sad truth is that men make 40 percent more than equally educated women. Despite "female liberation," male–female salary discrepancies are greater now than they have been since the 1930s! Quite simply, a man's time is generally worth considerably more outside the home than is a woman's.

Also, from conception through birth, men are biologically excluded from a primary parenting experience; if the child is breast-fed, a woman frequently remains the primary parent well into infancy. This pattern often continues. The "exclusion" can be minimized—a father can feed a baby formula or be there during feedings—but it also can be maximized. When Dolores had her baby, she would rarely let her husband hold the child, and when he did, she would circle him as though awaiting disaster. Consequently, her husband held the baby less often.

There is little use denying the fact that most housework and caretaking are still done by women, whether or not they work outside the home and whether or not there are children. A Harvard-based project on Human Sexual Development surveyed 1400 mothers and fathers in Cleveland. While most people agreed that men and women should share housework, 90 percent of the wives and 85 percent of the husbands said that the wives did all or most of the household chores. In fact, less than 3 percent of the households reported that the father did most of the housework while only 12 percent claimed to share the work equally. While our sex-role attitudes have changed, our sex-role behavior appears to be less malleable, for both sexes.

Even when husbands try to participate, wives may criticize them ("No, you don't hold a baby like that!") or do things for them ("Don't bother! I'll do it!"). Sometimes this is done inadvertently—this sort of behavior has been so frequently modeled that women are often not even aware of behaving this way. Sometimes women feel threatened when a man performs well around the house, and keeping him helpless ("Poor Harold! If I didn't cook for him, he would starve to death!") gives women a feeling of importance. Thus, many men may be rewarded when they appear bumbling in the house ("My husband makes bombs for the Pentagon," said one wife, "but he can't seem to learn how to make a scrambled egg").

There are also many interpersonal reasons why men do not often share a goodly amount of parenting. One person in a couple may tend to "weasel out" of commitments, making sharing almost impossible. Some couples don't work well together. Friends, family, and neighbors may criticize either or both of you. Your values and standards may be different than those of the other. If you both have careers, the chances of either of you advancing are reduced; after all, you're probably competing with people for whom work may be primary.

The Advantages of Sharing

Despite all these difficulties, even because of them, many men and women are committed to discovering ways of sharing parenting. Listen to Alan:

> I don't want to be like my father. When we were all grown, then, all of a sudden, he wanted to relate to us. But we had our own lives—he was a stranger. I know he worked hard and loved us and all that, but I never saw him when I grew up. Now he's sorry, because he lost touch with the soft parts of himself. Not me. I'm going to share parenting with my wife. I'm going to keep in touch with the values I think are important. I'm not trading fatherhood for a nicer car.

There are other advantages to sharing parenting. Caretaking, no matter how loving, can become tedious and repetitious, but it is much less so when shared. Sharing allows both of you to do more of other sorts of things while parenting, and advantageously, you will both have more in common. This bond can minimize the gap that often occurs when one of you is engaged solely in working and the other solely in the home. There is likely to be considerably less resentment than is fostered by traditional situations for both parties (He: "All she does is sit around all day while I'm working!"—she: "All he does is flirt and gab all day while I'm stuck in this house"). Both of you will have opportunities to behave in a variety of ways that you may not have tried before. The possibility of one of you coming to monopolize or overwhelm the child will be lessened. If both are working outside the home, one of you won't be completely debilitated by having to do too much. You'll both work hard, but not so hard as not to be able to enjoy life or each other.

Even if parenting is going to be a secondary endeavor for one of you, it is important for you to acknowledge that it will still take time—unless you want to be a stranger to your child and partner! Also, studies have found that fathers have a very important role in their child's development because of the physical nature of their play and style of interaction. Next time, watch the differences between the way men and women interact with children. We think you will find that most men are very physical in their style of play, often throwing infants in the air (and catching them!). They tend to be less verbal than mothers and more tactile. In fact, one study found that most infants chose playing with their fathers rather than with their mothers when given a choice.* It seems that even though most fathers spend relatively little time on caretaking, they spend very important time interacting.

You need to have energy left over from your work to enjoy playing and talking with a child, rather than retreating behind a paper. You need to enjoy family-centered tasks, so that you don't resent spending your spare time in undesirable ways. You also have to be willing to share your partner. Most secondary parents have told us that their biggest resentment was giving up the attention and devotion of their partners. While there are obviously huge differences between the way parents divide their energies, children require and deserve attention; there is only so much to go around. If you don't participate in parenting when you are home, you will be separate from your parenting partner. And later, you'll have a more tired, and perhaps resentful, partner.

Are You Willing to Share?

The decision to share parenting is not an easy one. The following questions have been designed to help you and your partner decide if

---

*Clarke-Stewart, K. A., "And Daddy Makes Three: The Father's Impact on Mother and Young Child," *Child Development* 49 (June 1978):466–78.

you would be willing to share the experience, how much you would want to share, and in what way.

1. *If total child rearing time equals 100 percent, how much of a percentage will each of you do?* It's amazing how few couples verbalize the expectations. She: "We are going to share child rearing, right?" He: "Yes." She: "50-50." He: "Well—maybe not quite 50-50." She: "Oh? 60–40?" He: "70–30?"

Of course, these are estimates, but they are revealing estimates. Many partners have seriously misunderstood how much sharing was going to be entailed. Surprise. Both of you should share your ideal percentages. You can also use examples of tasks you currently share: "I'll share child rearing the way we share taking care of the car, garden, house, bird."

2. *Do you or your partner enjoy doing things with children of various ages? Of both sexes?* If not, there may be times when one or both of you attempt to avoid parenting. One young mother mourned her husband's neglect of their daughter: "If Alice were a son, he would take her with him." Some men reported that their wives disappeared during their child's adolescence, and some wives couldn't remember if their husbands lived at home during the child's first three months. It can become a problem when you both avoid parenting simultaneously. Moreover, it can become a problem when neither of you sees the pattern as a temporary one, but rather as a fixed parenting script that doesn't change as the child does. If one of you dislikes parenting for a given age range, can you compensate for this in some way, recognizing that it is temporary?

3. *Can you count on your partner's verbal commitments?* This is a hard question to ask, but necessary. We sometimes want an agreement so badly that we pressure our spouse into half-hearted compliance, or we misinterpret gentle refusals. Some people do not feel bound by verbal agreements, as Lisa stated: "My husband said, sure, we'd parent together. But we don't. I don't know why I believed him. He was always telling me he'd do things—and he means it too. But he never quite gets around to doing anything. Being a parent, either."

A few couples have written contracts stipulating exactly who is responsible for what and for how long. In this way, one's roles are clear to all; written agreements are more public and permanent than spoken ones. ("But you agreed to doing the nighttime feedings!" "I never said any such thing.")

A contract specifies:

Those responsibilities for which each partner is responsible.

What will happen if each partner does what is expected.

What will happen when neither partner does what is expected.

How and when either partner can renegotiate.

The contract is signed by both parties and dated; some people even have it witnessed. One couple went to a lawyer. You might wonder who would want a baby with someone you had to take to a lawyer? But only in modern times and among few cultures have people avoided establishing elaborate contracts when expanding kinships. The affluent are careful in arranging inheritance matters well in advance. Spouses have frequently had recourse to legal protection from each other, and the extent to which they do so is determined mostly by class and culture.

Most couples prefer to share parenting less formally. Some feel a contract takes all the fun out of parenting—like "setting time limits for foreplay." But how seriously is your partner committed to the sharing he or she agrees to? Does she or he follow through on these sorts of commitments? Or does he or she forget? Or deny making them? Or have so much else to do first? Or change his or her mind frequently? We don't like to be this objective with loved ones, but sometimes it is easier to accept someone's differences from the beginning than to cast them in a script they will not and do not play.

4. *How evenly do you and your partner share work responsibilities?* If you already have children, what percentages of child rearing tasks does each of you do? Do you expect a change? Why? Both of you have changed, and parenting will be different this time. In what way? If you do not have children but have pets, who is the primary caretaker? How much of the responsibilities and joys do you share? Said Mary, "If I waited for my husband to feed the dog, we would have a very dead dog." Is this pattern likely to continue with a child? If one of you is already working disproportionately hard, how will a child affect this ratio? Do you have an accurate assessment of you and your partner's contributions? Betty had been married 18 years and told us that she resented how hard she worked. She had a part-

time job plus the major responsibility for the home and children. When her husband came home, he would sit down and expect to be waited on. He was resistant to any change in this pattern, claiming he had worked hard enough all day.

In order to assess whether Betty really had a justifiable complaint, we asked her to compare her and her spouse's working hours per week. One reason for doing this is to counteract the natural but inaccurate tendency to exaggerate one's own working time and to minimize another's; this assessment also controls for the fact that "women's work is never done." Rarely do married women (in most households) come home and plop down with a paper for the evening. Because they are usually the first up and the last to bed, they feel as though they work many more hours than their husbands, even if they have spare time during the day.

The following exercise measures the time both of you spend on necessary work activities. Include only activities that are *essential*— if you enjoy working on cars as a hobby, include only that time necessary to run a car. If your going to night school is necessary for your career, it counts—if not, it doesn't, even if it will benefit your career in the long run.

Exercise

Hours in paid or necessary employment activities (include transportation and dressing time):

	You	*Partner*
Monday	_____	_____
Tuesday	_____	_____
Wednesday	_____	_____
Thursday	_____	_____
Friday	_____	_____
Saturday	_____	_____
Weekly Total	_____	_____

Hours in house-related chores, weekly:

	You	*Partner*
Laundry	_____	_____
Bills	_____	_____
Food shopping	_____	_____
Food preparation	_____	_____
Cleaning	_____	_____
Garbage	_____	_____
Lawn, garden	_____	_____
Repairs	_____	_____
Cars	_____	_____
Other necessary chores (clothes shopping, etc.)	_____	_____
Weekly Total	_____	_____
COMPLETE TOTALS	_____	_____

When Betty added up her hours, she was shocked to discover that her husband put in significantly more working hours than she did—it was only that she tended to work the most when he was home resting. When she saw that the problem was distribution rather than amount of work, she no longer resented the situation.

After evaluating the amount of time both of you spend on work activities, ask yourselves what is likely to happen when a child appears? How are you going to try to balance the increased time demands?

5. *How often and well do you work together?* Pick an example, like having to wash the car or run a party. Which of the following portrayals best describes you? (There may be more than one.)

When we're together, we don't do anything but relate to each
other.

If we have to do something, then we do it together, happily.

We enjoy working together on most things.

We try to work together, but often end up arguing.

He or she does it, and I watch.

We both do different things at the same time.

I do it, and he or she disappears.

What I do, I do—what he or she does, we do.

These styles often continue into parenting. If you expect a different
style to emerge, how will it develop? Why should your style change?
How will you help it to change?

After considering these issues, if you do want to share parenting,
consider whether you want to parent jointly or to alternate responsibility. In joint parenting, you both try to be with the child and to
share responsibilities as much as possible. If the child is sick, for
example, you may discuss who stays home. In alternate parenting,
you alternate primary responsibility in some systematic way. Unlike
joint parenting, each of you clearly has the most responsibility at
different periods of time. While both include sharing, they require
very different kinds of arrangements and interactions.

If you are people who value being together, joint parenting is ideal
if you have very flexible schedules. You are probably going to need
money for supplementary child care in order to get out together occasionally. One of the happiest situations we have seen involved a
young couple who owned a hobby store. Both worked together in
the store, and when the baby came, they built a little crib for him
next to the cash register. The child was always playing with some
adult and was as happy and curious a child as we have seen. If he
needed some special attention, one or both of his parents would
take care of him. All were delightfully happy. His proud father an-
nounced, "He's the only six-month-old who reaches for money!"
Of course, these are unusual circumstances (in the past they were
quite typical!) since fewer couples today have such opportunities
for sharing.

Even if time and scheduling problems can be arranged for joint parenting, several issues should be considered as to how well you work together. Try and answer these questions:

1. *Will one of you (or both) try to take over whatever task you both undertake?* Three women were preparing dinner during a recent party. One said the following, "Have you ever noticed how well we work together? You can't do that with my husband. As soon as he's involved, he has to take over and order me around. He never just helps." Everyone agreed, with one replying, "In fact, my husband's more of a pain in the ass than a help. It's easier to banish him from the kitchen than to try to work with him—or should I say *for* him?" Will this conversation apply to your parenting together?

2. *Do you hold different standards for performance or value different things than your partner?* One husband said that nothing he did around the house pleased his wife. When he washed the dishes, she proclaimed them dirty and so on. If you are parenting together, will you tend to share the same priorities? Does the house have to be in perfect order? If your child gets into a chocolate cake, will one of you, laughing, find a camera, and will one of you, screaming, throw the baby into a bath?

3. *How differently will you parent from each other?* Very often, significant differences in social class, education, religion, and ethnicity become obvious and difficult to manage when you parent. This problem is so important that the entire next chapter will be devoted to it. When you have differences (and no matter how well matched you are, you will!), how do you resolve them? Are these differences likely to continue when parenting? If so, how will you both deal with the situation?

4. *Will the time you spend together now change if you parent jointly?* You may want to test your tolerance of each other *before* a third party enters the scene.

Alternating Sharing

Some couples, no matter how loving, cannot or do not wish to parent jointly. Instead they prefer to share parenting by alternating primary responsibility. In this way, they both can continue to parent and work outside the home—without having a third person taking care of the baby. Jimmy and Gloria decided on the alternate arrangement. Jimmy works weekdays and his wife, a nurse, works weekends. "This way we raise our own baby," explained Gloria. How well do they like the arrangement? Jimmy: "It's fine for the baby, but it's hell on us. We never get together anymore. We haven't been out in months. And then it's rarely as a family—it's me and the baby, Gloria and the baby, or me and Gloria. It's not good." (Of course, this situation gets less extreme as the child gets older and stays awake later at night.)

Others alternate daily. Judy and Harry are both academics. Each takes turns getting up with the baby. They scheduled their courses on different days and parent accordingly. They sometimes switch the baby back and forth two or three times daily. Said Harry, "It's awkward sometimes. I'll be lecturing and suddenly, Judy will come in with the baby because she has to deal with something else. But generally, it's wonderful. The baby is comfortable with us both and is an integral part of our lives."

Some couples with similar careers get one position for both of them. They may alternate every six months, or semesters if academics. This arrangement is quite common in Scandinavia and is on the rise here. (It causes some complications in terms of benefits, but they can be ironed out.) Alternate parenting is becoming an option for divorced and separated parents who chose not to appoint one parent with primary custody.

How can you arrange alternate parenting? Scheduling should be worked out as clearly and flexibly as possible, *in advance*. Try it on paper and discuss how you both would feel about it. How much time will you and your partner be apart? How often will you be able to socialize or go out without the baby? How often will you be a family? Problems can develop if you have very different styles because when you're all together, everyone may get confused. But for many, alternate parenting is ideal. One father told us that without this option, he never would have tried a homemaking role. He had agreed to give it a try for three months. His conclusion? "I love it! I think I'll stay home permanently!"

PARENTING MOSTLY BY YOURSELF

Sometimes your partner or you reneges on the sharing. Or you split. Or one of you dies. Or you didn't have a partner to start with. Or you're changing partners. Or your partner was never interested in sharing very much. You are doing most of it yourself.

Being a primary parent means adopting the primary responsibility for the welfare of the child. This responsibility can vary from a 60–40 sharing arrangement with your partner to being a single parent. The vast majority of homes in America are parented mostly by one parent—usually, but not always, the mother. There are also increasing numbers of single-parent families (unmarried, divorced, widowed, separated, deserted, and so on).

As a primary parent, you have to consider certain issues unique to this situation. Do you know how primary you will be? If you have a partner, what is it that he or she will take responsibility for? Sometimes one parent "trades" the right to have a baby for sole responsibility. You have to be very careful when you are "blackmailed" into primary parenting. Tina was 32 and wanted a baby badly; finally, her husband agreed, but only on the condition that she "take care of it." He would contribute economically, but he did not want to be expected to do anything else unless he so decided.

Many couples accept similar sorts of compromises when there are considerable differences between them. After all, "I really don't want a child! I feel I'm already sacrificing my wife—or at least some of her." Yet no one can help resenting such a situation. You may even end up covering for the other parent. People usually don't tell their children, "Your father's a creep and never does anything for you." Instead they try to leave room for the other parent to change— and in so doing, they anxiously try to mold the child into patterns acceptable to the partner. Others don't want their child to know about problems the partner is having, or may try to hide the fact that the partner may dislike the child. Ethel agreed to bear a child if her husband would be the primary parent and buy her a dog (honest!). Said her husband, "I never knew where she was coming from. One day she might decide to take our son out or play with him. The next day she would go into a rage if I asked her if she wanted to do anything! Then I would try to make things seem okay. How can you explain this to a child? I don't even understand it."

What will your partner do? Will he or she call babysitters? Drive to school? Feed? Clothe? Under what conditions? One husband told us, "Ellen will do 60 percent, and we'll hire a nanny to do my 40 percent." Ellen was not amused. It is important that you have a good idea of what parenting will be like with this partner and whether both of you can live with the arrangements without too much resentment.

The primary parent model can work very well. Many couples assume that the mother will take the role of the primary parent and she often does so, thus enabling the husband to devote his time to other necessary features of family life. In other situations, the woman has no steady partner. Does this affect the child? Studies have found that there are consequences of having no older male in a household when a child is under five years of age. Of course this does not have to be the *father*—an older brother, uncle, or grandfather seems to suffice. Boys without early male models tend to be either more or less aggressive than others. Girls tend to have difficulty in relating sexually to men when they get older; they may be uncomfortable and unsure of how to flirt or handle sexual advances. If the father (or male figure) leaves after the child is older than five, these problems are less likely to develop. However, this absence can be altered by arranging for the child to have regular interaction with an older male model.

Less evidence has been gathered on the effects of a father raising a child by himself. There were only 450,000 single male parents in the United States as of 1976; in Canada, 20 percent of the single-parent families are headed by men. Of these, most fathers will either remarry or arrange in some other way for a female caretaker for the child.

When the Father Is the Mother

We spoke to some men who had decided to be the primary parent and found that they often reached this decision by considering personal predilections and economics. At present, only 15 percent of the families with mothers in the working force are managed by the father. Many of these are not by choice, but as a temporary measure during unemployment, or because of a disability. It is unknown how many men actually choose to be primary parents.

A British study of motherless families found that 60 percent of the fathers reported considerable depression, difficulty sleeping, and less concentration at work.* Studies have found that single fathers find the most difficulty in the same areas as do mothers: difficulty in balancing work outside the home with parenting, isolation and a poor social life, depression and stress, and ignorance about children, homemaking, and parenting.

The portrait is considerably altered when the father elects to be the primary parent or when there is a supportive partner. We interviewed two such men. Edna and Tim are both professionals. The wife is a lawyer and the husband a marketing consultant. Tim: "My wife loves her work more than I do! She even makes more money than I and is well on her way up the administrative ladder. I love kids, and I like staying home, cooking, and cleaning, and so on. I'll probably see a few clients on a part-time basis and raise our child."

Linda and Steve live in Hawaii. Both are postal clerks. The mother explains, "At first I stayed home with our child. But I felt cooped up and short tempered. But Steve loved to play with the kid so we said we would try and switch roles for a month. Our boss agreed, and it's worked splendidly."

While the primary fathers we interviewed were very happy, they enumerated several points of difficulty for those who are considering primary fathering:

How ambitious are you really?

Are you trying to flee into the home role or have you chosen it because it fits you well?

Will you, later in your life, regret and resent your reversal of traditional priorities?

---

*Keshet, Harry Finkelstein and Rosenthal, Kristine M., "Single Parent Fathers: A New Study," *Children Today* (May–June 1978).

How are your friends, family, and community likely to react?

The postal clerks, for example, experienced considerably more social disapproval and criticism than the professional couple, who were often admired for being unconventional. Both men said one of the major difficulties they faced was dealing with the community. "I'm the only young man in the park," laughed one. "You get lonely, and you try to talk with the young mothers. It's like walking on eggs, though. Their husbands don't like it one bit and sometimes, just to get them jealous, the women may imply an interest you don't have. I almost got punched out last week."

There are several questions that men should consider before deciding whether to take on the responsibility of primary parenting:

1. *Are you willing to respect your partner's right to pursue her career in her way?* Of course, this question should apply to women also, but we do come from a society that downplays women's careers. Women, generally, are more oriented to security than upward mobility (for obvious reasons, we think). Will you respect your partner's right to make decisions about her job as you would if you were the primary worker? Obviously, we do not mean that you shouldn't have input into career decisions, but rather that when you exchange roles, you don't lay your "abandoned" ambitions on her shoulders.

2. *Is your partner willing to respect your right to be a primary parent in your own way?* Will she be criticizing your cooking, cleaning, laundry, and the way you spend your day? Will she be able to let you take responsibility for things she may have done in the past? ("A cinch!" claim many women until they try it!)

3. *Will both of you feel comfortable with the exchange?* Will you suddenly realize that you are attracted by soft, feminine women and be turned off by your wife's orientation? Will she realize that she is turned on by successful, competitive men while you are being supportive and gentle?

4. *What tasks are you including in parenting?* Cooking? Home repairs? Car repairs? Laundry? Is your workload going to be bal-

anced? Can each of you do, or learn to do, these tasks adequately? Said one mother, "John said since he had learned to care for an infant, I could learn to tune the car. 'No thanks,' I told him—'I'll take it to a garage.' He got all upset!" She probably could have, maybe even should have, learned this task. But it is also possible that it was not worth learning for her—many men and women have others tune their cars. If her husband feels strongly about this issue, they can trade tasks of approximately equal time demands, or they can exchange money items equal to the cost of the tune-up. When you change roles, it is best to address each of your limitations and your strengths and then try to arrange responsibilities accordingly.

The Problems of Being Primary

Some primary parents are so busy doing other sorts of things that they have little time for parenting. Sometimes this is by choice. Susan, a mother of five, is rarely home. She can often be found on the tennis courts or shopping. When she is home, she is likely to be sunning herself or reading. She hires local teenagers to care for the children, who are clean and well dressed but who can often be heard calling for her.

Sometimes the demands of being a primary parent can seriously disrupt your career. Listen to Sharon, a lawyer:

It isn't fair that many of us have to choose between being a professional or being a parent, but there you are. To be both, you need extraordinary amounts of energy. I don't have it, that's all. Yes, I've fallen way behind because I'm a mother, even though we use day care. Listen, I come home every night and have to clean and cook and parent. My male colleagues go home to a warm dinner, read the paper, and work on briefs. In the morning while I'm cooking and driving kids around, they're sitting on their commuter trains getting chummy. And when the kids are sick or there's a problem, I have to deal with it. It's not only the doing—it's the thinking, the worry, the distraction. There are men in my office who are fathers, but it isn't the same. It's a much smaller piece of their lives. By the time my kids are old enough, I'll be too old to really make it. Hell, I'm not sure making it is all that important, anyway. It's just that people ought to know that it takes a lot of work to make it—and a lot to be a good mother. And I don't have enough energy to do both.

Primary fathers have the same limitations. They are less likely to be promoted; in fact, one English study documented a 44 percent decrease in family income three years after the mother's absence (although she contributed only 12 percent of the income).

Other people find work interferes with parenting, but they have no choice. One young divorcée has an executive position in an insurance firm. Her daughter, Nicole, is one and one-half years old. "I hate not being able to bring up my own baby. But I have to work overtime to support us, to give her a chance to live in a nice neighborhood and to go to a good school. So I drop her off at the preschool at seven. My mother picks her up at six. When I get home, about ten or so, she's fast asleep. On weekends, I sometimes work or else I have errands to run. So it goes. I love her, but I'm almost a stranger to her."

Some people find the prospect of single parenting so aversive that they do not want children for fear of becoming a single parent. "I'm afraid," confessed one 25-year-old woman. "If we were to split, then I would be alone with a kid. Who would want me then? I couldn't do anything. It would make me feel so dependent. Now I do what I want, and if he doesn't like it, then I am free to move on without too many complications." When asked how she and her husband got along, she replied, "Great." At our curious expression, she explained that "lots of people get along great and then divorce. You can't tell!"

Our social climate is much more supportive of unmarried parents than it has been in the past. More and more subcultures in our society readily accept, even respect, the unmarried parent (one study related this to the increase in premarital teenage pregnancies). This attitude is quite a change, given our heritage in regard to bastards and "shamed women." There are many free community agencies (listed in the telephone directory) that counsel unmarried persons regarding whether or not to keep a baby.

Some unmarried fathers are now requesting custody of their children, and some people even plan on being unmarried parents. Said Jill, age 23, "I don't want a man. I don't want to get married. But I do intend to have a baby." Will she be comfortable with the reaction of her family? Her friends? Employers? Community? Is she looking forward to discomforting, maybe shocking, someone? Has she worked out parenting strategically? Marriage will be less likely as an unmarried mother than if she doesn't have a child or is a divorcée. How will being a "bastard" affect the child? Most of these children miss not having a father and suffer some cruelty and name-calling by peers. However, they have no more problems than children whose parents divorced early in life. There is still shame attached to being a child out of wedlock—especially if the father is unknown. However, it is lessening among Americans in general and has virtually disappeared in some subcultures. Most children experience, but survive, the stigma.

Other single parents are homosexuals; they have chosen to raise a child (either by adoption or otherwise). The effects of being raised by a gay person or couple have not been well studied, mainly because these people often do not identify themselves. Also, until recently, homosexuals changed partners very frequently; within the last few years, however, gays are forming more stable relationships, even getting married. Currently, the courts are trying to decide whether or not homosexuals can have custody of their children; until recently, it was one of the few reasons for which judges would remove a child from the biological mother.

One's sexuality, however, is not related to one's parenting abilities —a gay person can be a marvelous parent. If you are gay, how discreet are you? What would you tell a child? How much lying would be necessary, and could you adapt to either that or coming out? How would you feel about your child's sexual orientation? If you think you would be a good parent, check with your state homophile league on current laws. Then at least you'll know the rules.

So far, we have outlined the lifestyle changes necessitated by parenting. But having a child changes more than the activities in which you engage. It also has profound effects on your relationships with other people: with yourself, your partner, with your other children if you have them, with your parents and in-laws, even with your friends and neighbors. These interpersonal changes are the subject of our next chapter.

ADDITIONAL READINGS

Caplan, Frank. *Parents Yellow Pages: A Directory.* New Jersey: Princeton Center for Infancy, 1977.

Elkind, David. *A Sympathetic Understanding of the Child: Birth to Sixteen.* Boston: Allyn and Bacon, 1971.

Galper, Miriam. *Coparenting: Sharing Your Child Equally.* Philadelphia: Running Press, 1978.

Keshet, Harry Finkelstein, and Rosenthal, Kristine. "Single Parent Fathers: A New Study." *Children Today.* May/June 1978.

Klein, Carol. *The Single Parent Experience.* New York: Avon Books, 1978.

Moore, Raymond S., and Moore, Dennis R. "How Early Should They Go To School?" *Childhood Education,* May/June 1976.

Olds, Sally Wendkos, "When Mommy Goes To Work . . ." *Family Health/Today's Health,* February 1977.

Parke, Ross D., and Sawin, Douglas B. "Fathering: It's a Major Role." *Psychology Today,* November 1977.

5

Interpersonal Considerations

Relationships with other people change dramatically when you parent. The time, energy, and economic demands discussed in previous chapters can produce changes in the ways you behave toward others. Additionally, values and priorities often change, which lead to changes in the way you perceive yourself and other people. And people treat you differently as a parent; in fact, you may even treat yourself differently!

This chapter has been divided into seven sections in order to discuss these interpersonal changes:

1. *The meaning of parenthood.* In this section we talk about one of the most elusive and intense experiences of parenting—the relationship between parent and child. How important and positive a relationship would it be for you?

2. *Will a child bring you together or.* . . . When you parent, you may discover some profound differences that can strain even the best of relationships if you are unprepared for them. This section has been designed to help you anticipate, and either avoid or prepare for, these differences.

3. *When two become three, three become four, four.* . . . Family dynamics, for both parents and children, change with each child you have. This section looks at some of the characteristics of different size families to help you assess how many children you and your partner want, if any, and the best way to space them.

4. *Other family members.* Parenting, or not parenting, changes relationships with your parents, siblings, and in-laws. It can precipitate crises we thought we had resolved years ago and initiate con-

flicts and unions that surprise us. Some of the more common changes
are discussed, along with ways of handling them.

5. *Your friends and neighbors.* Most of us are social beings, and
parenting (or not parenting when others are) often disrupts our
friendships and interactions with our communities. This section
looks at how this may happen to you and what you can do about it.

6. *Looking ahead.* Parenting spans so many years that we cannot
afford to be shortsighted. The reluctant parent of today may become
the enthusiastic parent of tomorrow and vice versa! While it is difficult to project ourselves into a changing future, there are fairly consistent patterns to the changes that we adults experience as we age.
In this section we will discuss how people's feelings about themselves
as parents, and nonparents, tend to change as they get older.

7. *Twenty questions for consideration.* We will ask you and your
partner some personal questions to help you evaluate some of the
concerns raised in this chapter.

It is not easy to predict how you are likely to behave as a parent.
Those of you with children have the best available basis for making
predictions, as long as you keep in mind changes in yourself, your
partner, and your environment, all of which can greatly affect your
next parenting experience. For those of you who have not parented,
prediction is more difficult. However, there are sources of information
that will help you develop a reasonably good idea of the interpersonal
changes that would accompany parenting for you.

One informational source is how you relate to children. If you
don't know how you and your partner behave *together* with children, it is important that you find out. After all, many people treat
children quite differently from adults, and their behavior can be
quite a surprise to someone who has seen them only in adult company. You can borrow your nephews and nieces (your relatives will
be grateful, and you will also benefit!)—or volunteer to work at a
local park, camp, or school. Share a skill with a Cub or Girl Scout
troop in your neighborhood. Certainly, you should explore opportunities to observe you and your partner's parenting styles with
children of different ages and sexes.

A second most important source of information is how you were
raised. Most studies have found that we tend to parent as we were

parented. We especially tend to behave as did our same-sexed parent. Therefore, the more differently you and your partner were raised, the more different you are likely to be when parenting. Now this doesn't mean we *have* to behave like our parents—only that we will tend to. Our parents are our first, and often only, models, so it's understandable that we would tend to behave as they behaved when similar sorts of situations arise. Of course, we can and do change. But we think people tend to overestimate how consciously they control their own behavior. Parenting is so complex and involves such a large, varied repertoire that much of what we do is "automatic." Those parents who do try to make major changes often report being exhausted by the constant self-monitoring required. Through sheer exhaustion and frustration, many of them are turning to books that advise them to "rely on their instincts." But when most parents "do what comes naturally," they usually do just what their own parents did!

A third ancillary source of information is how you treat your pets. We have found that there are general similarities between the way some people treat their pets before they have children and the way they treat their children. Of course, there are vast differences between children and pets, but both set the occasion for cooperative caretaking and require that couples address differences concerning discipline, affection, tolerance, and play.

We believe that all of us (with or without children) can get a useful approximation of how well we and our partner are likely to respond to being parents in the near future. We can explore and discuss differences we are likely to encounter, and we can then assess more accurately whether this parenting experience will facilitate or disrupt our relationships. Even more importantly, if we decide to parent, we can prepare by recognizing and minimizing many of our differences and sources of conflict *before* a baby is born.

THE MEANING OF PARENTHOOD

"A parent–child relationship is what I most fear missing," confessed one childfree woman. Even those with children share similar feelings.

Said Jan, mother of three, "Every child I don't have is a special person I won't get to know."

There is little question that in our culture the parent–child relationship is unique in its intensity, permanence, and quality. Those of you with children know the hard-to-describe feelings of a parent. You also know how different the feelings can be for different children. No two children are alike, and loving each equally does not mean having the same feelings for both. For those without children, the relationship can better be imagined by remembering how you felt about your parents as you grew up. It may also be useful to observe the parent–child relationships around you. What kinds of interactions do you see among parents who are similar to you with children of different ages and sexes?

It is obviously difficult, probably impossible, to portray the complexities, intensities, and ambivalences of something as individual and changing as a parent–child relationship. In this section we will simply describe how some parents report feeling about their children. These parental feelings are hard to put into words, but considering them is essential in making a parenting decision. After all, for parents they comprise one of the most important of life's experiences. While some of us may elect to travel a different path, we should address the good, and bad, feelings we will be missing before we make our decision.

Mothering

Mother–child relationships have been a favored subject of research and fiction. Mother–son interactions were described by Freud as the most perfect relationship in the world. (Of course, his was the son's point of view.) The mother secures the penis she has been denied. If one translates "penis" as a symbol of control, power, respect, and potential (rather than as an anatomical feature), penis envy is still a reality. Mother–daughter relationships have been portrayed in some excellent films ("An Unmarried Woman," "Autumn Sonata") and books. *My Mother, Myself,* by Nancy Friday, is very provocative.

It is clear that for many women motherhood is the most important role in their lives, often valued far more than the relationship with their partners. *The Washington Post* (Nov. 1971) published a Harris poll which found that 53 percent of the women interviewed experienced their major life satisfaction from being mothers. Only 23 percent reported major satisfaction from being wives—1 percent more than the 22 percent who achieved major satisfaction from housework!

Several mothers we interviewed said being a parent was the most wonderful, significant event in their lives. "Sure, it's a lot of work," said one young mother, "but my children are my very favorite people, my dearest friends." Another said, "I can't even imagine a life without my children. It would be unlived." But not all mothers feel this way. "I adore my daughter," said one mother, "but I get so tired of being leaned on and used all the time." And Elona told us, "I am too old, too tired. I would rather be working." Dependency seemed to be a major theme in their feelings. The women who disliked the mother role hated the never-ending "me-ness" of their children. The less satisfaction they received from giving and helping, from being backstage instead of centerstage, the less positively they felt about their relationships.

Are there differences in the relationships of mothers with sons than with daughters? Most said very definitely, yes. The mothers of sons often said they were thrilled by a man's potential—"Few women have not experienced the pain or limitations of being female," said one mother. "To have a son who won't feel those things is very exciting to me." Almost 86 percent of a freshman class of 103 indicated that their mothers gave preferential treatment to the males in the family. Some of these preferences were minor: "In my house, the men were always served first, the best, and most." Others were major: "I could stay out as late as I wanted to, use the car, and go to college. My older sister got nothing."

The change in women's behavior—their increased ambition, participation in sports, access to birth control, financial independence—makes mother–daughter relationships especially rewarding and/or difficult. "You see yourself in a daughter," said one mother. "I feel about her like I feel about the best piece of myself. I want her to flower, to be more of herself than I got to be of myself." In past generations and cultures, the birth of a daughter was seen as unfortunate. Girls were of little economic or social use; their own mothers grieved. Said an Italian grandmother, "When my first daughter was born, there was none of the thrill I had with my son. I knew what her life would be. She cooks, she cleans, she serves a man, and has his babies."

For American-born women of today, there are more options. "I'm thrilled to have a daughter," said one woman. "The world is changing for her. She has so many opportunities, so much to choose from." But she also confessed some apprehension: "It's more difficult raising a girl now. It's harder to make decisions when there is so much talk about change and so little of it in actuality. How do you handle birth control? Little League? I think your goals, society's goals, are much clearer for a boy."

Fathering

Father–child relationships were, until recently, rarely discussed. There was almost a conspiracy of silence about how fathers felt about their children. Being a father was treated as an aside—"He is president of X Company, a member of X society, a water skier, hiking enthusiast, and father of eight." The research on fathers is scant, even though the majority of researchers have been male. Studies have found that men tend to sex stereotype children more than do women. Most fathers we interviewed who had both sons and daughters felt very differently about them.

The father–child relationship has been very variable through the centuries, with fathers sometimes having minimal contact with their offspring. Today, more fathers seem to want to be personally involved in relationships with their children. More and more college freshmen males report signing up for child development courses in order to "be a better father when the time comes." As more men and women share roles, fathers may contribute more to their families, and receive more in return. Said one recent father, "How can you describe what it feels like to look at your child? I know millions of people have children, but it feels as though no one could ever feel the feelings I feel—joy and fear and hope and pride, all mixed up. A smile is a miracle."

Father–son conflicts have been extensively discussed, but usually from the son's point of view. More is said of the child's desire to overthrow the father than of the father's desire to maintain control, and more is said of the child's fear of castration than of the father's urge to castrate. Along with these conflicts, which most men have experienced from at least the son's vantage point, is the inordinate pride and pleasure many fathers take in their sons. "My joy," said one father about his child. (*Kramer versus Kramer,* a novel by Avery Corman, beautifully explores a developing father–son relationship.)

Fathers and daughters also have complex relationships. Most studies have found that successful women share a history of having very close, warm relationships with their successful fathers. And women whose fathers are not present during their early years often have a lot of difficulty relating to men during adolescence. There is probably a mock flirtation between fathers and daughters that is useful, but may be very uncomfortable for some fathers. The fathers we interviewed sometimes didn't know quite what to do with their daughters. When daughters become adolescents, many fathers experience sexual crises. "Thinking of pimply kids trying to hump my daughter obsesses me," grieved one father. "It's changed all my feelings about men and women. I'm suddenly confused."

Many fathers, especially cynical ones, reported very positive feelings toward their daughters. Their girls were the embodiment of goodness, and with them they could safely be indulgent, gentle, and tender. Men are much less competitive with daughters; even their play is less physical and more communicative. Said one father, "My daughter is my number one companion. When I come home from work, I can't wait to hear her stories about school and what she's learned." Contrast this with the father who said bitterly, "Relationship? Oh, yes, I'm the guy who brings home the bacon between *Sesame Street* and *Star Trek.*"

The Simple Joys of Parenting?

None of these encapsulated descriptions captures the intensity and complexity of parent–child relationships. The sacrifices parents lovingly make for their children (sometimes of their own lives) testify to the depth of their feelings. There is little doubt that of all the features of parenting missed by nonparents, the parent–child relationship is the least replicable. Childfree people can establish close relationships with relatives, or neighbors, or foster children, but they are not the same as the relationship that evolves in the caring and rearing of a child, whether or not it is your own "flesh and blood." (While biological parenthood may be important, many parents of adopted children claim that they feel as strongly about them as they do their biological children, sometimes even more strongly.) It is the rearing of a child that is irreplaceable and which in our culture defines the parent–child bond.

To balance this view is the realization that the parent–child relationship may not necessarily be primary (although it is usually important), and it may not necessarily be positive. Pronatalists sometimes portray parenting as a biologically determined event of absolute primacy. While it may be so for some parents, it is not so for others, sometimes for entire cultures. One Peace Corps volunteer in Africa was astounded by the fact that most of the tribal women she talked to were not sure of how many children they had borne. In the past, many fathers were equally ignorant of their number of illegitimate progeny. In other cultures, babies who were either deformed or female were killed by their mothers; in others, firstborns were sacrificed, either to deities, other tribes, or in service to nobility. Despite the supposed primacy of parent bonds, parents surrender their children often and willingly—to custom, religion, or politics.

Today more and more parents are physically leaving their children much of the time in preference for another partner, a career, or a change in lifestyle. Parents are people, too, and as we'll discuss in a later section, they change as they age. Their priorities and goals shift, as does their environment. Sometimes, their relationships with their children may be less critical than other features of their lives.

The U.S. Census Bureau predicts that 45 percent of all children born in 1977 will spend a significant period of their lives with only one parent. Some parents even run away. While the majority are fathers, the number of runaway mothers has increased from 1 percent of the total runaway parents in 1976 to 5 percent in 1978. The problem has become so significant that states such as Michigan spend 12 million dollars yearly to track down runaway parents—and their child-care payments.

Even for nondeserting parents, the parent–child relationship is not always sufficient unto itself. Although many parents report that the infant and preschool years are the most rewarding, these years are also the most common ones for maternal depression, anxiety, child abuse, and divorce. For most of us, however, the search for happiness, meaningfulness, and fulfillment does not end with, but may include, parenthood.

The primacy of parenting is also affected by changes in the child's needs as he or she ages. The parent–child relationship is usually primary for everyone during the child's early years. By the age of one and one-half, most primary parents are ready to let their children have the freedom they need and want. By six or seven, the child is forming many significant relationships outside the home. Many parents are depressed by this independence, sometimes without realizing it. Parents often start, or increase, involvement in other activities at this time. Adolescence is frequently tumultuous, with adolescents and parents trying to work out the transition to adulthood. Often mother–daughter and father–son conflicts are hot and heavy. Letting go is difficult. But later on these conflicts smooth out, and even closer ties may be established. Adult years are years in which the relationship is less important, at least in our culture. (In others, the parent–child relationship stays primary.) While the rewards of parenting may extend throughout life, certainly they are concentrated in the early years.

Along with not being primary, parent–child relationships may not be all positive. In many instances, parents feel either ambivalent, or actually hostile, about their children. "I hate you," young children scream at their parents—and mean it. The parents assume a veneer of emotional consistency that is only superficial. In our interviews with parents, we were constantly surprised by the extent of the ambivalence parents reported. Parents with the most beautiful children, with whom they apparently had joyous relationships, confessed to many moments of regret. They found it hard to communicate the fact that they loved their children, sincerely and deeply, and yet, simultaneously, wished they had not had them. These ambivalent feelings can be affected by numerous factors.

Parent–child fit is critical to how good a relationship will be. The jangly, problem child can tie the mellow, slow-moving parent into emotional knots. (Some parents have excellent relationships with all but one of their children.) How well a parent parents is also critical to a good relationship. Whether or not the parents set limits that both they and their child can live with will determine the way they will relate to each other (much more is said on this in chapter 6). Some children have problems that estrange their parents. They may fall short of parental expectations or violate parental values. Many children have grown up believing that their parents thought they were not worth the trouble. Some of these are "good kids"; others have, or have caused, significant difficulties. Said Angela, "If I had known my boy would turn out like this, I wouldn't have had him."

Also important is how much we enjoy what it is we must do as parents; this can be distinct from our enjoyment of the child for whom we do it (as discussed in chapter 4). The importance parents attribute to relationships relative to possessions, ambitions, and leisure is critical. Parents who value these sorts of things more than relationships may feel that their children deflect energies and resources they prefer to direct elsewhere.

Another important factor in parent–child relationships is your relationship, as you perceived it, with your parents. For most of us, it is the best known parent–child model and the one we fall back upon so often. Earlier we asked you to consider the quality and tone of your relationship with your parents as you grew up. It may have occurred to you that your memory might not jive with that of your parents. Most studies have found that the parent–child relationship is quite different when evaluated by parents and children. Children usually report having less attention, more physical punishment, stricter rules, and more problems than the parents report. Of course, a relationship varies with the person experiencing it. How do you think your memories of childhood with your parents differ from theirs? Answering this sort of question is good practice in putting ourselves in the role we are thinking about assuming.

However important our relationship with a child, it does not exist in isolation. People say that love is not a pie that can be divided into only so many pieces. This statement is probably true, but loving behavior is less expansive. You have other relationships to consider, and how well you handle them is another important factor in the quality of parent–child interactions.

WILL A CHILD BRING YOU TOGETHER OR . . .

Many couples are concerned with the effect that parenting will have on their relationship. This is not a concern to be taken lightly. The purpose of many modern marriages is not primarily procreational. We select partners for a variety of reasons, such as companionship, romance, and/or stimulation. As a result, some people feel pulled between being a partner and being a parent. Said Anne, "It's like being torn apart by wild horses. Our son has tantrums when I'm with Jim, and Jim has tantrums when I attend to my son. I'm not a wife and mother—I'm a wife and *then* a mother. I can't be both at the same time."

Changes in Your Sexual Relationship

Parenting, or not parenting, often profoundly affects sexuality and, consequently, marriage. Sexual problems are the second most commonly reported cause of divorce (money is the first!) because many parents fail to prepare for and adapt to the sexual changes that accompany parenting.

One area of sexual change is physical and physiological. There are biological consequences to becoming a parent that can significantly alter our sexual responsiveness and attractiveness. (See pp. 43–50, which detail the physical changes accompanying pregnancy and birth, as well as give suggestions for dealing positively with them.)

A second area of change involves changes in our moral values. We think of our parents as asexual, and when we become parents, we may model this behavior along with others. Often the face we present to our children gets carried into our bedroom. We share a culture in which the ultimate insult is to impugn the sexual mores of one's mother. Recently, in a human sexuality class, we discussed how it felt to realize that your parents "did it." One 20-year-old student said, "Not my parents!" And so we find pregnant women who say, "I don't want to make love any more. It's like there are three of us. It's obscene." And there are fathers who confess, "I can't get it on with my wife any more. She smells of talcum powder, and she's so motherly!" Freud suggested that these associations—talcum powder, babies, motherhood—trigger Oedipal conflicts. Men may emotionally respond to their wives as they did, long ago, to their mothers—with desire that has to be repressed.

One way of minimizing these sorts of problems is to have a place, perhaps your bed, in which your relationship as man and woman is primary. Talk about the baby elsewhere—and get the baby out of sight while you are romancing. Some parents bring the baby to bed with them; this is fine, unless you are experiencing the conflict we are discussing. If you are, keep your bed for yourselves. Moreover, parents may stop behaving in romantic ways toward each other. Since our behavior in bed is a synopsis of daily interactions, parents can touch each other, even in front of children. A kiss, or hug, has never perverted any child we know of. (Of course, you can take this to extremes! The children of one California couple were taken from them because they made love in front of them!) But the parental role ought not to obscure your relationship as lovers. This "conflict" can start even before you parent, as it has for one man who said, "The only time my wife wants to make love is to make babies."

A third area of sexual change when parenting is adapting to lessened privacy. Parents are often disturbed by crying and may feel either put off or worried. Said one mother, "I feel guilty if we're making love and the baby cries. What if she were to die? How could I ever forgive myself?" Common turn-offs are: "What if the children come in?" or "Ssh! The children will hear!" The best prevention is to plan your environment so as to maximize sexual privacy. Install door locks. Design a safe, separate space for the baby. One couple used a one-way intercom so that they could be unrestrained without fear of either disturbing the child or not being able to hear the crying.

Sexuality also changes because child rearing is exhausting. Parents of young children report a lot of fatigue, depression, and anxiety, all of which can reduce sexual activity, even interest. Sometimes you can minimize exhaustion by reducing strain. Is your sex life worth that second job? Can you share more, or hire a helper, even briefly? You can avoid talking about child problems in bed. And when you are too tired to make love, you can snuggle, cuddle, and be lovable.

A good sexual relationship is more often a product than a cause of a good relationship. Most parents who have a satisfying sex life report having had one before becoming parents. They emphasize the importance of communication, tenderness, affection, and reassurance. If one's sexual pleasure changes dramatically when parenting, it may be a reflection of interpersonal pleasures or difficulties in other areas. Said Allen, "You feel more committed. Sex is better than ever when you know its potential, that it's more than a plaything. You may get to do it less, but it means more." Yet other parents are so embattled and conflicted over their new roles that their resentment and ambivalence get expressed sexually. We hope that by exploring these possible conflicts now, many of you who decide to parent will be less likely to experience these sorts of problems.

Changes in Loving

Sometimes, the couples who are the most afraid of parenting are the ones who are the most happily married. As one man explained, "We are so happy together. We're afraid of rocking the boat, of risking what we have for an unknown quantity." A survey of over 2000 adults found that the majority of parents reported being the happiest before children arrived and again after they had left home. The study also found childfree marriages to be happier than those with children. Yet another study found that of 46 urban, middle-class couples, 38 reported extensive or severe crises in adjusting to their first child. One father of six criticized these findings: "That's no surprise," he scoffed. "Children test the fiber of a relationship. It doesn't surprise me that some childless couples who stay together are happy. One way of avoiding not being able to cut the mustard is not to buy any! But I hardly think avoiding life is happiness!" Compare this response to that of another father. "If I had known how much my wife and I would have to give up of each other, we'd never have had the baby. It will be years before we have the time and energy to devote to each other that we had before."

Many couples we interviewed reported that the kind of love they felt for each other changed when they had a child. The character changed from being romantic, stimulating, and verbal to being supportive, helpful, and active. How happily couples adapted to these changes seemed to be partly based on the kinds of sharing they did before parenting. The parents who found the changes most disturbing were those, like the man interviewed above, who were very into each other as a romantic, fun-seeking couple. The more you relate in ways that would exclude a child, the more distracting the child will be.

We should consider, however, how children can benefit, rather than detract from, some relationships. While some marriages falter from a lack of attention, others fail because of too much. We modern Americans expect a lot from our partnerships—economic stability, romance, sexual delight, emotional support, togetherness, and so on. The relatively recent emphasis on marriage for love has been accompanied by a skyrocketing divorce rate (one out of three!). Children can provide a couple with something to attend to beside or in addition to each other. Said Jerry, "We are so much happier now with the baby. Jan was always leaning on me, making demands. She thought we should act like dates, instead of husband and wife. But she wants me to be successful, too. She couldn't see that making money and romancing her 24 hours a day were not compatible. Now with the kid, she's occupied. We have something to share other than her living off my experiences." And Candy: "We were always arguing. It wasn't that we didn't love each other—maybe too much. Always pushing at each other. Now we parent instead."

Unfortunately, more often children are incorporated into parental problems. Rather than deflecting arguments, they become a part, even a cause, of them. Recent research by Dr. Frances Grossman and her colleagues at Boston University has found significant correlations between the reported happiness of couples before and during pregnancy with how well they and their infants adjust to each other. Parents who reported problems in their relationships had infants with more sleeping and feeding difficulties, which might serve to further increase the strain on an already strained relationship.

Still, some people buy the myth that children will bring them closer to the other parent through some sort of mystical gluing process. Many are willing to take a chance. Said Dolores, "Perhaps a child will help us weather this period. Perhaps not, but I've decided that I'd rather be a divorced mother than a married nonmother." We asked her whether she was aware of how most divorced parents fare: that they comprise 84 percent of all divorces; that a year after alimony and child support costs have been awarded, fewer than 40 percent of the wage earners are still sending the money on schedule; that divorcées make even less money than single women (fewer than 4 percent can afford to hire household help); that remarriage and dating are more difficult; that divorcées with young children report so much stress that one-fourth of them in one study worried about having a nervous breakdown; that children of divorced parents have more problems than those whose homes are intact; that children often turn against and criticize their mothers when their support is most needed. "Nonetheless," Dolores insisted, "I'll run the risk. I just don't find a man–woman relationship all that satisfying. Not that it isn't nice. It's just that being a mother will be much more important to me."

Most people juggle a number of roles in their lives—as a spouse, home-worker, worker, fun-seeker, and, perhaps, parent. How partners prioritize these roles has profound effects on how they relate to each other. If one of you is a dedicated career person and the other a dedicated fun seeker, you can run into conflicts. Frequently, couples learn to adapt to each other's priorities. This accommodation may be one reason why studies have found that the happiest parents have children between their third and eighth years of marriage. It takes a few years to adjust to each other, but after being together for many years, you develop interactive patterns that may be difficult to change.

Changes in Expectations of Yourself and Your Partner

Many couples who seemed content enough before they became parents seem considerably less so afterward. Ted was tight-lipped when he told us, "All Cindy seems to care about now is money. She's always on my back. We live just as well as we did before the kid. But now she wants to join a country club, or buy her clothes at Bonwit's. It's like I'm supposed to just provide now that she's decided she likes the good life!" And Alice: "All of a sudden, my cooking isn't good enough, the house is a mess—the other day he asked me why I didn't iron his shirts! Why, now, with the baby to take care of, is he laying this trip on me?"

Neither of these changes has very much to do with the child itself. It has more to do with the fact that having (or even thinking about having) children prompts us to reevaluate our lifestyles and ourselves. We have to look ahead, and we may not like what we see. The life we live may be satisfactory on a daily basis, but when we take a longer view, we may have to confront the fact that we're grown up; that we're aging—that options are fewer. That we are unlikely to achieve what we once thought we or our partners would achieve. That we've made the wrong choice—of partner, career, whatever—and that it's too late to go back. That is why some parents become bitchy, critical, anxious, and dissatisfied, and why many couples who were once content living modestly are suddenly discontent when they have a child. It is facing their lives that is disconcerting to them, and they often turn against each other. We tend to marry people very much like ourselves (except in sex, usually!)—and it's often easier to focus on someone else's shortcomings, even if we share them.

It would be shortsighted to ascribe this self-evaluation solely to parenting. We can confront our "inadequacies," however we define them, with or without a child—on a thirtieth birthday, or upon a change in jobs, or the promotion of a friend. But when we watch our children, we often see mirror images of ourselves. How we feel about us becomes a very important part of how we feel about a child. If we don't like ourselves, we express this to our children when they behave like us (which they do). If we don't like or respect our partner, we are likely to express this much more openly to a child, who, after all, has considerably less counter-control. We have found that happy people who become happy parents tend to have happy children. Parenting can give us more of an opportunity to express our good feelings about ourselves than to create good feelings where there were none. We believe that liking yourself and each other (via therapy, education, or any self-improvement program you wish) is a prerequisite to an enjoyable parenting experience.

One possible source of good feelings about yourself and your partner is whether you achieve those goals you think worthwhile. But parenting, as we pointed out in the last chapter, is not something most of us can do in addition to what we're doing now. It's something we do *instead.* One mother told us that she had spent all her energy on her kids and regretted never having done anything important. How sad that she felt this way! People have very different goals and very different ways of judging importance. Grown women and men measure their lives on how many muffins they can sell, yards they can jump, students they can help, money they can make, songs they can sing. Each of us has to derive for ourselves some idea of the kinds of things we want to do during our life. Then we can consider how well these activities fit with the kind of parenting experience we want. Can we accomplish our goals before, during, or after parenting?

Some goals are incompatible with parenting—but not as many as we think. Too often, people believe having a child means they can't do this and shouldn't do that, not because it's dangerous or unhealthy, but because parents don't do things like that! Part of this conservatism has to do with our expectations of parents and our modeling of our own parents. Women who ride roller coasters and wear jeans to dinner parties may become mothers who refuse challenges and worry about local gossip. Males find themselves becoming judgmental and punitive. Another part of this conservatism is based on the belief that children require a very narrowly defined lifestyle. Not true. Children grow up in very different cultures all over the world and are remarkably adaptive. Of course, there are consequences to a child having unconventional parents—but there are also consequences of having conventional parents, especially unhappy ones. Middle-class parents who live a suburban lifestyle "for the sake of the children" may not be doing their kids a favor. Yes, children have needs, and, yes, they do better in some environments than in others. But, as we'll see in the next chapter, it is not the number of toys, or size house, or even school district that is critical to a child's development. Many of the "sacrifices" parents have made for their children have benefited the children themselves very little.

The most difficult time for children of unconventional families is between the ages of 8 and 13. They often are very conforming and want their parents to be likewise. However, this is temporary and by no means universal. Said one anthropologist, "The fact that we lived a somewhat strange life was torture for our daughter when she was 11 and 12. She wouldn't invite her friends to our house because we had weird masks on the walls and because I didn't look like Betty Crocker. But before that and after, she has been really proud of being different. She thinks other kids are really deprived."

Many prospective parents are afraid that their children will be ashamed of them if they are not embodiments of the cultural ideal. This fear is realistic—even when you *are* the embodiment of the cultural ideal! During late childhood almost all children are ashamed of their parents—because their parents are "too fat," "too old," "too sexy," "not attractive," "too attractive," "too loud," "too quiet," and because they "have an accent" or "dress funny." This kind of parental rejection is part of growing up, of taking another perspective, and for many children it is unavoidable, perhaps even beneficial. Parents are floored because they respond to their own feelings of incompetence. "My kid sees right through me," they think. Parenting can wreck havoc with our self-esteem when we think parents are supposed to be perfect. Perhaps this is a continuation of our childhood view of adults, especially of our own same-sexed parent.

Some of us take until adolescence to see our parents' faults, and until middle age to forgive them for having any. As Roger Gould commented, "A child's idealized image of an adult can become the adult's painful measure of himself."* When some of us become parents, we expect to be, or try to be, or want to be, perfect. We spend a lot of energy pretending we are. We may even keep our children from knowing us too well so they won't find out our "secret." We may put off parenting until we have approximated an unrealistic ideal, or become uncomfortable with ourselves as parents, or we may criticize our partner for not living up to our idealized version of our own parent.

One way of minimizing these problems is to make friends with children before you have your *own*. If you can be comfortable interacting with kids with minimal role playing, you are more likely to continue this with your own children. If you can't change scripts, perhaps you want to find out why or do something else that won't be as trying.

Differences and Similarities in Parental Investment

Parents sometimes differ markedly on how much of a personal investment they put into a child or children. There are potential difficulties in investing too little, of course, and of approaching parenting cavalierly. Child neglecters, for example, bear children and then let them pretty much take care of themselves. Of course, our definitions of neglect vary with the times and the neighborhood. A child who has not been cleaned or fed in several days is neglected. But what about a suburban child whose parents will not drive him anywhere? Or the child who could not get money to go to the movies with his friends because his parents are house-poor?

There are also potential difficulties in investing too much in children. The stereotyped Jewish mother is reputed to have unwavering, relentless ambitions for her son, often expressed as the DLD syndrome (doctor, lawyer, or dentist). However, this is far from a Jewish monopoly. Parents who are disappointed in their own lives and who feel they have missed important opportunities try to provide these same opportunities for their children. Many parents believe that

*Gould, Roger, "Adult Life Stages: Growth Toward Self-Tolerance." *Psychology Today* (Feb. 1975).

their children should do "better" (however defined) than they did;
while this attitude is laudable, well-off children have quite a task to
fulfill. Some are paralyzed by the challenge; others are denied the
right of selecting for themselves an acceptable lifestyle. Another
danger of over-investment is that the parents expect to be "paid
back." Abusive parents are very frequently those who have invested
heavily in a child. They expect, or demand, returns from the child
that are not forthcoming—sometimes because the child is too young
or unsuited to the role the parent wants played. While most parents
have expectations for their children, problems often arise when these
expectations are very high, inflexible, and narrowly defined.

Difficulties also arise when there are differences in parental investment. As Tim stated: "I never see my wife alone anymore. The kid
is welded to her, like a third arm. I feel like an intruder." Or Ellen:
"Jim spends all our money on our child! I haven't been out in
months, but if she sees a toy she wants, it's hers!" If one of you was
the object of unremitting devotion and the other of benign neglect,
you may discover considerable differences in how you prioritize
your children. These differences sponsor jealousy and estrangement.
The most common complaint of recent parents is how much of their
partner they lost upon parenting.

Certainly, balancing a child's needs with those of a spouse and/or
other children is extraordinarily difficult. We believe that failure to
do this well is a major cause of family discord. A seemingly simple
solution is to share parenting when you are all together. If you interact while parenting, you are less likely to see the child as a distraction; but this interaction requires that you also have time to interact
with each other as a couple, without the child present.

Finding the right balance is different for each of us each time we
parent. An important consideration is how much time and attention
you need and want from each other. Couples who are independent
(she is at night class, he is bowling; she is in the sewing room while he
is in the family room) adopt more readily to a primary parent model
than those who are into togetherness. (Lamented one such couple,
"We have looked everywhere for a double toilet seat.") Unless the

together-oriented couple shares parenting or gets extensive child-care support, changes in their relationship will be extensive.

We have found that people who tend to be overprotective and intense about their pets often tend to be the same way with their children (of course to a greater degree). One couple had a cat that they wouldn't let out of the house for fear of it being hit by a car (even though they lived in a relatively quiet suburb). When the cat started urinating on the floor, they locked the cat in the basement where it spent the last four years of its life. Their child was also over-protected and subjected to constant, worried surveillance. Perhaps you know of other people whose investment in their pets was similar (although usually less intense, of course) to that in their children.

A more useful pattern for determining parental investment is to find out how invested each set of parents was in each of you. Children of self-sacrificing parents tend to sacrifice for their children, which is not surprising given that many such parents tell their children, "You'll do the same for your kids!" To not do so, then, can make you feel very guilty. Some people don't want to parent because they think parenting equals endless, unrequited sacrifice—of time, of love, of energy, of money. Not so. There are many more degrees of freedom than are investigated by most of us. Perhaps you don't have to live in the best suburb. Perhaps you can work, even travel. Perhaps you don't have to sacrifice—only give and take.

Children—Little Adults, Slaves, or Nobodies?

Another major source of disagreement between partners is over standards for children's behavior. One position, the *continuous model,* means that you want to foster in children the same qualities you want to see in them when they're adults. In centuries past, children dressed just like adults, and they performed adult tasks to the best of their abilities. For example, if a man picked big stones out of a field, his son was expected to pick up the little stones. It was also acceptable for children to engage in those activities enjoyed by adults —drinking, smoking, gambling, chewing tobacco, even sex!

The opposite point of view is called the *discontinuous model.* This model believes that children should behave quite differently from adults—they should be seen and not heard, respectful of their elders, obedient without questioning, exempt from work or responsibility. For example, a skit on television recently portrayed what would happen if a "typical" couple treated their dinner guests as they treated their own children. The guests were met with: "Let me see your hands," "Sit up in your chair, young man!" and "Don't talk with your mouth full."

Naturally, most of us have a combination of these extreme models. The difference between your model and your partner's, however, can be the source of considerable problems. We recently interacted with one couple who exemplified this difference. The mother encouraged her children to enter into discussions with us, to ask questions, and to join us in activities. The father glared at them whenever they spoke out and asked them to "run off and play because this was adult time." It was disconcerting to see the children encouraged by one parent to do what the other one disliked, but this happens more frequently than one would imagine. Interacting together with children is a good way of finding out if your standards are very different. If so, you can discuss them and perhaps reach a compromise.

Differences in Religion and Culture

Frequently, differences that are easily accepted between partners are problematic if and when children arrive. Few prospective parents address the question of how they want to raise their children in terms of religion. Many agnostics experience different feelings when a child is involved. "Children need faith," or "children need to belong," or "children need to be something" are among the more common reasons parents offer for becoming involved in church activities. If one of you does not change, you are likely to see the other as hypocritical and conforming. Similar conflicts can occur if you have a differing commitment to your church. Said one young man, "I remember the fighting on Sunday morning. My Mom would get us dressed and ready for church, and my Dad would be scoffing and laughing. Then I would want to stay home and he would say yes and she would say no, and off they would go with us kids picking sides."

When you are of different faiths, the decision becomes even more emotionally charged, especially if your parents and in-laws get into the act. There are holiday conflicts, biblical differences, discrimination concerns. Said one mother, "Our different religions didn't seem important when we got married—or now. But it will be if we have a child. I don't want my kid to be a. . . . I don't want to hurt my husband but that's how I feel. And it surprises me." Talking this problem over before you have a child will enable you to consider your differences, if there are any, more calmly and objectively.

Little Boys Are Made of . . .

One topic many prospective parents neglect to discuss is differences regarding how boys and girls should be raised. Of course, they usually discuss sex preferences. They may even deliberately try to have a girl or boy in the manner detailed in chapter 1 (see p. 65). But we find that many parents fail to address substantial sex-related issues until after the child is born; then they are surprised to find gaping differences between them. We believe this is a topic well worth considering before you decide to parent, so that you can better estimate how you are likely to react and whether some compromise is possible *before* the child is put in the middle.

Studies have shown that children assume well-defined sex roles by the age of two. Mothers, unknowingly, handle their sons significantly more often than they do their daughters. Furthermore, while their physical contact with sons is likely to be caressing, with their daughters they are more likely to be fussing and correcting. Fathers play more with sons than daughters, and the nature of play is more physical and competitive. Yet, despite the extent of differences between the rearing of males and females, studies have found surprisingly few consistent differences between the sexes. Boys are more aggressive than girls, from about 18 months on. And while girls have better verbal abilities, males have superior spatial and mathematical skills. However, these differences are not found until adolescence, and there is every reason to suspect that environmental influences are significant. Yet most of us were raised, and will raise our boys and girls, differently. For example, some people (you?) would:

Teach a girl, but not a boy, to cook, clean, and do laundry.

Play football, baseball, golf, hockey—but only with a boy.

Have different allowances, curfews, and standards of conduct for sons and daughters.

Send a boy to college, but not a girl.

Pay for orthodontia and plastic surgery for a girl but not for a boy.

Encourage boys to be doctors and girls to be nurses.

Buy dolls for girls and erector sets for boys.

If you both agree on a particular general approach, you can avoid the double messages so many parents communicate about sex roles.

Differences in Tolerance Levels

Most parents will tell you that parenting is stressful, whether or not they judge it worth the stress. (By the way, some stress can be positive, as when you win a marathon. We call this *eustress*—and parents get lots of it too!) Most parents tend to minimize the stresses of parenting. As one prospective father told us: "I would be much more comfortable about fathering if the fathers I knew didn't deny the changes I see happening to them. Oh, kids aren't that expensive, they tell me, or they're not that much work—and then I see how they're hustling for money, or exhausted from being up all night, or arguing with their wives. Maybe kids are worth it, but I'd feel much more comfortable if they would talk about the 'it' they're worth."

You can count on stress with children: fevers, crying, bedwetting, measles, fights, injuries. There is always the possibility of serious illness, accidents, or emotional difficulties. The way you and your partner respond to stress is exceedingly important in how well you come to enjoy parenting, as well as how healthy your family will be. We know stress can be physically and emotionally destructive. We also know that when people can't handle stress adaptively, they feel guilty, anxious, and even more stressed. We can find ourselves in a vicious circle from which escape is most difficult.

How well you handle the stress of parenting is partly a function of the kinds of things you respond to as being stressful. People often have very different boiling points in different situations and under different conditions. Would these sorts of events tend to anger you or your partner a great deal?

noise
things out of order
dirt (spilled liquids, urine, crumbs, mud)
breaking things
interruptions
many things occurring simultaneously
disobedience
stupidity (as you define it)
being ignored
having to repeat yourself
someone not following directions
dependence (clinging, whining, following)
independence
a job poorly done

A second factor in how well you handle parenting stress is you and your partner's irritability level. Some people are more easily upset and disturbed than others. While your environment is very important in determining how "high-strung" you are (look at your parents!), there are significant differences in irritability even among newborns. For example, Dr. Daniel Freedman has reported that Navajo Indian infants quietly accept being strapped to a cradle board, whereas Caucasian babies protest vigorously to the same treatment.* A husband told us in great admiration that in 30 years of marriage and 6 children, he had never heard his wife so much as raise her voice! Anyone who is hot-tempered will find this statement incredible! If you are very excitable, and your partner is as calm as a proverbial cucumber, you may either balance each other or get involved in

---

*Freedman, Daniel G., "Ethnic Differences in Babies." *Human Nature* 2, no. 1 (January 1979).

intense conflicts. If one of you reacts with aplomb while the other is in a fury, the child is confused, the calm parent becomes upset, and the angry parent feels misunderstood. Everyone's behavior is understandable, but divisive.

Also important is how well you respond to stress and how well your coping style fits with your partner's. We have found that some people under stress turn to escape routes (drugs, lovers, partying, contemplating their navels); others turn to their loved ones (Comfort me! Take care of me!); and yet others push people away or lash out at people and things around them ("Leave me alone!" or, "It's your fault!"). Obviously, if you turn to your partner for comfort, you don't want him or her to be behind the bar getting drunk. And, if you have a child in trouble, you both don't want to be getting drunk together!

The most dangerous response to parental stress is lashing out, especially if you lash out at the child. As we mentioned earlier in this book, child abuse runs in families. If you were hit often as a child and find yourself responding physically when angry, it is possible that you may abuse your own child. You should be especially concerned if either you or your partner abuse each other. Studies have indicated that 80 percent of abused children come from families in which someone was physically abused even before the child's birth. If either of you batters a loved one, you can get free help in many cities from groups who are learning other ways of dealing with anger. Join! Some people think parenting will help them increase their tolerance and self-control, and if they are well controlled to start with, it might. But children specialize in testing limits (it's a major way of growing), and you can count on them getting you angry. It's how well you control and express your anger that is important. We have seen too many anguished, guilty parents who should never have tested their self-control on their bruised, frightened children.

To increase our tolerance levels and improve our coping skills before we parent is essential, not only for the child's welfare, but for our own and for our marriage. Millions of parents suffering the physical and emotional consequences of stress take sedatives, drink alcohol, sleep too much or not enough, cry often, are depressed, anxious, and resentful, and behave badly to their families or themselves. Current approaches to the stress of parenting and to the child abuse that sometimes accompanies it tend to occur *after* the fact. Then, of course, problems are more serious and complex, and it is more difficult for people to learn new ways of coping with the situation. But we can learn to change before we have children, or elect not to have them.

Spare the Rod and Spoil the Child?

We have just discussed differences in tolerance levels; now we will address discipline—that is, the deliberate use of control over children. One area of disagreement is whether and when physical punishment ought to be employed. People feel very strongly and very differently about this, yet we are amazed by how few prospective parents discuss their attitudes.

Some people oppose any corporal punishment with the argument that parents are modeling the use of force and violence, while others believe that the use of physical punishment is essential to maintaining control and respect. Obviously, problems develop if you and your partner are in different camps, not only because of the effect that punishment has on children, but also because of the effect it has on the other partner. Said Ellie, "I sit in the kitchen and shake when I hear my husband hitting Tim. The poor baby is crying and shaking, and he's hitting him! I hate him at those moments." After her husband leaves the room, Ellie goes in to comfort Tim. This sort of pronounced discrepancy between partners can wreak havoc on their marriage and their offspring. Other "Ellie's" respond by trying to cover up the offenses of their children. If this happens frequently, it can foster enormous resentment, deception, and anxiety and even increase the number of misdeeds committed. A more positive way of handling the problem would be for Ellie to tell her partner how his punishing the child makes her feel. Then they could discuss whether there are any alternative disciplinary measures that would be as effective but less upsetting. We believe that by initiating such compromises *before* a baby is in the picture, you are more likely to do so if and when you have a child—and more likely to know whether or not you can agree upon and carry through such compromises.

Another conflict over discipline occurs when you assign the punitive role to one parent, typically the father. While children certainly survive the "wait til Daddy comes home" approach, we do not believe it is a particularly good model. Punishment should occur as close as possible in time to the behavior you want to punish. By waiting, you are inadvertently punishing your child's seeing his father come home. "To this day," said Jamie, "I remember the sheer dread of hearing my father's car pull in the driveway." And Jamie's father recollects, "I hated playing the mean role. As soon as I'd come home, my wife would start in on me—'you know what your kids did? Jamie did that and Ellen did this.' I hated to see my own kids afraid of me. But I hit them because it was the only thing I knew."

Some parents use disciplinary measures other than, or instead of, corporal punishment. They withdraw their love, or a privilege, or embarrass the child, or lecture, bluster, and call names. Some even play a "look-what-you're-doing-to-me" method of exerting control. This technique was best demonstrated by a mother who used to bang her head against the wall whenever her daughter upset her. This tactic is a good way of endowing a child with guilt—it has also been known to produce headaches. Most of us employ the techniques we know best—that is, the ones used on us! A method favored by one partner may be shocking to the other, especially if you were raised very differently.

A third major area of disagreement over discipline is the amount of control parents exert over their children. Some people are more permissive than others and are willing to let things pass that would infuriate others. Said Jerry: "When our dog urinates on the floor, my wife goes 'naughty, naughty!' I say that's not even punishment, and she says, 'Well, dogs pee!' It drives me crazy."

In some homes, children are free to behave at will, whereas in others, they might just as well be on a leash. Obviously, most of us fall somewhere in between, but how far apart we are is what is important. Listen to Martha describe having her stepchildren to dinner: "They have carte blanche right to interrupt us, to make demands, to fuss over food, to be the center of attention, and my husband lets them! I was taught manners and to eat what my mother served me! It's a relief when the kids leave!" Most studies have found that happy parents enjoy observing more than controlling. They don't try to mold their children into acceptable products, and they are able to let a child explore and make mistakes, especially at the important age of one and one-half when motor skills are advancing rapidly. But happy parents also set limits. It's hard to enjoy your child if he is a spoiled brat! It's finding the balance between permissiveness and control that is difficult and different for each of us. Taking a child for a weekend, or longer, is an excellent way of discovering your differences in this area.

HOW MANY CHILDREN?

Just as having a child will influence your relationship with your partner, it will also affect your relationship with your other children. If you don't have others, you have to make some tentative decisions about how many you want and the best way of spacing them, especially if age is becoming a factor.

One evening we had a couple over for dinner who had been married for two years. The wife told us she was eagerly awaiting a very large family—at least six, she said. Her husband almost choked on his baked potato—he was planning on two! We have since discovered that many couples don't address this issue—or take each other's replies seriously—until one of them tries to have a child.

Family size in the United States has been steadily decreasing. Similar decreases are found in most industrial countries with high standards of living, a literate population, and female paid labor. The United States birth rate had decreased from 18.4 babies per 1,000 people in 1970 to around 15 by 1973. The average family size had fallen from 2.6 in the 1950s to 1.7 in 1977. Lurking behind these statistics are individuals grappling with whether or not to have another, or any, child.

A *Redbook* poll of 80,000 women is one of the largest samples of what women think about having a baby. (Unfortunately, only women were surveyed, and there is likely to be a bias toward the sort of woman who reads *Redbook*. Also, what people report as their reasons may or may not be accurate. Nonetheless, the sheer size of the survey is impressive.)

Staying a Twosome

Only 6 percent of the married women who replied to the *Redbook* questionnaire indicated that they didn't want children (although 12 percent of the single women planned to be childfree). What were their reasons? See table 5-1 below. From our interviews, men seemed to share the priorities named in the *Redbook* questionnaire, but with more emphasis on the economic features of parenting and with an additional concern about taking energy away from the marriage.

The percentage of voluntary childfree couples has doubled from 5 percent to 10 percent in the last decade. Since many of these couples have not yet passed childbearing age, it is hard to predict how many will still be childfree in ten years. Even the couples themselves may not know. Some plan to be childfree and then change their minds (as did one couple who were selected to represent the ideal childfree lifestyle in a national magazine. A few months after the article appeared they gave birth!). Others plan to parent, but

TABLE 5-1 WOMEN WHO DON'T WANT CHILDREN

REASON (RESPONDENTS COULD CHECK MORE THAN ONE)	PERCENTAGE OF CHILDFREE RESPONDENTS
Being childless suits my lifestyle.	91
Having children involves too much responsibility.	65
Children would interfere with my career.	52
There's too much uncertainty in the world.	50
I don't think I would be a good mother.	49
Husband doesn't want children.	40
Children are too expensive.	36
I don't like children.	31
There's too much uncertainty in my marriage.	24
Other.	45

Source: Safran, Claire, "What 80,000 Women Feel About Having Children." *Redbook Magazine* (May, 1978).

never quite get around to it. In a recent study, only 9 of 56 older couples who had chosen to be childfree had agreed to do so before their marriage. Dr. Jean Veevers, a Canadian sociologist, found that two-thirds of the childfree women she interviewed got that way through a series of procrastinations.* First, they postponed having children for a specified period, and then they became increasingly vague about when to have the child. The third stage occurred when they acknowledged that they might not have children. The final decision to remain childfree came later, and sometimes was not even discussed. Life just went on, and contraception was employed until age rendered the matter moot.

Some couples who procrastinate do so for specific reasons. They wish to obtain things that they consider prerequisites to parenting. According to the *Redbook* survey, what women thought were the most important requirements are shown in table 5–2.

TABLE 5-2 BEFORE HAVING A FIRST CHILD

WHAT'S IMPORTANT TO ATTAIN (RESPONDENTS COULD CHECK MORE THAN ONE)	*PERCENTAGE OF RESPONDENTS*
A happy stable marriage.	54
Financial security.	43
My emotional maturity.	42
My husband's emotional maturity	32
My own readiness to take time out from work.	21
The chance to have traveled or experimented with different lifestyles.	21
A certain degree of progress in my work.	15
Work that is flexible enough to make my being a working mother easier.	9
Enough money to afford good child care while I work.	9
My first child was not planned.	22
None of the above.	7
Other.	5

Source: Safran, Claire, "What 80,000 Women Feel About Having Children." *Redbook Magazine* (May 1978).

*Veevers, Jean, "Voluntary Childlessness: A Neglected Area of Family Study." *Family Coordinator* 22, No. 199 (1973).

Sometimes, these prerequisites are never attained, and the couple remains childfree or has a child (or children) regardless. Sometimes, these requirements are met, but then new ones are created; having a baby is then postponed until it is abandoned.

Some couples who procrastinate into their thirties decide to have no children rather than to have only one. Said one woman, "I'm 35. Let's face it, I really could only have one now. But I hate only kids! They're spoiled rotten. I'd rather have none." Is she right? Are only children more difficult?

Having an Only Child

Studies of only children have found that they tend to be high achievers, verbally sophisticated, and intelligent. They also have a greater tendency to take care of their parents (you!) in old age (perhaps this is a form of the bystander-apathy effect—the more people who are around an accident, the less likely each is to offer assistance). They have no more problems than others and are as socially adept. Many parents worry that they may be depriving their only child of siblings with whom they can play. Certainly, this can be true—some people find that siblings are their very best friends. However, many other siblings are indifferent, or actually hostile, to each other.

Some studies have found that an unusually high proportion of people from large families choose to have an only child—presumably because their own experiences had not been all that wonderful. Said Allen, "I have four brothers, all of whom live within twenty miles of me. I have no idea where they actually are. I couldn't reach them even if I wanted to." Another group that has a high proportion of only children are only children themselves—presumably because their own experiences had not been all that terrible. The *Redbook* survey previously described reported on why women said they would want only one child (see table 5–3).

More men than women in our interviews said that they preferred one child. Economic factors were very important, but interpersonal interactions were a main source of concern. "Two children are too distracting," said one father. "With one child, you can parent together and still relate as a couple. With two, there's just too much activity."

TABLE 5-3   WOMEN WHO WANT JUST ONE CHILD

REASONS (RESPONDENTS COULD CHECK MORE THAN ONE)	*PERCENTAGE OF THOSE ANSWERING*
I can have a closer relationship with one child.	69
Emotionally, that's all I can handle.	65
It's less disruptive to my career and lifestyle.	62
Financially, that's all I can handle.	53
My partner doesn't want more.	39
I'm uncertain about the future of my marriage.	30
Medical reasons.	29
My marriage ended after having only one child.	22
I want to try everything once—but once is enough.	20
Other.	33

Source: Safran, Claire, "What 80,000 Women Feel About Having Children." *Redbook Magazine* (May 1978).

If only children are spoiled and difficult, it is because their parents make them that way, not because they are by nature different from other children. The parents of only children tend to be older, and the child may either be desperately wanted or not wanted at all. Said one 58-year-old father of a 7-year-old, "He's not spoiled! He knows he's a late-life accident, and he's damned lucky to be here." Ironically, though, many unwanted children are the most spoiled, in part because of parental guilt and in part because giving in can be less troublesome than sticking to your rules. There are certainly many things parents can do to increase the chances of an excellent only-child experience, such as arranging for playmates and being as involved in another activity as they would be with a second child. (For more details, read the excellent book, *One Child by Choice,* listed at the end of the chapter.)

When You're Having More than One

Those of you who already have at least two children know that the second child means a considerable increase in noise levels (which go up exponentially with subsequent children). But the second child is considerably easier to raise (barring special needs) because you have many of the necessary paraphernalia and because you know much more about children. Confided a second-time mother, "Now I can spot first-timers. Every whimper the baby makes they figure he's dying. By the second one, you know what's normal. You're much more relaxed about everything." Your standards are likely to be lower, and you both tend to be less strict. "My kid brother gets away with murder," is a typical, and often justified, complaint of firstborns. The relationship and issues surrounding a second child are likely to be different than those of the first. Each child is unique, even as an infant, and the challenge of shaping and adjusting to this new person can be just as exciting or trying as it was the first time around. The *Redbook* survey found that women who wanted more than one child offerred several reasons (see table 5–4).

Many men and women we interviewed saw the ideal family as two children, a boy and a girl. Said one father, "Watching our kids interact is the most beautiful sight in the world. When Kathy kisses her baby brother, it is all the love of mankind wrapped up." Many parents commented on the joy of sibling interaction. But if we examine the somewhat romantic and loving sibling relationship a little more closely, we find many other strong emotions, both positive and negative.

Many parents tell their firstborns they are going to have a baby to keep them company. They then appear amazed when (and if) the child reacts coolly, even hostilely. Sibling rivalry is no misnomer. One recent mother described a scene: "My four-year-old asked if she could kiss the baby and we said 'of course.' So she did, watching us all the while. But as soon as we moved away, she was trying to punch him in the head." It is difficult to distinguish when a child is deliberately trying to hurt a sibling, or whether it is just curiosity. For example, two- and three-year-olds tend to poke at babies' eyes quite viciously, but they do the same with dolls (and mommies!). Certainly there is passionate ambivalence, which parents are naive not to expect. And some siblings fight quite vigorously, often throughout childhood, sometimes throughout life. The universal parental cry "why can't you get along with each other?" is almost universally ignored. (After all, didn't you fight with your siblings, if you had any?)

TABLE 5-4 WOMEN WHO WANT MORE THAN ONE

REASONS (RESPONDENTS COULD CHECK MORE THAN ONE)	PERCENTAGE OF THOSE ANSWERING
A second child will be company for the first.	48
Emotionally we feel we can afford more than one child.	40
Financially we feel we can afford more than one child.	30
I love having lots of children around me.	22
I came from a big family and enjoyed it.	22
My husband has always wanted to have more than one.	18
It's easier to raise more than one child.	14
I was an only child and had a lonely life.	6

Source: Safran, Claire, "What 80,000 Women Feel about Having Children." *Redbook Magazine* (May, 1978).

Rivalry is increased when parents have well-defined ambitions for their children. If you have a rather narrow band of acceptable behaviors, you are likely to pit your children against each other, and you will fail to recognize and encourage individual differences. This failure can lead to increased rivalry, jealousy, and feelings of inferiority, particularly in the younger child. While firstborns match only children in their high levels of intelligence, ambition, verbal skills, and achievement, second-borns do not. They tend to be less direct and more manipulative, less ambitious and more easygoing. (This is, of course, a generalization and not true of *all* second-borns!) Additionally, most children tend to be egocentric. As soon as one child has something, the other child wants it. They fight over toys, food, television, and, of course, you.

Children are rarely cooperative before the age of seven or eight, even though studies have shown that they can be if contingencies have been carefully arranged. More generally, they squabble and prefer combat to cooperation. One father of a five- and four-year-old told us the following:

> I bought three stamps—fragile, special delivery, and air mail—and set up a mock post office. I put a slit in a Pampers box. I thought it would be fun to play mailman and process all these letters. So I took our old envelopes, and we sat down at the table and started to run them through. Well, kids don't work that way. One wants the other's stamp, the other wants mine, and round we go. After that was settled, neither

one would let the other stamp his envelope. And then no one would deliver anyone else's envelope. Needless to say, it was even worse than our national post office!

Would this sort of experience, frustrating as it might be, interest you? Would you have enjoyed it anyway? Try it again with some changes? Or would you tear the envelopes into little pieces and ship the kids to Minnesota?

With three children, you have the problem of the middle child, who often reports feeling neglected. Children, like adults, seem to prefer dyads to triads, so that two will often "gang up" on the third, most commonly the youngest. We all know stories about such childhood tortures, as portrayed in a commercial in which two older brothers decide to test a new cereal on their youngest brother—"Let Mikie try it!" Here's another example:

My brother and I saw this cowboy movie in which Indians tied up this guy with wet rawhide and left him spread-eagled in the sun. As the rawhide dried, it shrank. We were curious to see if it worked, so we got some rawhide and tied up our kid brother in the basement. But we got bored sitting around and so we went out to play for a while, meaning to come back soon. Of course we forgot all about him. It's a good thing my folks came home when they did.

This sort of thing is less likely to happen when there are four children relatively close in age because then they tend to break into two dyads. Of course, now you have mock wars between them! Most research has found that IQ scores tend to decrease with each child born, even when social-class factors are controlled. Some psychologists attribute this drop in IQ scores to decreased access to adult models; they theorize that the much-publicized drop in national test scores may be attributed to the sibling position differences in the population taking the test. Many of our school-aged children are second- and third-borns as opposed to the firstborns who took these tests in the 1960s. More data is being collected on this issue.

Researchers have found that the amount of stress reported by a family increases enormously upon the birth of the fourth child. This additional stress significantly increases the chances of divorce, psychological problems, and economic pressure. However, this is not always the case. Some parents thrive with large families. We have found that after four children, the entire family style must change if parents wish to be anything but exhausted. In four-plus-child families that are happy, everyone has very well-defined roles and responsibilities. Cooperation is valued more than independence. Older children care for the younger ones; chores are divided according to age, sex (among most families, anyway), and ability. Differences are encouraged, since it is easier for everyone to have, for example, a different instrument than to take turns on the same one. At the same time, it is more difficult to change roles once you have assumed one, since everyone depends upon your continuing. Children have more financial responsibility, for obvious reasons. In fact, as one mother of five told us, "Actually, it's less work than a small family because your expectations are different. You're a facilitator in a large family—a kind of environmental manager and organizer. In a small family, you tend to do everything yourself and try to cover for everyone else."

Spacing Children

The spacing of children is also important in deciding when to start having them. Obviously, if you want a large family, you can't postpone childbearing as long as you would if you want only one. Most experts suggest an ideal of three years between children because of the physical demands of pregnancy, birth, infancy, and toddlerhood. Parents of closely spaced children report greater stress and fatigue than those whose children are more widely spaced. Also, siblings who are only one or two years apart seem to experience more rivalry and negative feelings toward each other, especially if they are of the same sex. There are also overlapping college expenses, which may be prohibitive.

When siblings are more than four years apart, it is easier for the parents, but it is also easier for the children to lose contact with each other. When one enters elementary school, the other leaves for junior high; when one enters high school, the other is leaving for college; and so on. If siblings are more than six years apart, they are so separated that the second child conforms to the characteristics of a firstborn—that is, the effects are almost as though you have two separate families.

Extreme age differences between siblings are also confounded by changes in the ages and attitudes of the parents. Obviously, family spacing is a flexible decision. An important consideration is to avoid having children so close in age that your health, energy, and resources are strained, or so far apart that they have difficulty relating to one another.

OTHER FAMILY MEMBERS

Few events change family bonds as much as parenting. A child provides a new vehicle for communication. Said Helene: "My mother and I never got along until I had the baby. Then she was my best friend. She has been so supportive and helpful. She loves to babysit and she's so devoted. It's like we discovered a relationship we didn't know we had." Because when we parent we behave so much like our same-sexed parents, our understanding and tolerance of them may increase. The parent's prediction "wait til your child does this to you" rings true. We now understand what they felt. And our parents are usually helpful, as are grandparents and siblings. Hilda's sister, 38, recently had her first baby. "We can really talk now," said Hilda. "Before we had nothing in common anymore; we had gone our separate ways. Now we share our children. It's great!" In fact, when new parents do not have much support from others, they report considerable anxiety. One study found that highly anxious pregnant women were likely to be isolated from sources of female support— from friends, sisters, a mother.

Sometimes, relationships with family members deteriorate rather than improve. The child may become a pawn in a raging intergenerational battle. One developmentalist noted that grandparents and grandchildren get along so well because they share a common enemy. In some cultures, people interact only with every other generation, so that children are kept with their grandparents and away from their parents. This custom probably serves to reduce the tension between generations that so often accompanies extended families. Said one

Chinese woman who had grown up in prerevolutionary China: "We lived in a five-generation household. It was not good—too many arguments, jealousies, resentments. It is better for each generation to be on its own, in its own home."

Our relationship with our parents may deteriorate because they disappoint us. We view having a child as one of our best options for winning their approval. Confessed Julie, "I just told my mom I was pregnant. I had dreamed of this time and how happy I could make her. And she was happy, thrilled even. But I cried when I got off the phone. Somehow I just thought it would be—more. It was like when I brought home a good report card and she said, 'That's nice, dear.' It wasn't worth the work."

Another source of difficulty arises when you dislike your parents or strongly resent the way in which they raised you, and deliberately keep your child out of their influence. If you feel this way about your in-laws, the problems may be even more explosive. Parental difficulties worsen if you already argue about your parents, or if one or both of you has not learned to be assertive with them. Some of the most outspoken people we know become as wishy-washy as vanilla tapioca when they are with their parents. As a result, they may avoid or resent them.

Parenting is a role crisis for most of us, and it tends to evoke very strong feelings about the same-sexed parent. We may even avoid parenting so as to avoid fears of becoming like our own parents. Coming to terms with this part of ourselves is one of the most difficult adjustments to parenting. It is helpful to establish good relationships with your parents before you have a child, if it is possible. They will be more likely to help you, you will be more likely to ask for their help, and the child will have exposure to an older person (which can be advantageous). Additionally, it is easier to learn to be assertive, to compromise, and to set limits before a child is put in the middle. If getting along well with your parents is not possible, you may wish to consider substitute support systems—uncles, aunts, neighbors, and so on.

YOUR FRIENDS AND NEIGHBORS

Although your friends do not determine whether or not you have a child, they certainly will influence you. In our interviews, we found that childfree couples associated mostly with other childfree couples, whereas parents associated with other parents. The transition from one set of friends to another was usually gradual but pronounced and often fraught with discord.

Making and Breaking Friendships

Just as married couples find less in common with their single friends, parents and nonparents find their lifestyles diverging. Jason complained, "Up until last year, we had a great time partying and socializing. Now everyone but us has kids—they can't do this or that. What's the fun of finally being able to have a good time if no one can share it with you?"

Many of us begin to feel uncomfortable when our friends select a different life path. We feel estranged and insecure and often pressured into going along with a group, or rebelling against it. It seems that the older you get, the harder it becomes to remain unconventional. Some people who are dedicated individualists often feel as though opting to parent is a final capitulation to middle classdom. "I don't want to be a father just because I'm afraid to be different," said one man. But most nonparents are as conforming, or not, as parents. And children are not possessions that mark one's social class, like a lawn or Cadillac.

Parenting is as conventional, or unconventional, as the parents. Nonetheless, "There's a barrier that comes up between you," said one pregnant woman. "I guess it has to when you choose to do something that others choose not to do." This dilemma also applies to childfree couples, who feel as though they have less and less in common with those who elect to parent (and many times they do have less and less in common).

Childfree women often feel isolated and cut off from other women, especially more traditional housewives. As Lana said: "I never really had many close women friends since I've been married.

216

I used to scoff at them, with their talk of formulas and diapers. But now with the baby, we really have something to share—we can help each other in important ways." Mothers also feel this gap: "What do I have to offer?" they may think. We are reminded of the great story in Gail Sheehy's *Passages* about a mother at a dinner party. She is trying to impress her husband's boss, sitting beside her, with her intelligent and up-to-date chatter. When she looks down, she sees herself cutting up his steak into chewable pieces.

Different Lifestyles

Another source of discomfort between parents and nonparents is that the rewards of each lifestyle are so often different, even incompatible. Said Debbie, childfree, "It's so awkward to talk with my best friend. I know she and her husband are struggling with the baby, so I feel terrible telling her how we're planning our vacation and the plays we saw and so on. Then she tells me about her daughter's bath and formula and feels terrible because she doesn't want to proselytize motherhood. You feel uncomfortable sharing each other's good times, and soon you share less and less." This awkwardness is intensified by our own ambivalence. The mother talking to the successful, well-traveled professional woman vocalizes only the best experiences with her children to deny any resentful thoughts she may have. The childfree person may emphasize freedom and pleasure to deny questioning whether they are worth being without a family. And, thus, unknowingly, both make each other feel regretful and uncomfortable, often without even knowing why.

Some parents become very isolated when they parent, especially if their households have been set up to exclude others and to maximize privacy. What was a haven for the worker may become a prison for the housebound unless you arrange your environment beforehand. Consider your access to playgrounds, parks, and neighbors. It is in the parks and schools and Cub Scouts that parents often establish relationships with others. (There is no reason why you cannot participate in these activities, even without children, although people are likely to be surprised.) Another idea is to look into the possibility of joining cooperatives and play groups.

We have talked about the problems that can develop between parents and nonparents. When your friends and you are parents, the experience can be less than pleasant. Since parenting is such a personal and comprehensive activity, many people find themselves ill at ease with the parenting styles of other people. Said Eva, "I can't stand to be around my own best friend now that she has the baby. She lets the kid get away with murder. Of course, I don't say anything, but I'm starting to avoid her." When parents parent differently, they also may have different children. The parents compete, kids squabble, and friendships are strained.

It is sometimes easier to meet people as a parent, especially other parents. As a woman, you are less likely to be responded to in a sexual way when you are with a child. A man is less "available." People are nicer much of the time. Said one father: "You find a major change in the way people treat you when you have children! People are so much kinder. They shower you with presents and attention—even the crotchetiest people can become warm and generous when there are kids around!" Certainly, children can function as social facilitators in virtually all strata. But there are many cultural differences in the way people react to children. While they are the center of activity in Italy, China, Israel, and other countries, this is not always the case in our country.

Children will require—or facilitate, depending on your point of view—interactions with other people that you can more easily avoid by not parenting. On the other hand, nonparents who want to experience these kinds of interactions can, to some extent, but they will probably have to make concerted efforts to do so.

LOOKING AHEAD

"Having a kid is just something you do. It's a task, like getting a job or cleaning a house. I mean, you can enjoy it, but that's not why you do it. It's work. And I'll be glad when it's over."

"It's life's main purpose, I think. All of God's creatures procreate. It's an empty existence without children."

Parenting changes our feelings about ourselves. It is a role that contributes to the way in which we evaluate our self-worth and the meaning of our existence. But the values we have when we contemplate having children are likely to be very different than the values we develop over the subsequent years.

For some people, not procreating may damage their feelings of sexual worth. Of course, we recognize that it takes only one sexual encounter, good or bad, to produce a child; nevertheless, people (especially fathers) with many offspring are viewed as potent and highly sexed. On a "You Bet Your Life" television program, the inimitable Groucho Marx was interviewing a contestant who said he had ten children. Groucho looked at him with raised brows. "Ten children?" he repeated. "Yes," said the man proudly, "I love my wife." "Well," replied Groucho, "I love my cigar but I still take it out once in a while."

For women, the prospect of being "barren"—even by choice—can be dreadful. "I feel almost guilty," confessed one nonmother, "not using all this equipment I have." For women, procreation is viewed as one of their prime directives. It is very possible, however, to lead a full and varied life without experiencing the sexuality associated with progeny. Many artists, athletes, scientists, gays, physicians, teachers, priests, nuns, and popes have lived satisfying and happy lives without having had children.

We used to believe that once we reached adulthood, we crystallized into some stable and static creature called an adult. But, as Roger Gould reminds us, "While children mark the passing years by their changing bodies, adults change their minds."* We have found that there are certain patterns many of us follow as we age. But these changes can be so subtle that we may fail to observe them in ourselves. We are reminded of the story about a man who entered a doctor's waiting room. Sitting there was a middle-aged man who looked vaguely familiar. "Excuse me," said the first man. "Do I know you from somewhere?" "I don't know," the man replied, "my name is John Jones." The first man then recognized him as his

*Gould, Roger, "Adult Life Stages: Growth Toward Self-Tolerance." *Psychology Today* (Feb. 1975).

former classmate at Harvard. He was shocked at the sight of this once famous athlete and ladies' man! How old he looked! "Good to see you again," he replied, extending his hand. "I'm Phillip Ames. I knew you at Harvard." "Oh yes," said John Jones, looking at him carefully. "I remember now. What class was it you taught?"

As the Years Go By

The Twenties. Studies have found that many adults change their values and priorities in similar ways. In our twenties, we tend to focus on establishing intimacy. Love is the center of everything. Young marrieds, without children, report being the happiest of over 2,000 people interviewed. In our late twenties, many people expand their circle of intimates and invest more in the future. There is a lot of energy and idealism, ambition and grandiosity, so it is sometimes called the "roaring twenties." Most studies have found that women who have their first child after the age of 25 report being happier than do younger women. Even so, they, like their younger counterparts, are very likely to describe themselves as being tied down and to express doubts about their marriages. These same negative findings are not found in childfree women of the same age.

The Thirties. In our thirties, values tend to shift from intimacy to individualism. Friends, so important in our twenties, are considerably less so now. There is frequently the realization that a good marriage, even if you are fortunate enough to have one, is not sufficient for happiness. Parents in their thirties are generally much more dissatisfied with their financial situation than when they were in their twenties or than they are likely to be in their forties. However, childfree couples over 30 report very high life satisfaction and less financial pressure than most. Marital satisfaction tends to be lowest from the midthirties through the forties (it is the most common period for extramarital affairs)—but only among those who have children.

The thirties are pressure years for both career and family issues, especially for those who have had extended schooling. Said Terri, "At 30, you feel adult. You don't have much more time to get started. You want your schooling to pay off, but it isn't. You want a family, but you're not sure you're ready. You want to experience being your own person—but you don't want to become a parent at 40 either!" Jerry, age 36, told us, "It's not so much that I don't want kids. It's just the timing. I'm too old now. I mean even if we had the kid by next year, I'd be 37. I'm just getting my practice established. I'll be almost 60 by the time I finish putting the kid through college. What if he or she wants to go to graduate school? I'll be ready to retire before I've ever had time and money to spend on myself and my wife."

The thirties are often years of realism, of coming to terms with what we have and trying to maximize our pleasures. Many people in their thirties find that they don't work as hard as they did in their twenties. "I'm not sure why," speculated one nurse-administrator. "Nothing seems quite worth it. You start to really, personally, not idealistically, but personally, question the worth of much you've worked for before." Parents in their thirties report similar feelings. "We should have had kids earlier," said a 37-year-old father. "Now we question our every decision. People in their twenties just do, they don't know any better. And they're more patient, not as self-centered."

By the middle to late thirties, we can feel and see that we are aging. This prospect can frighten us into going backward. We "regress"—that is, we try to recapture certain qualities common to our youth by behaving as we did when we were younger, or by mimicking the behavior of other young people. Those of us without children may see parenthood as a way of turning back the clock. This kind of regression is also appealing to those of us who already have children. Said Betty, age 38:

> Last year we almost had another child. I was feeling old and dried up. I thought, oh, a baby! How young and fresh, to be a young mother again and to wheel the little carriage up and down the street! And then I said, hey. I'm not going to be a 21-year-old mother again. I'll be a 38-year-old mother! I'll be me as I am now, but with a baby! I decided that in a few years I would feel the same way I'm feeling now, with or without the baby, but I'd be 43. Would I want another then?

What Betty was asking was had she defined new goals for herself, or, lost and confused, was she regressing to past goals that she knew, for her, were not going to be satisfying for very long?

Regression is also tricky because our memories of the past can be very inaccurate. A number of studies interviewed mothers of school-aged children about their children's infancies. Many of them remembered their infants as being easy, happy, fun, and so on. However, when the children's pediatric records were consulted, it was found that many of these same mothers had complained weekly to health-care professionals about all the troubles they were having with their "problem babies." If you remember your children's preschool years as wonderful, consult your baby books and your pediatrician. You may find that such experiences are considerably more rejuvenating in memory than they were in actuality.

Just as you can't turn back the clock for yourself, you can't turn it back for your partner. Some people think that if they have a child, their partner will behave more as he or she did earlier in the marriage, and sometimes they do. Listen to Phil, "I hope Jan gets pregnant soon. She's in law school now, and she may think she's happy, but she isn't. She's become a bitch, competitive, high-strung, ambitious. I think a baby will remind her that she's a woman. She'll be soft again, you know, and accept herself for the wonderful person she is." Is or was, we prodded. Isn't it possible that the "maternal, feminine" woman he had known ten years ago was exploring an alternative style? Wasn't it presumptuous of him to assume she was fighting her "real" self, which a baby would magically release?

The Forties.   If the thirties and early forties are years of pressure and regression, the mid- to late-forties are years of resentment. No matter what we decided, we think it was wrong. Parents regret parenting and the "mistakes" they are sure they committed. Their children are usually adolescents, who can often make the most confident parent feel outdated and incompetent. In fact, most parents report adolescence and youth the least satisfying part of parenting. Unfortunately, it often corresponds to a time of heavy self-criticism. Parents blame themselves and each other for investing so much in other people, even their children. They feel cheated and betrayed and may react by becoming ambitious, self-centered, and determined.

Career people feel exactly the opposite. They regret having put so much into their jobs. They are no longer "up and coming," but fighting off younger people just to maintain their status quo. They feel replaceable and insecure. Frequently, it is at this time that they turn to their families. But often their children are grown and perhaps estranged. If there are no children, there are the same kinds of regrets and self-blame as we see with other past decisions. We feel out of touch with new styles and vocabulary. We feel fixated and guilty for avoiding what now seem to be greener pastures.

The Fifties.   Happily, we tend to feel much better about the whole thing in our fifties. Intimacy again becomes very important. Friends become even more valued than during the twenties. Couples tend to become more romantic (no—sexual desires have not disappeared!). We give up the discontent that haunted us in our forties and opt for a mellow fatalism.

The Sixties.   As we enter the late fifties and sixties, we tend to become more individualistic, less cooperative, and more "interiorized" (that's a nice way of saying selfish). The happiest old people are those who are invested in the world, who are active and involved with others, especially in a supportive way. Many parents are now grandparents, and some enjoy the experience more than parenting. "Children are investments," confided one grandmother, "but grandchildren are the dividends." An old Chinese tale relates the blessing of a monk to an old man. "May you die," blessed the monk, "then your son, then your son's son." Why do you so curse me?" mourned the old man. "Curse?" replied the monk. "To die in such an order is the greatest of blessings."

Others feel quite differently. "I wish my grandchildren would just leave me in peace," said one old woman. "All my life I've been waiting on children. I had hoped this would be my time to spend on me—finally." Many grandparents feel imposed upon and taken advantage of by their children; one elderly couple said they were actually moving out of state to get away from their family's demands.

Lawyers report that it is not uncommon for children to seek ways of prematurely gaining control over their parents estates, or to try to prevent late-life marriages that would alter the conditions of their inheritances. And hospital staffs report cases of suspected parental abuse.

To Be Old, With or Without Children

Fewer and fewer adults are taking their parents in to live with them, in part because modern lifestyles do not readily adjust to the needs of the elderly. Nevertheless, it is one thing to be young without children; it is quite another to be old without children. Your friends are likely to spend considerable time discussing their children and grandchildren, and this can precipitate strong feelings of remorse, guilt, and depression. Your own parents may be dead or dying; as a result, you may feel cut off and disconnected.

If you had chosen not to have children, you usually have invested yourself more heavily in work, community, travel, possessions, or a partner. As you age, though, your access to such activities becomes more and more limited. You retire. You can't travel as much, especially when health is an issue. If you don't have any money, just feeding yourself can be difficult. Communities have often changed around you. If you don't have an advocate (a role children often play for their aged parents), you are likely to be enmeshed in the red tape of bureaucracy and overworked social workers. Some couples chose not to have children because they wanted to devote themselves to each other. Yet data show that most women outlive men by an average of eight years. (Why? No one knows for sure.) Since most women marry men older than themselves, they can expect to be widowed eight or more years.

When you are elderly, especially when you are widowed, you may be very aware of the absence of children you did not have. However, many communities have programs for "foster grandparents," in which parents adopt an unrelated older couple as grandparents. Such programs give older couples without children an opportunity to at least approximate a grandparenting experience. Even grandparents may desire such services, especially if their adult children move far away, to another state, even another country, and grandparenting consists of yearly snapshots and occasional phone calls. Dr. Angus Campbell has written, "Grown children do not always pay much attention to their dying and sometime lonely parents; perhaps a widowed person is better off with no expectations about children than with shattered ones."*

It may be that great changes will occur in the behavior and life-style of the elderly in the near future. As we mentioned in chapter 3 on economics, the competitiveness that has plagued us since the baby boom is almost certain to continue until death. If the low birth rate in our generation continues, it is likely that the majority of us will be working well into our late sixties—maybe even early seventies—since our society is unlikely to have the resources to support us, workers to replace us, nor (given inflation) are we likely to have savings enough to ensure our own economic independence. As a consequence, the elderly of the future may be a far more important political and economic force than at present—it certainly will be a larger one. Our access to career, travel, and material goodies may continue well into old-old age. The elderly of the future may still be actively involved in their vocations and avocations, rather than (or in addition to) trading news about the vocations of their offspring. The extended family may be the only way our society can adequately care for the elderly, and those of us without caring children may be in heavy competition over inadequate, overtaxed resources.

Many of us weigh our anticipated life satisfaction in old age more heavily than during other stages. "Right now, I'm very happy being childfree," confessed one typical young woman, "but I don't want to regret it when I'm old." Somehow, we think regret is better when you're young. Perhaps it is. But along with the "cape diem" (seize the day!) ethic, many of us are concerned with planning for the distant future. After all, many of this generation have put off adult careers in favor of 10, 15, even 20 years of preparation! It is not reasonable to expect the old-age satisfaction of having parented to

*Campbell, Angus, "The American Way of Mating—Marriage, Si, Children, No." *Psychology Today* (May 1975).

compensate for a 20-year experience you dislike. Because parenting affects so many of our years, it is important not to be either short-sighted or telescopic in our decision.

TWENTY QUESTIONS FOR CONSIDERATION

The following questions have been designed to sponsor thought and communication between you and your partner. While there are no right answers, you may benefit from discussing and hopefully compromising the differences that occur between you.

1. What would you change about the way you were raised? Keep the same?
2. Can you share opinions on what you think about the way your partner was raised?
3. How happy are you with your current sexual relationship?
4. What kinds of goals would each of you like to achieve in the next three to five years? How well do they fit with parenting?
5. What kinds of things do you and your partner think parents owe their children?
6. Do both of you think children should be obedient? Work outside the home? Be responsible for chores? Participate in adult discussions?
7. What religious values, if any, would you want to foster in a child?
8. What would each of you do with and for a daughter but not a son? A son but not a daughter?
9. What do you think was the most stressful event you and your partner have faced? How well did you handle it, independently and together?
10. Under what conditions do you think it is justified for parents to physically punish children?
11. What general limits do you think parents ought to insist their children follow?
12. What roles are most important to each of you? (Rank from 1 to 5, in order, the following roles.) Consider how you allocate your time to each.

    _____ Spouse

_____ Homeworker

_____ Worker or career person

_____ Recreation

_____ Parent

13. What are your five favorite activities as a couple? Least favorite? How would parenting affect these activities?
14. How many children do each of you think would be best for you? Why?
15. How involved would you want your own parents to be in the raising of your child if you were to have one?
16. What do you think will be the most significant change in your current lifestyle if you parent?
17. If you parent, what social activities will you have to change or give up?
18. How has your relationship changed with couples who have had children since you've known them?
19. How have you and your partner changed in the last five years? What was important to you then? Now? Can you see a pattern to these changes? Can you make a tentative five-year prediction?
20. What features of parenting with your partner do you think you would most dislike? Like best?

ADDITIONAL READINGS

Bernard, Jessie. *The Future of Motherhood.* New York: Penguin Books, 1974

The Boston Women's Health Collective. *Our Children: Ourselves.* New York: Random House, 1978.

Campbell, Angus. "The American Way of Mating—Marriage, Si, Children, No." *Psychology Today* (May 1975).

Corman, Avery. *Kramer versus Kramer.* New York: Random House, 1977.

Friday, Nancy. *My Mother, Myself.* New York: Dell Publishing, 1978.

Hawke, Sharryl, and Knox, David. *One Child By Choice.* Englewood Cliffs, N.J. Prentice-Hall, 1977.

Huyck, Margaret H. *Growing Older.* Englewood Cliffs, N.J.: Prentice-Hall, 1974.

Kagan, Jerome. "Parent Love Trap." *Psychology Today* (August 1978).

Safran, Claire. "What 80,000 Women Feel About Having Children." *Redbook Magazine* (May 1978).

Sheehy, Gail. *Passages.* New York: Bantam Books, 1977.

6

Competency Considerations

In this chapter, we will help you determine how well prepared you are to meet the basic needs of children. We will talk about what "doing it right" means and why it is important for prospective parents to consider this issue. We will then examine those features that seem critical in fostering health, intelligence, love, and confidence. In our final section, we emphasize that nobody's perfect, neither children nor their parents; but there are certain kinds of difficulties that are likely to sponsor problems in children. Knowing them is important to making a good decision about whether or not to parent at this time.

YOU WANT TO DO IT RIGHT

People who choose to parent want to do it right. They want to be competent at one of the most important roles in their lives. They hope to rear children who are healthy, intelligent, loving, and confident. These goals for children are shared by almost all of us, regardless of culture, class, or race. The time to explore the factors that contribute to the development of these qualities in children is now—before you make a decision and before a child is conceived.

Many people have a very narrow interpretation of what "doing it right" as a parent means. Even experts have not been able to agree with each other over the best way to parent. The Group for the

Advancement of Science summarized the recommendations of parent experts over the past few decades:

1910: Spank them
1920: Deprive them
1930: Ignore them
1940: Reason with them
1950: Love them
1960: Spank them lovingly
1970: The hell with them

We have no worthwhile data demonstrating any of these "methods" to be better than others (this is especially difficult because our criteria change with the recommendations!). Instead, we believe that there are as many ways to be a competent parent as there are competent adults and children. By knowing the degrees of freedom open to you, you may consider parenting less of a test to be passed than as a developmental experience. This insight may influence your decision to parent.

Despite the broadness with which we define competent parenting, children do have basic (and we think, inalienable) needs and rights. People should be informed about them before they decide whether or not to parent. You would not buy a car until you knew what was required to keep it in good running condition. Thus, it may be that neither you nor your partner would be likely to be very good parents at this time. You may have certain problems that would make good parenting exceptionally difficult; or you may already have a child with a problem for whom a sibling would present additional concerns. You may be under stress that you can cope with as a couple but not as a family.

Professionals talk about "high risk families"—that is, families who have a high probability of having troubled, problem children. Too often, these parents do not find out that they are even taking a risk until after they have a child in trouble. Had they known beforehand, they may have decided to delay or avoid parenting, or to institute some changes in themselves or their environments before they had children.

This self-appraisal leads us to one of the most important reasons for knowing about competent parenting before you reach a decision. You can make changes before you actually parent. In this way you will be able to see if you can change, and if you like the changes. Change will be considerably easier than when you are in the midst of parenting, certainly easier than when a child has been incorporated into the problem. By knowing about these potential difficulties beforehand, you can make certain kinds of decisions that would make problems less likely to occur.

Despite the best laid plans, children can, and usually do, have problems—they do not come with warranties. Sometimes, the parents are at fault, either directly by treating the child a certain way, or indirectly, by providing the child with a certain kind of environment. Sometimes, the parent is not at fault at all. Parents are not perfect, nor, even if they were, do they exercise perfect control over the many experiences that influence a child. Children are different, right from the start, and parents are different with each child at different times (parents change too). Generations change, as do peer groups and schools. As children develop, they experience certain crises and difficulties from which they cannot, and probably should not, be insulated. Furthermore, your standards and values may not be your child's; so, if you want a carefully defined sort of child, or if you want to inculcate values like stamping a coin, or if you want to earn a sense of your own self-worth vicariously through the achievements you have designed for your offspring—reconsider. You might be better off considering alternative, nonparenting activities in which you are likely to have more control.

People who think parenting ought to be embarked upon cavalierly ("Don't worry about it! Do what comes naturally at the time") are ignoring how difficult it is to be a good parent—and how important. Furthermore, our competence as parents is critical to our feelings of self-esteem. Parents of troubled children are often guilty, anxious, and depressed. Marital problems also increase when there are problems with children, and parents often blame each other. Parents will tell you that they can almost feel their children's pain. The claim "it hurts me more than it hurts you" is often true. Additionally, problem children are often not particularly likable, even by their own parents. All of these factors make a good parenting experience extremely important for your own and your partner's happiness.

Competent parenting is also important for the child's happiness. Almost all adults who have personality problems had these same problems as children. (Not all children with problems grow up to be adults with problems, though.) Most of us carry on many of the problems, and strengths, of our own parents. It is not overly speculative to anticipate that our children, if we have any, will tend to do likewise. By the age of three, there are marked differences between children that are likely to persist throughout their lives unless there is extensive intervention. While people can overcome poor beginnings, it is certainly easier to have a good start. Most recent evidence supports the view that it is possible to recover from even the worst kinds of early experiences, barring irreparable physical damage. Guatemalan, Vietnamese, and other severely deprived children orphaned by war, famine, or pestilence have thrived when placed in good environments; but evidence also supports the view that while a bad start is reversible, a good start is not! Fortunately, children who develop well early in life seem to be able to cope with conditions that can destroy others.

Given the importance of competent parenting, we ought to evaluate ourselves before we reach a decision about whether or not to parent at this time. How likely are we to be good parents and to have a child who will be happy and productive? What kinds of things could we, or should we, consider working on if we want to prepare to parent well?

RAISING A HEALTHY CHILD

What are the most important factors in having a healthy child? Recent studies indicate that the three most important contributions to the health of children are nutrition, sanitation, and immunization. These factors are important long before the child is even conceived since they affect the parents' health as well.

It is important that parents stay up-to-date on the basics of good nutrition and act upon them (see chapter 1). Do you eat well-balanced meals? Do you read nutritional columns in the newspapers? Parents have the major responsibility for meeting the nutritional needs of their offspring. Poor early nutrition has been considered a factor in mental retardation and a range of physical problems.

Early overfeeding has also been identified as a major source of problems with weight control throughout one's life. People who were overweight before the age of five find it much harder to lose and keep off extra poundage, which may be one reason that obesity seems to run in families. If you are both heavy, your child would have an 80 percent chance of being fat; if only one of you is overweight, the chances drop to 40 percent; and if neither of you is heavy, only 20 percent. If you are both overweight and decide to parent, you may wish to consult with a nutritionist or diet therapist about ways of minimizing your child's chances of having a weight problem.

It is also important that parents provide sanitary and safe living conditions. Open sewers, rats, dumps, abandoned buildings, poor air quality, accumulation of dirt, insect infestations, and so on are all health hazards. How able are you to provide a clean, safe environment for the raising of children?

Contact with medical personnel is a third critical factor in a child's health. Do you have regular contact with physicians and dentists? If not, this is one behavior that should change well before pregnancy. Good prenatal care is essential, as is careful medical evaluation immediately after birth. During early childhood, children benefit from having their hearing and eyesight checked regularly (you would be amazed at how often sensory impairments in children are missed). They also require immunizations. (Recently, parents and schools have become lax in enforcing immunization programs. Epidemiologists warn of the possibility of new outbreaks of once common diseases like polio that could ravage an uninoculated population.) Regular contact with a good pediatrician is one of the major sources of child-care information for most parents.

Do you have regular contact with a dentist? If not, this, too, should change. Dental care is very important, virtually from the moment of birth, if not before. Recent studies have found that half of our children under 15 and 90 percent under five have never been to a dentist. Infants should be taken to see the dentist as soon as they have all their baby teeth, usually by the age of two. In 3 to 4 percent of all children, there is a problem with crowding of the baby teeth. This problem may be especially likely if both of you have spacing problems with your teeth. Early intervention can avoid uncomfortable and expensive orthodontic work later. Children should continue to visit the dentist once a year by the time they are six years old. You may want to find out whether the water in your town is fluoridated and, if not, to consult with your dentist. A recent study administered fluoride pills to 20 pregnant women and to their infants from birth. These children are now ten years old and have had no cavities, or observed side effects, to date.

What is the major problem dentists have with children? Listen to Dr. Louis Chertoff, a practicing dentist for 30 years. "The worst enemy is fear, and it starts long before they ever even see a dentist. Parents who are afraid pass it on." Good teeth run in families, as does good dental care and regular contact with a dentist.

RAISING AN INTELLIGENT CHILD

As prospective parents, you want to assess the likelihood of having a child who will do well in school, who will have good language and spatial skills, and who will think abstractly. Most of us place considerable weight on these skills.

School Success

Modern American society places more emphasis on formal education than probably any other society in the history of mankind. We spend more on education than we do on national defense. Almost one-third of our work force is involved in education—and even more would like to be. Schools are a personal, as well as national, priority. Many people attach considerable significance to how well a child performs in school, sometimes to the exclusion of other equally valuable achievements. After all, school is only one very special kind of environment in which many capable, talented children do not perform well.

Parents sometimes view their children's going to school as a job; how well the children perform is a reflection of the worth of their parents. Kenneth Keniston, the provocative Harvard sociologist, has pointed out that children are sometimes expected to produce good grades and high IQs as farm children were expected to produce crops.* Parents may also believe that good grades determine a child's success in life, not knowing that this assumption may not necessarily be so. For example, a recent study found that A students at a given college were no more successful or competent following graduation than were C students.

Certainly, though, school success is very important in how you feel about a child and how a child feels about himself. The grades he gets, the concepts he learns, the way teachers feel about him, and the judgments of his peers are critical. How can prospective parents evaluate their chances of having a child who will do well in school?

School success tends to run in families. The best predictor of how well a child is likely to do in school is the parents' socioeconomic status. The more money you earn, the more education you have, the more respected your occupation, the better your child's chances of being successful in school. You probably realize that your occupation does not actually cause a child to do well in school (getting a promotion will not put your child on the honor roll). Rather, a family's socioeconomic class correlates with the child's having opportunities to learn those things that lead to success in school. Parents of all socioeconomic levels can and do provide these kinds of opportunities once they have identified what they are.

One of the most important ways in which parents influence their children's school performance is in their selection of schools. Schools that have involved teachers, parental participation, and an eager student body promote learning (for more detailed guidelines, please see chapter 3). You may want to look into the schools in your com-

---

*Keniston, Kenneth, "Do Americans *Really* Like Children?" *Today's Education* (Nov./ Dec. 1975).

munity. Are they the ones where you would want to send a child? If not, how would you arrange for acceptable schooling?

Personality variables are also important in how well children do in school. Since most teachers are from the middle class, they tend to respond positively to attributes valued by the middle class—being physically attractive, competitive, attentive, following directions, sitting still, and seeking adult approval.

Among the intellectual skills needed for good school performance, the most important are probably language skills. The better the child can listen, speak, read, and write, the better he will tend to do in school. How these skills are learned is the subject of our next section.

Language and Spatial Skills

The way we speak affects whom we meet and what they think of us. Language may play a critical role in memory and may be necessary for certain kinds of complex thought processes. As you might have guessed, language skills also run in families. In order to learn language, children benefit from having a good model. They will learn the vocabulary, sentence structure, and communication style of their parents. Children can supplement parental models with books if they have good reading skills. Since boys generally have more reading problems than girls, a good male model can be very important. Parents can also provide books, the absence of which is a hallmark of families with language difficulties.

Spatial and mathematical skills are also important in functioning intelligently. Being able to read a map, put an engine together, and balance a checkbook are useful life skills. What sorts of experiences promote these abilities?

It is preferable if parents can provide a large, safe, object-filled environment. Can you provide one? Indoors? Outdoors? These sorts of spaces encourage children to move and explore. It seems reasonable that the more we explore space around us the better we understand and operate in it. We have found that children whose motor activities are restricted score considerably lower on spatial and motor skill tasks than those from cultures in which physical exploration is encouraged. However, some cultures restrict infants to their mothers' laps or cribs until eight or nine months of age; these children develop as well as nonrestricted infants as long as their physical restrictions are lifted at some relatively early age. Most researchers point to the period between one-and-a-half and three years as very important in the development of spatial and motor skills. It is at this time that toddlers are capable of independent locomotion and exploration. Letting a child go during these years is important. If you were planning to plop a child in a crib or playpen all day, or hang him off the wall in a harness—reconsider!

The development of mathematical skills may also lie in experience. The Swiss developmentalist, Jean Piaget, has theorized that our sensory and motor experiences form the rudiments of conceptualization. Certainly, when we have trouble understanding abstract principles we are helped by concretizing them. We learn about gravity by watching things fall and about quantity by building, counting, and piling. Without these experiences, comprehension is more difficult. Arranging these opportunities for learning is one of the major roles we think competent parents ought to assume.

Thinking

The development of reason is of great interest and importance to all of us. When parents are prepared to notice how children think, they are more likely to establish realistic standards and to present interesting activities. Dr. David Elkind, noted developmental psychologist, has written that the most common mistake parents make is to assume that children have different emotions from adults but think the same way. In fact, the opposite is true—children feel pretty much the way we do but think quite differently. Infants respond to the world as though "out of sight, out of mind." A very young infant has to learn that hidden objects can be retrieved. Most young babies will act as though a toy does not exist if a screen is placed in front of it. Dr. T. G. Bower found even stranger examples of infant reasoning—a toy is placed in one of two transparent cups in front of the child. The child retrieves the toy from the cup on the right two consecutive times. If, on the third time, we put the toy in the other cup, the infant will still look in the original cup—even though the toy is in plain view! A major reasoning advance in infancy is the child's understanding that objects exist independently from his perception of them.

Between the ages of 2 to 5, children become a little more sophisticated. They are exploring symbols and developing language, but they still behave as though moving things are alive (like clouds!). They are egocentric and find it difficult to distinguish reality from imaginary events. By 6 or 7, children are able to deal with two categories simultaneously, but is is not until adolescence that they can think hypothetically and formally. (For more details, please consult the references listed at the end of this chapter.)

Parents can foster thinking by providing a moderate number of manipulable, multisensory objects. They can be very simple; children really do not need the specialized and expensive toys many people buy them. One grandmother told us her grandson was given a number of elaborate toys on his second birthday. She brought him an old pocketbook with buttons and strings stuck in its many compartments—with which he happily played all afternoon! Toys that require the child's input are more stimulating than ones that require only that a button be pushed.

Studies have found that children who come from empty, deprived homes in which there were few manipulable objects tended to be passive, easily discouraged, and have short attention spans; but the same was true for children surrounded by many objects! Children thrived when given an opportunity to investigate a moderate assortment of stimuli. Recent research suggests that lower-class mothers hold their infants more often than do middle-class mothers (perhaps because they have less child-safe environments). Since held children vocalize and explore less than those who are more independent, these mothers may be inadvertently limiting their children's learning opportunities.

Dr. Burton White, the reknowned Harvard researcher, reported that parents who assisted their children upon request, for a few minutes at a time, had more competent babies than those who either ignored their children or who supervised learning activities. It seems that providing and consulting about an interesting environment can help children learn.

Parents also can provide a model for how to think. Studies have found that children learn a great deal about reasoning when their parents explain their decisions. It does not seem critical as to whether the decision is reached via democratic, permissive, or authoritarian methods. We forget that children are not going to learn how adults think unless they have access to our decision processes. Research on moral development has shown that children whose parents explain their decisions are considerably more moral than those whose parents do not, possibly because when the parents are not present, the children can still model their thinking and independently arrive at an acceptable conclusion.

RAISING A LOVING CHILD

There are no recipes for love, no necessary and sufficient ingredients to be mixed in oven-tested proportions; but there are ways in which parents can be more likely to establish a loving relationship with their child. This fundamental relationship is very important to how much a child loves others (including you) and himself.

Time Together, with Time to Care

We have said that the quality of a relationship is more important than its quantity. True. We have said that 24-hour-a-day parenting is not necessary—may not even be desirable. True. But to have any sort of quality relationship, you must have time and energy to expend on it—whether it be with a friend, a partner, a lover, or a child. How much time may be variable—depending on you, the child, and how the time is spent. But having a child without planning, wanting, counting on hours a day with and for the child is unrealistic—even neglectful. (We hope you have considered the time commitments in chapter 4 on lifestyle considerations.)

Recent evidence points to the importance of children having permanent, interacting caretakers from an early age on. It does not appear to matter who the caretaker is, or even how many of them there are. What does matter is that the caretakers and child develop a warm, physical, and social relationship over a period of time. Dr. T. G. Bower of Glasgow University has suggested that children need to learn the subtle communication skills essential to intimate relationships. Parents can, of course, arrange for relatively permanent, positive relations with others in addition to themselves. If we want our children to be loving, we must provide them with loving models and with a language, both nonverbal and verbal, for communicating their love. For this reason, it is important that in arranging child care you are able to select warm, responsive, and relatively permanent caretakers for your child.

How we spend our time together is as important as the amount. We tend to like people we share good times with and dislike those with whom we suffer. This very basic principle is often ignored in family life. One woman put it this way, "Friends you invite to dinner, family you kick in the ass." If parents can increase the number of positive interactions between them and their children, it will help enormously in laying the groundwork for a loving relationship. How positive is the emotional climate in your home? Is there much yelling or squabbling? How might it be affected by a child's presence?

It Takes at Least Two

Love is positive interaction, part of which is physical contact. Do you enjoy cuddling a child? Having physical contact with people? Studies have found that it is important for infants and young children to physically interact with a variety of human stimuli—to be able to touch a face, pull hair, smell skin, kiss lips, look into eyes, hear laughter and speech. Physically aloof parents can sponsor resentment, guilt, and, not surprisingly, aloofness. "I can never forgive my mother," said one woman. "The only time she ever touched me was to hit me. She even got my sisters to clean or feed me. I know she sometimes went hungry so we kids could eat; but I can never feel anything for her because of the way she would pull back when I most needed her." Clutchiness can also be destructive. Babies are happiest when parents hold them close enough to be intimate, but freely enough so that they have the option of looking away.

The happiest parents are assertive. One father described parenting as "holding on, letting go, holding on, and letting go. You have to be able to do both very well and to know when, for each of you, you have to do one or the other."

Do you listen to what people tell you? Being a good listener is one of the hallmarks of a competent and happy parent. It is also the hallmark of a confiding and open child. Prospective parents can work on being good listeners. Observe what kinds of things make you open up and what you do, if anything, to shut off communication from others. Parents benefit by being able to read nonverbal cues. Read some articles or books to help you develop this skill. *Parent Effectiveness Training* instructs people in techniques of listening, which we think can be ever so useful before, or even without, children (see Additional Readings at the end of this chapter).

I'm Glad You're You

How many different kinds of people do you know as friends? People who get along with only a very specific kind of person can run into difficulty if their children are not that sort. Some developmentalists have divided newborns into three broad temperaments—easy, slow to warm (cautious, reserved, but will come around), and difficult. Sometimes these differences are exclusively infant-generated. For example, one foster mother has cared for 37 foster infants over a ten-year period. "But last year," she told us, "I just could not handle this one baby. He was so nasty and cold. Nothing worked with him—I tried everything. They could not take him away fast enough." Sometimes, differences arise between the parent and the child's temperaments. The passive, easygoing baby may be a delight for a calm mother and a source of concern for a hyperactive one.

The person who prefers stability, order, and predictability is likely to find parenting less positive than those who enjoy change, surprise, and novelty. Loving parent–child relationships are also common to people who laugh easily and often and who prefer watching to directing. They are also common to sociable people—that is, people who have good long-term relationships with friends, neighbors, and relatives. Sociable people are less likely to demand too much friendship from their children. Also, we can assume that sociable people at least have appropriate social repertoires, whether or not they engage in them with their families.

A loving child is usually loved. You can set the occasion for loving if you are willing to spend caring time together, to communicate, with empathy and understanding, and to focus on the positive things the child is and can do. Do these sound like things you and your partner would be likely to enjoy?

RAISING A CONFIDENT CHILD

How a child feels about himself is very critical to his chances of happiness. Of course, we all fluctuate in how we feel about ourselves, depending on a lot of internal and external events. Some theorists believe that it is during our early years that we form our most basic feelings about ourselves. If we feel poorly about ourselves, we are likely to avoid competitive activities and never show ourselves that we are better than we believe. How can prospective parents help promote a child's willingness to address challenges?

Belonging

Part of a good self-image is accepting yourself as a member of your cultural heritage and biological sex. The self-concept of black children increases when they are exposed to worthy black models and are admired for traits common to their race. The same principle is true of accepting one's sex. If you want to promote good self-concepts in children, do not insult a class of which they are a member; but this often means you have to be comfortable with who and what you are. If you, as parents, dislike yourself or each other, how much harder it will be for your child to like himself! Being acceptably happy with yourselves is one of the most useful prerequisites to competent parenting.

Showing How It Is Done

Children learn how to be confident by having a confident model, especially, but not exclusively, one of their own sex. Many successful women were very close to their successful fathers, or they had a childhood model they used to pattern themselves after. The more similar the model is to us, the more we learn from him or her.

Most parents are surprised when they discover that fears and insecurities run in families. A mother who is afraid of bees or spiders is very likely to have a child with such fears. These fears are usually learned by a child by the age of four or five. Those of us who are phobic (inappropriately fearful of certain events) know how crippling it can be. One woman was so afraid of dogs that for 25 years she rarely ventured outside her home without a companion! If you have such fears, you may be able to conquer them by yourself by using self-help books (listed at the end of this chapter); if not, consult with a behavior therapist, as recommended by your state psychological association or by the Association for the Advancement of Behavior Therapy.* Their success rate is extremely high, and the procedure is usually covered by insurance (check!). Conquering your fears is the best way to avoid passing such fears to your children.

The Importance of Control

Depression and anxiety are relatively common in children and adults and often accompany helplessness. To avoid or overcome anxiety and depression it is important for even very young children to be able to control their environments. All of us feel ever so much better about ourselves when we have some control over the world around us.

Dr. John Watson, a developmental psychologist, has found that just the exercise of control can make a child laugh. For example, a child lying in a crib has a musical mobile hanging above him. If the mobile is moved by another person, the child will laugh and watch

*The Association for the Advancement of Behavior Therapy, 420 Lexington Ave., New York, N.Y. 10017.

the mobile for a while; then he will "get used to it" and not respond to it for some time. Now, imagine the same child and the same mobile, but this time the mobile is attached to the child's left foot. The child "accidentally" moves his body until he discovers the necessary and sufficient mobile-moving behavior—he may, for example, flex his toes or jerk his foot. He will laugh and play with the mobile much longer when *he* is the one making it operate. Eventually, he will tire of this, too. But if one, sneakingly, now attached the mobile to his right foot, what happens? Sooner or later he jerks his left leg and looks up at the mobile. When nothing happens, he jerks his foot again. When nothing happens, he begins to reinvestigate until he discovers the control in his right leg. He will then laugh and play with the mobile quite intently.

Children can be given increased control as they learn to exercise it responsibly. Even at young ages, children can be given options: "Do you want to play on the swings or in the sandbox?" By structuring the environment carefully, parents can allow children to exercise control to the best of their abilities.

It is especially important for children to exercise some control over the way in which their parents behave toward them. When parents are inconsistent and unpredictable, there is no cause and effect relationship between what a child does and how he is treated. The parent who yells at a child today for what he rewards tomorrow produces enormous anxiety. When the nice daddy or mommy comes and goes, such children often feel unable to set the occasion for being loved.

It is also important to encourage a child to accomplish by himself what he can do for himself. The parent who picks up a climbing child and puts him into a seat deprives the child of the accomplishment of making it himself. When we conquer a mountain, write a paper, finish a race, we feel better about ourselves. So do children. Some parents love their children so much that they give them what they want and do everything for them. Despite the most loving of intentions, such parenting can rob children of a history of overcoming problems—and the pride that such achievements produce.

Crime and Punishment

Children who are punished frequently, especially by love withdrawal, tend to feel very badly about themselves. All the conditions associated with the punishment become anxiety eliciting, even the child's own thoughts and feelings.

If your parents used a lot of aversive control (hitting, yelling, threatening), you also may tend to behave this way. One way of counteracting this tendency is to take a child development course, which can help by teaching you to anticipate and understand a child's behavior instead of punishing it. For example, the year-old child who keeps knocking food off the tray is not doing so to provoke mommy; he is learning what happens when things fall down. One clever parent tied a spoon onto the child's tray, which he could throw down at will; since it was metal, it made a better noise than oatmeal and was easily retrievable—so much better than yelling or hitting the child.

Have You Praised Your Child Today?

A father of eight told us, "I am devoted to bringing out the best in each of my children!" Most of us have strengths and weaknesses. The most successful among us have learned to strike a balance between the two.

The skills of early childhood are often far more disparate than in later life; a 15-month-old who is walking very well may be a long way from talking. Neither skill is predictive of his adult functioning. By the age of six or seven, the child's abilities tend to even out (but not always; a continued large disparity in skills is considered a learning disability). Strong interests and skill areas become well established during middle childhood, but there is every reason to believe that these are modifiable well into adulthood. Parents can do a great deal to sponsor self-confidence in a child by focusing on the child's strengths. One parent told us, "The number one rule in our household is that each one of us is worthwhile. We will not tolerate any self-deprecation, even as a joke. My kids fight, but never do we allow them to call each other 'stupid' or 'ugly.' We decided long ago that our kids were not going to inherit our insecurities."

The only time in which parental pride can be destructive is when the child does not control the source of the pride. If the parent defines the skills the child must develop, the child may not have them. The parent who reveres only good grades is really valuing the teachers' assessments (valid or invalid) more than the child's learning; and if the pride is rare but effusive, children can become very afraid of losing parental approval, afraid enough to stop trying to earn it.

To develop self-confidence, children need what adults need—control of their environment, praise instead of punishment, a good model, encouragement to tackle difficult problems, and someone who is proud of their successes, as they define them. How likely is it that you and your partner will provide these things?

HELL—NOBODY'S PERFECT!

In the previous sections, we have talked about how parents can promote qualities like health, intelligence, love, and confidence; but no matter how dedicated you are, well prepared, skillful, loving, or intelligent, you can expect to have problems as a parent. Problems are as much a part of parenting as arguing is part of marriage.

Developmental Problems

Age 0–2. Eating problems, irregularities in sleeping patterns, weaning, and excessive crying, often aggravated by teething, are all common during the first two years. Infants are also very susceptible to respiratory diseases and infections (especially of the ear). The first year of life shows a higher health risk than any other until the age of 65. The majority of babies who die weigh under five and one-half pounds at birth and die of infection. (Lower-class babies are more at risk than those of the middle and upper class.) Other common problems are rashes, which require scrupulous and consistent treatment, and fears of strangers and maternal separation.

Age 2–4. Tantrums, negativism ("No!"), and thumb sucking are typical of the next two years. Constant supervision is a necessity. In addition, respiratory diseases, running noses, flu, high fevers (103 degrees and up), and sore throats are usual. Toilet training is a major issue for most parents. The recommended age to begin training varies according to cultures and individuals. As a general rule, girls can be trained earlier than boys because they develop slightly faster. Bowel control comes considerably before bladder control. The optimal age for the average child is 16 months. Recent advances in learning theory have provided a relatively short-term, reliable, and pleasant toilet-training procedure that can eliminate the shaming and battling so common to techniques in the past. This well-tested procedure is clearly outlined in the book, *Toilet Training in Less Than A Day,* by Drs. Azrin and Foxx (referenced at the end of this chapter). Nevertheless, nighttime wetting is frequent, as are regressions to pretraining behaviors when children are under stress (as when a new baby enters the home).

Age 4–6. Common problems in this age group involve aggressive and destructive behavior. This is also the age for nightmares and fears of the dark, wild animals, and monsters. Many children have imaginary playmates. The child is often jealous of the same-sexed parent and is learning how to "divide and conquer." The child sees morality in terms of being caught and has little notion of intentions. Over one-third of the children over the age of 4 have bed-wetting problems.

Age 6–8. Adjustments to school are often difficult, with some children evidencing considerable school anxiety. Other children become very important in the child's functioning, and peer groups are often cruel. Many childhood diseases (rubella, mumps, measles, scarlet fever, polio, chicken pox, and so on) occur during this age, and tonsillectomies and appendectomies are not uncommon.

Age 8–10. The majority of children bite their nails during this age range. Children are often extremely conforming and often cruel to their parents. One Jamaican mother confessed, in tears, that her 9-year-old asked her not to come to school because he was ashamed of her accent. Your appearance and behavior is important to them as a way of securing approval from their peers. Some have dubbed this time as the Age of Rejection. The physical phobias of early childhood tend to now become more social and interpersonal. Children, especially boys, tend to become willfully unkempt and physically boisterous. Boys and girls often dislike, even hate, each other.

Age 10–12. Preadolescence is a time of wild mood swings, extreme conservatism, and judgmentalism. Parents are highly criticized. There are often problems with stealing and drugs (most cigarette smokers start between the ages of 11 and 12!).

School is often seen as boring and repetitive. Boys and girls tend to hate each other, and children form close attachments with one or two friends. Twenty-five percent of all adolescents are fat, possibly storing up body fat for the growth spurt to follow. Their appetites are huge, but they often respond to food with: "Uck! What's *that*?"

Age 13–18. During early and middle adolescence, exceedingly rapid body changes take place. Changes in body size are accompanied by changes in sexual characteristics—menstruation, pubic hair, breasts, penis enlargement, wet dreams, and so on. Most adolescents are ignorant of the body changes that will happen to them—and are frightened. One young woman upon seeing her pubic hair thought she was turning into an ape! While the sequence of development is the same, the speed of development varies. During this age, one 14-year-old can appear childlike while another appears adult. Girls develop two years faster than boys, which also generates problems. The most difficulties are experienced by late-developing males, who are often rejected by females, picked on by males, and treated as children by adults. (Age of maturation is inherited; if you and your partner were late bloomers, your child is likely to be!).

Speed of development also varies across generations. Developmentalists have found that in the fourteenth and fifteenth centuries, women began menstruating at the age of 14 to 15. Inexplicably, the age increased until by the 1800s, women in the United States were menstruating at around 17 or 18. Since there is usually a period of at least a year after the first menstruation in which girls are sterile, many of our foremothers could not bear children until they were almost 20. In the 1900s, however, the age of the first menses began to decrease rapidly, until now the average age is 12.8. It has apparently stabilized, but as it stands, young girls today are capable of having babies at a younger age than any other in recent history! Venereal disease and teenage pregnancies are reaching epidemic proportions and are compounded by ignorance and fear.

Conflict with the parent of the opposite sex is common and intense. There is much fighting, often about adult privileges. Sloppiness, preference for loud music, and selfishness are also common. Boys and girls are discovering each other with the consequent pleasures and pains experienced by all generations. Late adolescents can participate in many adult activities—but they are essentially inexperienced. The result is a grownup who "suddenly" does something very stupid or shortsighted from the parent's point of view.

Money is a major source of concern for most families with adolescents. There are also parental difficulties in adapting to the independence of young adults. Conversely, more and more students are going on to graduate schools, perhaps increasing the years of dependence even longer. Developmental studies are finding that between the ages of 18 to 24, people (especially college students) become more liberal, tolerant, and unconventional. Sometimes, there are parental value conflicts. However, many become more conservative and conventional after graduation. Despite the publicized generation gap, 80 percent of the adolescents in one major survey strongly agreed with the basic principles and moral values of their parents.*

Adulthood.   The problems of an adult may also be the parents' problems. Issues about marriage, grandchildren, and lifestyle can be painful (and enjoyable!). No matter what the age, there will be the spats, worries, and joys unique to parent–child relationships. Recently, we were telling a 50-year-old mother about a couple who had sold their house and cars, bought a sailboat, and sailed around the world. Her first response was, "Oh, their poor mothers!"

*Conger, John, "A World They Never Knew: The Family and Social Change." *Daedalus* (Fall 1971).

Special Needs Children

We have talked about some of the common developmental problems that occur in a normal child's life. Now we will talk about problems with children who are not "normal." Most of our characteristics (height, appearance, intelligence) cover a large range, with the majority of people falling in the middle, and fewer people on the extremes. For example, our average male height is 5'11", and most males are somewhere around that, with a few who are 5'4" and a few 6'6". Most of us have IQ's of about 100, some 50, some 150. The term "special needs" is now used to describe children who are on either side of the average for various reasons. Of course, a major consideration is how much deviation in a given characteristic a given culture tolerates before the characteristic is judged above or below average.

The term "special needs" evolved because it does not label a child by his handicap and because it emphasizes what can be corrected, not what is incorrect. Congenital (at birth) special needs infants occur between 24.4 and 40 per thousand births (depending on what statistics you look at). If we were to define special needs children as those who would benefit from the assistance of specialized personnel, over 60 percent of our nation's children would qualify. More conservative estimates are that about 20 percent of our children have identified special needs in the following areas: about 1 percent are visually impaired, including the blind; 6 to 8 percent are hearing impaired, including the deaf; about 5 percent have speech problems; about 5 percent are crippled; about 3 percent are mentally retarded; and about 10 percent have learning disabilities. The percentage of children with emotional problems is extremely variable, depending upon your definition.

When we think about having a baby, we do not imagine a handicapped child. Yet, many prospective parents fear the possibility, even after having done the best they could to increase the chances of a healthy baby. In Sparta, deformed babies were killed; in other cultures, they were locked in attics and hidden in shame. They were doomed to useless and often miserable lives. But today, advancements in prostheses, education, surgery, medication, therapy, and architectural design have increased the chances of even severely handicapped individuals living happy, productive lives.

Our society has been progressing toward including special needs children with others as much as possible. Even those of our children who do not have identified special needs will be in classrooms with children who in previous generations were kept in separate rooms, even separate schools. This trend is called *mainstreaming,* and it is one of the major educational movements at the local, state, and federal levels. We will probably be more comfortable with special needs children when we have the chance to interact with them and to learn that they are children first, before they are handicapped. After all, we all have special needs to varying degrees.

Special needs children provide a special parent experience. Said one mother of a blind child, "He has been the most growing experience in my life. He has been able to do things that surprise us. And he so loves life, even without seeing it. Watching and helping him grow has been a blessing." We think prospective parents should do everything in their power to ensure a healthy child, but we can balance our remaining fears by realizing that many people have found very special joys in special needs children.

Threats to Parenting Competence

Parents are not perfect. We all know that. And while there are ways to be a bad parent, they are fewer than you think. Here are some of the problems that we think can threaten your parenting competence.

A Poor Relationship with Your Partner. It is likely to worsen when you parent. Have you considered what it would be like parenting with your partner now? Being a single parent? If you want a child soon, have you considered some marital counseling? Some good talking and compromising? Divorce is unpleasant for both parents and children, and the younger the child at the time of the split, the more problems that result for everyone.

A Drug Problem. Drug abuse tends to run in families. If both of you have alcohol problems, for example, your child would have an 80 percent chance of also having problems. Along with the risk of passing on an alcoholic propensity is the even greater risk of becoming a neglectful or abusive parent if either or both of you are heavy drinkers. If you are in this position, why not attend an Al-Anon meeting and speak with the family members of alcoholics? If you have a problem with another drug (even cigarette smoking tends to run in families!), join a group in your area or seek medical or psychological help. We think you will agree that it is preferable for you to control you or your partner's drug problem before you decide to parent.

Poor Temper Control. If you or your partner are very hot-tempered and if you get physically or emotionally abusive, you ought to change before you decide to parent. Contact a group in your area. Self-help groups dealing with home violence are springing up throughout the country (read the newspaper or call your state psychological association for some referrals). You can break the temper habit before you break the child.

Patty identified herself as a potential child abuser. "I want a child," she told us. "But I have nightmares about being abusive, like my mother. I have the same streak. When I get mad, I hit the dog or break things. Afterwards I'm sorry, but I can't seem to stop at the time." What did Patty do? She went into therapy to learn to handle her anger. When she got angry less often and less violently, she began to spend supervised time around babies and children, learning to handle them and herself in positive ways. If she continues to do well, Patty intends to have her baby. But, even then, her husband has agreed to assume primary caretaking through infancy (the most trying time for her). And they have resources on hand—a therapist, social worker, and babysitter—for the first sign of trouble. Said Patty, "I'm not going to abuse this child. And if I start, I've set it up so someone will stop me right away." Isn't this so much wiser than her sister, whose daughter was hospitalized twice last year, and is only now entering therapy?

Inability to Make and Keep Friends. One of the most obvious

signs of interpersonal problems is having no friends. We do not necessarily mean a bosom buddy, or enough friends to fill a symphony
hall. Do you know some people, however few, for any length of time
in a warm and sociable way? If the answer is no, why? Do you find
it impossible to get close, or impossible to stay that way? Some
social skills training (there are groups all over the country) can be
really helpful. When you can form close, long-term relationships,
you will be happier with yourself and others, and you will be less
likely to have unrealistic expectations of a child.

Long Bouts of Depression.   All of us get the blues but if you con-
sistently have entire days in which you do not see the point of getting out of bed and don't, can't eat or sleep, cry a lot, and think
suicidal thoughts—see a psychologist or psychiatrist. Often depressed
people think the child will give them a reason to keep going, and
sometimes it does; but too often, it does not. In fact, it may even
make you feel worse, since depression among parents of young children is common.

Frequent High Levels of Anxiety.   All of us get anxious and can
agree that it is one of the most unpleasant of emotions. If you are
highly anxious and irritable and have frequent difficulty sleeping or
eating, you could benefit from relaxation training. Most of us could.
If you often feel "tied up in knots," or you get pronounced physical
symptoms (difficulty breathing, upset stomach, palpitations, and so
on), you ought to reduce your tension before you parent, perhaps
with professional help. A screaming child is unlikely to help your
equilibrium.

Difficulty Holding a Job or Maintaining Yourself.   If you are having trouble just functioning, having a baby is likely to be disastrous.
Some people think a child will give them structure and discipline,
but this is something the parent, not the infant, has to provide. Find
out why you are having such a hard time; maybe you need help, or
maybe you need a change of environment. You need to be coping
with what you have, before you add parenting.

You or Your Partner Has Special Needs.   Many handicapped people are wonderful at parenting. Even blind and deaf people can parent well, but of course they have additional considerations. A primary consideration is whether your handicap is hereditary. If you have any doubt, you should discuss it with your physician, and then, perhaps, with a genetic counselor. If your handicap is not genetically based, you need to address what kinds of special provisions you will need to help you—equipment, child care, and so on. A conference with a rehabilitation counselor and/or a parent with special needs could be very helpful. Said one prospective crippled parent, "I keep thinking that if I have a child, he won't be able to accept having me as his father. That I won't be able to play baseball or run with him." He was focusing on what he could not do. What about all the things he could do? What about his empathy, energy, patience, optimism, and love? As we have said, there are many ways of being a good parent, none of which requires physical or psychological perfection.

Using Your Children to Fulfill Your Own Goals. Perhaps the most important, essential ingredient of competent parenting is being a good catalyst—one who is able to bring out the best in someone else. The more critical you tend to be, the more narrowly you define success and achievement, the more trying you are likely to find parenting. "I want to instill in my son an appreciation of music," "I want my daughter to be a doctor." "My kid will only go to the best schools." These were typical comments from people we interviewed. We all have expectations for the children we contemplate having, just as our parents had expectations of us. But we should have learned that it can be destructive to expect children to fulfill our own goals.

David Elkind, who made a study of middle-class delinquents, found common patterns to the family lives of regular offenders.* Almost all were in families in which the culturally implied contract between parents and children had been violated. The most common kinds of misuse involved parents using their children to fulfill their own goals. Enormous pressure was levied on the child to be the quarterback the father was, or to go to the college his father couldn't

*Elkind, David, "Middle-Class Delinquency." *Mental Hygiene* 51 (1967):80–84.

get into, or to contribute more than his fair share of time and labor to the household. Dr. Elkind saw the delinquency as a symptom of the family's pathology.

Other professionals have observed similar events. Erik Erikson has observed that young adolescents sometimes assume the roles their parents have selected for them without exploring other options. He called this a "crystallized identity." On the positive side, these children may grow up to be outstanding scholars, athletes, and achievers. But they are also the ones who may suddenly and dramatically break out of their conforming, quiet roles, through self-abuse, suicide, or violence against others. Other adolescents react to unfair expectations by assuming the role exactly opposite to what the parent desires, perhaps even adopting the role the parents fear most. Erikson calls this a "negative identity," since the adolescent defines himself negatively.

While some parents communicate their demands directly, others are less obvious.

"Whatever he wants. . . ."

"I have absolutely no expectations of my children."

Few of us are this tolerant. When we deny our preferences, we often give double messages—do whatever you want, but you'd better want to do what we want. Since few of us escape our histories, it is only reasonable that we acknowledge our hopes for our children, define them as broadly as we can, and adapt them to the child's strengths and interests. To achieve this sensitive parenting role means that we cannot afford to live through our children, as some of our parents lived through us. The best way to avoid this is to involve ourselves in additional enterprises that we think are worthwhile.

Parents Are People, Just Like Children

Some parents try to play "perfect." They are always trying to be right, to be in control, to be rational. Playing this script can be so exhausting that the child is resented or is expected to pay the parent back by becoming a certain kind of person (just as perfect!). Said Betsy, "I wish I could have known my mother as a person, but she wouldn't let me. What I knew was a starched, restrained woman without genitals or faults. She never told me her feelings or needs. She so catered to me that I never recognized she existed." In trying to provide a child with a perfect model, we may provide him with an inhuman one.

Parents are not perfect. Most of us are idiosyncratic. We are fond of saying that if you know someone who is not in some way weird, you don't know him well; and we change as we age and learn. As parents, there are other events in our lives (work, love) that can affect our parenting. And children change. One of the exciting (and for some frustrating) aspects of parenting is that the child never stays the same. Parents cannot have a stock supply of permanent answers to changing questions. Almost all parents and children get out of synchrony with each other sometimes, no matter how briefly. This imperfection may even be necessary or beneficial for both!

While some people are so intolerant of their shortcomings that they fear becoming parents, we hope that this chapter has convinced you that there are many ways you can be a good parent—and no one way to be a perfect one.

ADDITIONAL READINGS

Ackerman, Paul, and Kappelman, Murray. *Signals: What Your Child Is Really Telling You.* New York: Dial Press, 1978.

Azrin, Nathan, and Foxx, Richard. *Toilet Training in Less Than A Day.* New York: Simon and Schuster, 1974.

Beadle, Muriel. *A Child's Mind.* New York: Anchor Books, 1971.

Gordon, Thomas. *Parent Effectiveness Training.* New York: New American Library, 1975.

Maccoby, Eleanor Emmons, and Jackling, Carol Nagy. "What We Know and Don't Know about Sex Differences." *Psychology Today,* December 1974.

Peck, Ellen, and Granzig, William. *The Parent Test.* New York: G. P. Putnam's Sons, 1978.

Smith, Manuel J. *Kicking the Fear Habit.* New York: Bantam Books, 1978.

Sroufe, L. Alan. "Attachment and the Roots of Competence." *Human Nature* 1, No. 10, October 1978.

7

Considering Your Options

In this, the final chapter, we hope you are ready to make a deliberate and informed parenting decision, if you have not already done so. There are really only four possible alternatives: (1) you can procrastinate deciding (this is a decision too!); (2) you can decide not to have another child; (3) you can decide not to have a child at all; or (4) you can decide to parent, either again or for the first time. Which of these options is the best for you at this time?

WE JUST CAN'T MAKE UP OUR MINDS

Since incompleted tasks tend to be remembered better than completed ones, indecisiveness over parenting can plague the most stalwart. Baby commercials, children, thoughts of age may prompt you to reconsider the issue. Because this indecisiveness may be unpleasant, some are tempted to terminate the ambivalence with pregnancy. This kind of decision can create more problems than it solves, however, especially if you and/or your partner are strongly ambivalent. In order to gain the time necessary for a mutual decision, be particularly careful with birth control precautions as you address your indecisiveness. You may even want to discuss your feelings about abortion, just in case the issue arises.

The Roots of Indecision

Probably a major reason so many people are indecisive about parenting is that many of us are indecisive in general. Making decisions is rarely easy, especially making profound ones that are emotional in nature and subject to an unpredictable future. (Remember the anguish of deciding whether or not to marry? And at least then you knew *who* it was you'd be living with!) One troubled fence-warmer said, "It's just that I hate making irreversible decisions." Replied his wife, "So do I—but very soon not having decided will also be irreversible." There are biological limits to parenting (probably in the forties for childbearing and best sperm quality). The older you are, the less time you have left to vacillate.

Many couples try to avoid the issue by saying, "Well, we can always adopt." But you should know that healthy, normal infants are very hard to come by. Legal abortions and social acceptance of single parents have decreased the number of babies available. Adoption criteria are often judgmental (religious, economic, and social values are carefully considered), and older couples are less favored. In fact, many couples are on waiting lists for years without ever having an opportunity to adopt a child. As an older couple, you are more likely to be able to adopt an older, nonwhite, special needs child. But even then you will have to pass very rigorous and often conservative assessments by the agency. We do not mean to downplay the feasibility and worthiness of adoption; only that it is not the easy, secure process so many couples envision.

A second source of indecisiveness is that some people dislike doing the things parents do, but still want a parent relationship with a child (or an additional child). Can we decrease the parenting responsibilities (a nanny?) and increase the positive qualities of the relationship? Or, by income, temperament, or opinion are we relatively inflexible in the tasks we undertake and relationships we forge?

How much we are invested in other, seemingly incompatible, activities—travel, romance, career, possessions, other children—is another source of indecision. It is obviously difficult to weigh giving up some of these things for a child you don't yet have. Because lifestyle changes are among the most profound consequences of parenting, especially for the first time, it is important for you to consider this issue carefully. One suggestion that bears repeating is for you to spend a few days with children of different ages. Such an experience may help you to better judge how compatible or incompatible your style of parenting will be relative to your other activities and interests.

You may also be indecisive because you are afraid you or your partner might not be a good parent. While perfection is not a parenting prerequisite, there are some serious economic, emotional, and medical problems (like chronic drug abuse, severe anxiety attacks, a battering spouse) that deserve attention well *before* you parent. We hope the numerous suggestions in this book will encourage you to enter into therapy, consult a physician, or join a self-help group if you have a problem that can jeopardize either your ability to parent competently or the health of the child. The following excellent short questionnaire, written and distributed by the National Alliance for Optional Parenthood (NAOP), can help you assess your parental readiness.

Am I Parent Material?*

Does having and raising a child fit the lifestyle I want?

1. What do I want out of life for myself? What do I think is important?
2. Could I handle a child and a job at the same time? Would I have time and energy for both?
3. Would I be ready to give up the freedom to do what I want to do, when I want to do it?
4. Would I be willing to cut back my social life and spend more time at home? Would I miss my free time and privacy?
5. Can I afford to support a child? Do I know how much it takes to raise a child?

*This paper was prepared by Carole Baker, Executive Director of the National Alliance for Optional Parenthood, in cooperation with Elizabeth K. Canfield, Health and Family Planning Counselor, University of Southern California; Dr. Robert E. Gould, Prof. of Psychiatry, New York Medical College; Dr. E. James Lieberman, Associate Clinical Prof. of Psychiatry, George Washington School of Medicine; Anjel Martinez, Director of Special Projects, James Bowman Associates, San Francisco; and Dr. Burleigh Seaver, Research Associate, Pennsylvania State University, Institute for Research on Human Resources.

6. Do I want to raise a child in the neighborhood where I live now? Would I be willing and able to move?
7. How would a child interfere with *my* growth and development?
8. Would a child change my educational plans? Do I have the energy to go to school and raise a child at the same time?
9. Am I willing to give a great part of my life—at least 18 years—to being responsible for a child? And spend a large portion of my life being concerned about my child's well being?

What's in it for me?

1. Do I like doing things with children? Do I enjoy activities that children can do?
2. Would I want a child to be "like me"?
3. Would I try to pass on to my child my ideas and values? What if my child's ideas and values turn out to be different from mine?
4. Would I want my child to achieve things that I wish I had, but didn't?
5. Would I expect my child to keep me from being lonely in my old age? Do I do that for my parents? Do my parents do that for my grandparents?
6. Do I want a boy or a girl child? What if I don't get what I want?
7. Would having a child show others how mature I am?
8. Will I prove I am a man or a woman by having a child?
9. Do I expect my child to make my life happy?

Raising a child? What's there to know?

1. Do I like children? When I'm around children for a while, what do I think or feel about having one around all of the time?
2. Do I enjoy teaching others?
3. Is it easy for me to tell other people what I want, or need, or what I expect of them?
4. Do I want to give a child the love (s)he needs? Is loving easy for me?
5. Am I patient enough to deal with the noise and the confusion and the 24-hour-a-day responsibility? What kind of time and space do I need for myself?

6. What do I do when I get angry or upset? Would I take things out on a child if I lost my temper?

7. What does discipline mean to me? What does freedom, or setting limits, or giving space mean? What is being too strict, or not strict enough? Would I want a perfect child?

8. How do I get along with my parents? What will I do to avoid the mistakes my parents made?

9. How would I take care of my child's health and safety? How do I take care of my own?

10. What if I have a child and find out I made a wrong decision?

Have my partner and I really talked about becoming parents?

1. Does my partner want to have a child? Have we talked about our reasons?

2. Could we give a child a good home? Is our relationship a happy and strong one?

3. Are we both ready to give our time and energy to raising a child?

4. Could we share our love with a child without jealousy?

5. What would happen if we separated after having a child, or if one of us should die?

6. Do my partner and I understand each other's feelings about religion, work, family, child raising, future goals? Do we feel pretty much the same way? Will children fit into these feelings, hopes and plans?

7. Suppose one of us wants a child and the other doesn't? Who decides?

8. Which of the questions in this pamphlet do we need to *really* discuss before making a decision?

Listing Your Reasons for Having a Child

Another exercise that might help resolve your indecision is for you and your partner to independently list your reasons for having a child at this time. Then, on a second piece of paper, list all the reasons against having a child at this time. Be sure to include both you and your family's emotions. You will have to assess how much weight to lend to each item, of course, but studying the lists is often helpful in clarifying your dilemma. Said one prospective father after reviewing his list, "All my feelings were for having a baby, but all my materialistic concerns were against. Now I know I have to decide which I value more."

Compare your lists with your partner's. How are they the same? Different? What can you do to minimize the con's? If you are both leaning against parenting, what can you do to approximate the pro's as a nonparent? By the way, if either of your lists has almost no pro's or con's, reread this book! If there is one truism about parenting, it is that it is an intense experience with both positive and negative consequences. If we fail to consider both sides in our decision, we may later regret our choice and feel that perhaps it was made on an incomplete basis.

Exploring Your Differences

Postponing the decision about parenting is sometimes necessary when there are differences in opinion between you and your partner. It is likely that each of you has different feelings about becoming a parent at this time. Many indecisive couples we interviewed said they often seesawed on the decision. "When my daughter was two, my husband wanted a second child," confided one mother. "I said 'No way!' Now, two years later, I want one, and he says, 'Are you kidding?'"

Some people make a parenting decision based on their partners', rather than their own, feelings. One recent study by Judith Teicholz found that a number of the women she interviewed planned to remain childfree in deference to their husbands' wishes. Quite a few men we interviewed said that they had decided to have a child because "that's what my wife wanted and I wanted her to be happy." Certainly, the decision to parent ought to be mutual. But parenting is also an individual experience, especially for the one who is likely to be the primary parent. Given today's divorce rate, you may be a parent far longer than you may be your partner's spouse. Each of you ought to decide individually how you feel about being a parent, with and without your partner. Having assessed your own feelings, you can more honestly discuss, compromise, or negotiate a mutually acceptable decision as a couple.

One way in which you and your partner can better communicate your feelings is for each of you to come up with a percentage (out of a total of 100 percent) for parenting and a percentage against. Of course, percentages are going to be gross estimates, but they can be very useful in getting a handle on a topic in which words are often inadequate. By comparing each other's percentages you can get a better (not perfect, only better) idea of the extent of your differences. And you can get a better idea of your feelings as a couple by adding your percentages. For example:

	PRO	CON
Husband	80%	20%
Wife	40%	60%
Total	120%	80%

TABLE 7-1 PERCENTAGE CHART FOR INDECISIVE COUPLES

DATE

	PRO	CON
Husband	___%	___%
Wife	___%	___%
Total	___%	___%

Conditions under which husband would change percentages:
    More pro:
    More con:
Conditions under which wife would change percentages:
    More pro:
    More con:

DATE

	PRO	CON
Husband	___%	___%
Wife	___%	___%
Total	___%	___%

Conditions under which husband would change percentages:
    More pro:
    More con:
Conditions under which wife would change percentages:
    More pro:
    More con:

A second step in dealing with your differences is to discuss under what conditions each of you would tend toward being more pro or con parenting. The husband in the above example might ask his wife the kinds of things that would make her more than 40 percent pro being a parent. Perhaps some compromising and negotiating is possible.

If you want more individualized guidance than is provided here, consider contacting others to work with you. Friends can gather together and share their concerns, perhaps even do some of the exercises in this book together. While discussion can help some people, you have to be sure you trust and are comfortable with your friends. Professional guidance can be obtained through counselors and therapists specializing in these sorts of family decisions. In many of our larger cities, there are professionally run workshops that specifically address parent options. Check your state psychological association and yellow page listings for names. (Always be sure to check credentials.)

Deciding Not to Decide

If, after doing the exercises in this book, talking to children, observing yourself and your partner, and accompanying families, you still can't decide; decide not to decide. Schedule an appointment to rediscuss the issue and to reread this book in about six months to a year. Pick a date on your calendar and plan to meet in a certain location and time that is most suitable. By comparing exercises over months, or years, it should be clear as to which direction you are moving. Do you think this shift will continue? Reread your previous conditions for changing your tilt pro or con. Have they changed? Are either of you more willing to compromise or amend the conditions? If you still have not decided, do it again in six months, and if necessary, six months after that!

There is nothing wrong about not reaching a decision. The fact that you are ambivalent is understandable—after all, even parents are ambivalent! It is easier, and more reliable, if you make decisions for six-month intervals than for a lifetime. Being actively childfree for the next six months will provide one of the best bases for making another decision at that time.

WE HAVE ENOUGH, THANK YOU

Some parents have fears about raising an only child—they have heard that only children are spoiled, lonely, and neurotic. While some parents do spoil and cater to their only children, research seems to have found that there are no more of these problems in "onlies" than among others. The problem here is not with the child, but with the parents. Spoiling an only child can be avoided by not permitting yourselves to center exclusively on the child. Have a hobby or avocation. Provide playmates. Work outside the home. By permitting other activities to distract you as would a second child, you are less likely to have the "spoiled brat" most parents fear.

While other families have more than one child, family size has been steadily decreasing. In 1960, 25 percent of married couples wanted only two children; by 1976 the percentage had doubled to 50 percent. The average American family size has decreased to 1.7 children, the lowest it has been in decades. Whether this trend will continue is a subject of considerable debate.

If you have decided not to have another child, you ought to select a useful and reliable contraceptive that will not threaten your health over years of use. You may want to consider sterilization if you are positive about your decision, even in the event that something happens to your partner or other children. We also think it is important for you to consider why you want the child you have been considering. To nurture? To feel necessary? To seem young? To provide a playmate, or distraction, for your other child or children? To separate, or unite, you and your partner? To avoid the world outside the family? Once you have identified the functions you expect a child to serve, you may be able to substitute other things that will better serve those functions.

WE WANT TO BE CHILDFREE

Choosing to be childfree is a decision that brings both advantages and disadvantages. While you are still a minority (only about 10 percent of our population), your lifestyle is becoming increasingly acceptable. The following are some of the advantages you can expect:

1. You will tend to have a happier marriage and, if not, a less painful divorce.
2. You will have more economic security and a higher standard of living. You will be able to travel, eat out, and save (if you can) considerably more than if you were parents.
3. You will be able to devote more of yourself to a career, crusade or hobby. Or work less if you choose.
4. You will have more spare time to do with as you please. You can make love during the afternoon or go to matinees.
5. You will be able to be impulsive and poorly organized without being irresponsible to someone else.
6. You are less likely to be depressed and anxious, to quarrel, and to require psychotherapy.
7. Your bad habits will not be thrust on someone too young to deal with them.
8. You will work and worry considerably less than do parents.

The childfree men and women we interviewed emphasized their financial advantages, enjoyment of spontaneous activities, intense involvement in work or each other, and freedom to travel. There are also disadvantages to being childfree, many of which can be overcome, all of which ought to be considered.

1. *Birth control is an issue.* You must be careful in selecting a reliable and easy contraceptive. Sterilization is a possibility if you are positive about your decision. Otherwise, it may be a bit final. You ought to think about your feelings on abortion, just in case.

2. *Your peers and family are likely to disapprove or not understand.* How can you handle family pressure to procreate? Sometimes an honest answer, once, is best. Thereafter, a firm "it's none of your business" is in order. By law, you have the right to say this even to a

prospective employer—theoretically at least. Some people have found that an "oh, I'm sterile" works wonders and successfully avoids confrontations. You can expect your parents to be disappointed— and you can't blame them. However, it doesn't mean that you have to conform to their expectations or suffer their criticisms. You may have to help each other survive them.

The proselytizing of friends can be even worse because it's unlikely to be direct. Janice, 32 and childfree, described visiting her friend who had recently become a mother: "She is so overbearingly maternal," she told us. "And so defensive! Everytime I mention anything I've done, she has a baby story—or even worse, she doesn't look at me while I'm talking but directs a loving stare at her kid. I can't bear to be subjected to this silent competition." Meeting her friend outside of the home without the child might prove better for Janice. Additional solutions might be to seek out other childfree couples (through NAOP) or to strike up relationships with parents of older, even grown, children.

3. *People are likely to think of you as lazy.* To attempt to be a worker, homemaker, and primary parent—and to do these tasks well—requires enormous energy. As more couples work outside the home, there has to be less work done inside the home. In such circumstances, we cannot agree that being childfree means you are lazy. As one European woman observed, "I hear a lot about female liberation in America. But I've been all over the world, and I have never seen people work any harder or longer than American women. They are slaves to their jobs, their husbands, their homes, and their kids. That's freedom?" Said one childfree woman, "Who is to say that writing a book, or making a soufflé, or listening to music is lazier than having a kid? Many parents spend less time on their children than I do cooking!"

Being childfree may not mean that you are lazy; it may mean that you choose to put energy into something else. You may enjoy working very hard, traveling frequently, being dedicated to many hobbies, avocations, or sports, and/or being very couple-oriented while enjoying romantic pastimes in which children could not be included. It is true, though, that some people *are* too lazy to be good parents. We are all different and have different energy levels. What is comfortable for one person to undertake may exhaust someone else. And let no one kid you. Parenting is hard work, physically and emotionally.

Consequently, there are thousands of neglected children in the world because they require interest and energy that some parents don't have.

You can't use having children as a way of testing or proving how industrious you are. After all, who made up this contest? If you have very low energy levels and are frequently exhausted by doing little, see a doctor! Consider whether you have inner tensions that are exhausting you (fighting yourself is the toughest of battles!). If not, you may very well be the kind of person who prefers sedentary, passive activities; gets flustered and upset by too much activity or bustle; values order, quiet, and simplicity; loves sleeping late; and never quite gets around to doing things. There is nothing necessarily wrong with you. In fact, despite images of our primitive ancestors working enormous hours to merely survive, anthropologists find few cultures in which people work as hard and as long as we do! If you have limited energy, you just have to be selective about how you're going to spend it.

We believe you can also be too high-strung to enjoy parenting! You may be very intense, or easily excitable and irritable. Are you very nervous, perhaps have trouble sleeping or eating? Do you have frequent headaches, heartburn, or palpitations? Said one child of such a parent, "It was hell! It was like living with nitroglycerin. I could never sit down without her jumping all over me. Everyone who went into our house came out strung as tightly as a high wire." Such people would benefit by learning how to relax before they have, and overwhelm, their children. Parenting is one task at which you can't afford to either run out of steam or blow up!

4. *People are likely to think of you as selfish.* This can be true. You can be too selfish to be a good parent. You can value material things more than relationships (you can't understand why people bother with pets!), enjoy being the center of attention, prefer being taken care of and kept relatively free from responsibility, resent doing too much for others, or prioritize your own needs.

Said Sheryl, "I always use my work as an excuse. But it really has nothing to do with it. I just don't want to work any harder at anything. I just like to sleep on weekends and fool around in the kitchen and run around naked. And maybe that's stupid—but who cares?"

For most of us, though, there can be a point at which we are uncomfortable with our own selfishness. Erik Erikson, the reknowned psychoanalyst, theorizes that during adulthood, we face a conflict between *generativity* (putting energy into things outside ourselves for the benefit of the future of humanity) and *self-absorption* (putting energy into ourselves and our own comfort and pleasure). For most of us, happiness involves balancing the two. (Few childfree couples, when they are older and see their friends with grown children and grandchildren, are going to console themselves with, "Well, we got to sleep late in the mornings.")

Sometimes being childfree can enable you to give much more to others. If you were to take the time, energy, money, and devotion involved in parenting and spend even some of it on a worthy cause, you could serve humanity very well. In many ways, investing yourself in a humane cause requires even more discipline than does parenting, for a hungry baby beside you will scream until you feed it, while you can't hear the screams of all the hungry babies of the world who need your help. Being childfree does not mean you have to be overly (for you!) self-absorbed. There are many ways, other than and in addition to, procreating in which you can contribute to the welfare of our world.

5. *You can regret not having had children later in life.* This is true. But almost 70 percent of Americans responding to an Ann Landers survey regretted having had children! None of us can predict the future. As in all decisions, we gather as much evidence as we can and behave accordingly. In our golden years, we face a crisis Erikson has called "Integrity versus Despair," in which we evaluate how well we have lived our lives. Rearing healthy, happy, productive children is a major source of life satisfaction for many people. But many parents don't have such children. And there are alternative ways of achieving satisfaction. If you have actively engaged in activities that were of value to you and others, you can have integrity.

6. *You can get out of touch with the new and become an "old fogey."* Children keep you active in your community and bring a variety of people, directly and indirectly, into your home. They use new slang, wear fashionable clothes, and listen to current music. Without children, however, it is easy to become stagnant, isolated, and out of touch with other people and current styles and values. We have observed that people tend to fixate on the music, slang, dress, and style of their late teens. However, this isolation is not necessary; you can compensate by making a point of keeping up with style (not

just superficially, either) and interacting with people of different ages, but it requires effort, social skill, and community involvement. (Of course, so does parenting!)

7. *If your partner dies or leaves, you can end up alone.* You can also end up alone with children, but it is more likely to happen without them. For some, this prospect is scarier than for others. Often, the system grinds up our elderly (especially the poor and the infirm), and without children or an active spouse, you can be at its mercy. But often children are equally helpless, and the number of old people in institutions (parents and nonparents) is growing daily. But also growing is the number of families interested in "adopting" foster grandparents in their communities (perhaps you, when the time comes?).

Emotionally, we have to recognize that we are alone. We cannot crawl out of our bodies, at least not in this life, nor shield ourselves from life through others. The fact that we even think we can is a kind of infantile hope—that by attaching ourselves to a parent, or parent substitute, we will be safe. As adults, we must recognize that even parents are often powerless. You can evaluate this concern intelligently only when, and if, you address your fear of separation.

8. *You can miss the joy of watching a child develop.* You can approximate this experience by working (either paid or volunteer) with children in nurseries, day care centers, schools, Brownie or Cub Scout meetings, and so on. Adults who are segregated from children frequently become cynical and unenthusiastic; but again, this can be readily avoided.

9. *You can miss the special relationship that develops between oneself and one's offspring, including grandchildren.* There may be no substitute for certain kinds of parental feelings. But parental feelings are not all positive—only intense—and lovers, careers, and self-interest may take priority and may provide more satisfaction. You can approximate a parent–child experience by forming long-term relationships with children—children of relatives, friends, or neighbors. You can take in foster children or foreign exchange students. You can be a Big Brother or Sister, or join a Y. But these are only approximations of the actual parent experience that childfree couples have to knowingly relinquish.

To better appreciate the experience, observe as many parent–child relationships as possible, especially those in which the parents are similar to yourselves. If you still decide the benefits of being child-free are worth the disadvantages, focus not on what you are *not* doing as a parent, but what you *are doing* instead. To be rewarding, being "childfree" has to be much more active than being a "non-parent."

WE WANT TO PARENT

Over 90 percent of the world's adults are parents, with many of the remaining adults also trying to become parents. Obviously, parenting has many advantages, but they are difficult to specify because they are primarily emotional. Additionally, the unpleasant consequences of child rearing often are more obvious than the benefits; you can count on expenses, responsibilities, and work, while no one can safely anticipate a child's caring for him in his old age, or on a child's labor economically benefiting the family, or even on a child's growing up to be someone we enjoy.

A child's kiss smeared in jam, or a first word, may thrill parents while it does little for an uninvolved observer. For example, listen to a conversation between a husband and wife who were discussing friends who had recently had a baby:

> He: I can't believe her! All she does is wait on that baby.
>
> She: Yes. Cute kid, though.
>
> He: Not cute enough.
>
> She: Well, she seems delighted. I've never seen her happier.
>
> He: Are you kidding? That's just a front.
>
> She: No, I really think she's happy.
>
> He: Come on, how could they be happy? They're exhausted. They haven't been out since the baby was born.

Curious, we asked the mother what rewards she saw in parenting and whether they were sufficient compensation for her. She replied, "Oh, yes! Sure, it's a lot of work. And I don't get to be with my husband as much. But when my baby smiles at me—it's worth every minute of work I've ever done!"

While parenting is costly, the rewards are ample, even if they are difficult to enumerate. After all, divorced parents fight more often to get custody than to be free of it. Listen to Phyllis: "Sometimes I envy our friends who have a big house and fancy cars, who travel and shop at Bonwit's. But then I think—I wouldn't trade any of my children for all of it put together!" Another parent asked, "If children are looked upon as resource drains, then what are the more important things they are taking away from? I can't think of any!"

The parents we interviewed had a lot of different things to say about why they enjoyed being parents. For example:

> I love to watch my child grow. The changes he experiences open up a whole new world for me.

> I love being with my kids. I think the relationship I have with them is fantastic.

> It's like trying to describe why you love somebody. It's impossible, but if you ever have, you know what it feels like.

> The potential excites me. It's your own personal extension into the future.

Some people who elect to parent will do so for reasons other than their enjoyment of parenting or children. Some have children because they have few viable alternatives. Stated Janice: "I don't do anything well. I'm not pretty or smart or anything. What would I be if not a mother?" Other parents are searching for a sense of purpose, especially one that is future-oriented. One young woman who recently had a mastectomy told us, "I would have killed myself except for my baby. She gave me reason to go on, to refuse to give up." But for most parents, while children are important, even necessary, they are not sufficient as a raison d'être. Said Gerry, "I'm the same as before, only busier." Some believe having children is just one of the tasks of life, to be done well, but not especially enjoyed. Others prefer the status of the role over its function. Said Sheila, "I want to quit my job, but I can't just let my husband support me until we have a kid." For still others, a child is viewed as at least a potential source of unconditional love and devotion.

A child can also provide an excuse for not achieving other goals ("If it weren't for the kids. . . .") or a substitute for other goals (My kids are everything. . . ."). Some of us want to parent because we have difficulty establishing long-term relationships with others. Tending a baby can occupy us when we feel socially uncomfortable.

And a baby, especially an attractive one, can elicit admiration and envy from other people that we may not earn on our own.

Some parents think of their children as friends, even advisors (which of course they are not). Many couples relate to each other through the child. The child may signify their love, their biological investment in humanity, or instruments of control over each other. And parenting may set the occasion for you to do certain things as a family (like celebrating holidays) that you don't do as a couple. None of these motives are bad unless they obscure your recognizing what is entailed in parenting and how suited you are to enjoying the child.

Before Trying to Become Pregnant

Most couples postpone having a child, even when they've decided to have one, until certain prerequisites have been attained, among them a good marriage, economic security, and stability. We also think that before you even try to become a parent, you can do some very specific kinds of things to greatly improve your chances of having a positive experience:

1. *Wait at least a year after the birth of your last child.*
2. *Discuss the decision with your partner.*
3. *Discuss sharing of parenting responsibilities.* Percentages are helpful. (You'll do _____ percent; she or he will do _____ percent.)
4. *Discuss parenting values such as discipline, religion, sex roles, and money.* If you've had children before, what would you want to change in your parenting?
5. *Consider the consequences on other members of the family.* If you have another child, or children, do you have the personal resources to handle another child?
6. *Assess your relationship with your partner.* Is it stable, positive, and likely to remain so?
7. *Improve you and your partner's communication and negotiating tactics.* When you parent, you will discover differences you never dreamed of and must be able to resolve them well.
8. *Implement whatever behavior changes you want to make, such as learning to control your temper, conferring with a marriage*

counselor, and so on. Don't expect to magically turn over the proverbial leaf when you become a parent.

9. *Assess your financial status today and in the near future.*

10. *Consider you and your partner's career goals.* Discuss the likelihood of relocation, child-care provisions, time for parenting, and so on.

11. *Evaluate whether your present living quarters will be adequate (room, spacing, heat, hot water supply).* If so, for how long? Is there a safe and adequate outdoor and indoor play area? A nearby playground or park?

12. *Assess the public and private schools in your area.* Will a move be necessary and, if so, might now be a better time?

13. *Plan your transportation needs in the coming year.*

14. *Begin putting aside the funds necessary for furnishings, food, clothing, and other baby items.* (Keep in mind that you may get a lot of gifts, but there are no guarantees.)

15. *Be leery of accepting new responsibilities and obligations that may extend into pregnancy.* (This applies to men also.)

16. *If you are combining parenting responsibilities with work, plan how you can manage the relative proportion of each you desire.*

17. *Assess your life insurance coverage.*

18. *Check your work benefits for sick pay, vacation days, and optimum timing for benefits.* Also, check for leave-of-absence policies, possibilities of extended leaves, and paternity benefits.

19. *Consult your health policy carefully.* If you and your partner have separate ones, is it worth going under one versus the other? If you do not have a family plan, what is the best way of getting one and when? What pregnancy and birth costs do the plans cover (Prenatal care? At-home help? Complications? Consultations? Anesthesia? Obstetrical fees? Pediatric checkups?)? If you change policies, how long does it take before you are covered?

20. *Consult with your gynecologist at least six months before you try to become pregnant to make sure all is well and that there are no contraindications.* Be sure to tell him or her all the medications you use. (Please see chapter 1 for suggested questions to ask your doctor.)

21. *Keep careful track of your menstrual cycle.*

22. *Have a rubella (German measles) titre (test) at least three months before you try to get pregnant to see if you are immune.*

This test is done in a laboratory with your doctor's permission. If you are not immune, discuss the wisdom of inoculation with your doctor.

23. *Have all your medical and dental needs taken care of, especially those involving injections, pills, X-rays, and the like.* Pregnancy often increases cavities, so pay careful attention to your teeth.

24. *Terminate use of the birth control pill and substitute a non-chemical contraceptive for at least three months before conception.*

25. *Consult with a genetic counselor if you or your partner run a risk of inherited illness or deformity.*

26. *Eat well, follow a good exercise program (especially one focusing on breathing, flexibility, and strengthening lower body muscles) and get adequate sleep as long before conception as possible.*

27. *Discuss with your partner both of you limiting your drug use (including alcohol and tobacco) at least six months before you even try to become pregnant.* Preliminary evidence suggests that both male and female drug use may affect the health of the baby, so both of you should be involved.

By following these suggestions, you are increasing your chances of having a physically and emotionally rewarding experience.

Attempting Pregnancy

Having prepared yourselves physically and emotionally for conception, you can relax and enjoy trying to become pregnant. Many couples report a very special joy and closeness in procreative love-making. This sharing can set the occasion for even more sharing when pregnancy occurs. There are a number of things you can do while attempting pregnancy that are very helpful.

1. *Stop birth control with the consent of your partner.*

2. *Have frequent intercourse, since fresh sperm seem to be healthier and less subject to deformity.*

3. *Identify when you are likely to ovulate by using the rhythm methods detailed in chapter 1.* Pregnancy is most likely during this time.

4. *If you wish to influence the sex of your offspring, after discussion with your partner, consider employing one of the options specified in chapter 1.*

5. *Plan on conception taking about three to six months from when you start trying, longer if you are over 30 years old.*

Studies indicate that two-thirds of all pregnancies occur within three months after the start of unprotected intercourse. If the average couple has intercourse twice a week, then it generally takes about 24 times before conception is likely to occur. Within six months, 75 to 80 percent of women become pregnant, and by the end of one year, as many as 90 percent have conceived, with another 5 percent conceiving during the second year. The amount of time necessary for conception appears to increase once the woman is beyond her fertility peak (late thirties) and a male beyond his (midforties and on). Thus, the postponement of pregnancy may be a factor in the increase from 10 percent to 15 percent of infertility among couples of childbearing age.

When should you begin to worry about infertility? Generally, if you have been having regular unprotected intercourse for a year or more without conception, you ought to consult with a urologist or gynecologist. A man's fertility questions can be answered relatively easily by having a urologist perform a sperm test to see if he is capable of fathering a child. One common male problem is the development of varicose veins within the scrotum. This condition can be readily diagnosed and corrected by a minor surgical procedure.

Women's questions about their fertility are more difficult to answer. The problems are more varied, ranging from secretion of sperm-destroying cervical secretions (in 10 to 25 percent of infertile couples) to a failure to release eggs. For a man's difficulties, artificial insemination (by his own sperm, or a donor's) may provide a ready solution. For a woman, solutions may be more difficult: The much publicized test-tube baby (in which an artificially fertilized egg was implanted into a woman's uterus) will allow some infertile women to bear children.

For more information, or references of physicians specializing in fertility problems, call or write your nearest Planned Parenthood center. You can also send a stamped, self-addressed envelope to the American Fertility Society, 1608 13th Ave., South, Birmingham, Alabama 35205.

6. *Select a reputable laboratory for pregnancy testing.* It is best to confirm pregnancy as early as possible so that you can take extra precautions. Having a well-run, nearby, and free-of-charge laboratory

will allow you to test your urine whenever your menses are late. You can ask your doctor for a referral or check through the telephone directory. Be sure to check your choice with your physician or state medical association. Home pregnancy testers are also useful. A blood test can give you early (a week after conception) results, but it is expensive.

7. *Avoid unnecessary exposure to possible health risks.* This recommendation applies to both of you. While you, the man, are producing and storing the sperm that might produce a child, you ought to do what you can to protect your sperm from deformity. Avoid or at least reduce your exposure to X-rays, contaminated substances, drugs, including alcohol, perhaps even micro-waves. Take extra special safety precautions if you work around possibly dangerous substances. Women ought to do likewise.

8. *Decide with your partner upon a preferred birth style, including how you want the baby handled after the birth.* The consumer-patient is a relatively new model with advantages and disadvantages. The advantages are that couples can exercise control over the birth experience and have a wide range of safe, supportive options. The disadvantage is that few of us are knowledgeable enough to make sound medical decisions. With the right to choose comes the possibility of being wrong—and the consequences may be profound. (See chapter 2 for outlines of various birth options and how to select a style most comfortable for you.) The earlier you select a birth style, the better, because it will reduce your apprehension and increase communication. But please recognize that these decisions are never final. You should consult with your obstetrician and be prepared to make changes if and when unexpected events occur. The birth experience ought to be viewed as secondary to ensuring the health and welfare of all involved.

9. *Select an obstetrician (if you don't already have one) and a pediatrician.* We think it preferable to make a selection even before you are actually pregnant if the pregnancy is a planned one. In the past, most insurance companies did not pay for a first visit to the doctor ($25 to $35), but recent Supreme Court rulings may change this policy. You should check your coverage.

Selecting someone who you feel is competent and cooperative is very important in having a positive experience. We recommend that you and your partner consider going together to select someone supportive for you as a couple. (Some suggested questions appear in chapter 2, pp. 97–98). You may get recommended names from your gynecologist or family doctor, or from a respected friend or family member. Discuss with the doctor your preferred birth styles and see whether your views are compatible with your medical history and with the doctor's orientation. Do you relate well to each other?

You might also wish to select a well-respected hospital that specializes in maternity and explore its special staff plans (they are usually less expensive. (More is said about this option in chapter 3.) A good, consistent relationship with medical personnel becomes increasingly important as the pregnancy progresses. Most physicians, or midwives, see the pregnant woman, and her partner if he wishes, once a month up until the seventh month, then every two weeks for the seventh and eighth months, then weekly through the ninth month. During these exams, the woman is given a physical (her weight, blood pressure, and dimensions are measured and recorded), her history is checked for any difficulties, lab tests are performed, and advice and/or information is provided. We think it is helpful to go together, but if you do be sure to plan time alone for each of you with the doctor. Everyone has private concerns, even from his or her partner.

10. *Take a course on child development.* Do some reading on pregnancy, birth, and the care of infants.

During Pregnancy

Once you know you are pregnant, there are a number of things you can do to make the experience more positive. The greatest risk of spontaneous abortion and fetal deformity is in the first trimester, so your doctor should be contacted at the first sign of vaginal bleeding or painful cramping. Additional suggestions follow.

1. *Watch your drug intake!* All basic structures are forming and are very susceptible to damage, especially early in pregnancy. Smoking is particularly bad for the fetus during the last trimester.

2. *As soon as you know you are pregnant, consult with your gynecologist or obstetrician.*

3. *Eat well, sleep well, and exercise as directed by your doctor.*

4. *Decide whether or not you want a midwife, and if so, make arrangements.*

5. *Include the father-to-be in as much of the pregnancy experience as possible.*

6. *Discuss whether you wish to breast-feed and how you will schedule feedings.* Consider how the father can be included. If you decide to breast-feed, contact your local LaLeche League and ask your doctor for preparatory information.

7. *Sign up, both of you, for classes in childbirth at your local hospital or hospital of delivery.* Even if you are not planning a natural birth, knowledge can be very useful for reducing fear and in case of emergency. Read some books on birthing. Contact the International Childbirth Education Association for classes and information.

8. *Avoid undercooked red meat and cats that roam because both can communicate an infection called toxoplasmosis that is harmful to the fetus.* Also avoid parrots, parakeets, and pigeons.

9. *Enjoy sex with your partner as often as you wish unless it is physically uncomfortable for you or unless you are directed otherwise by your doctor.*

10. *Visit with your obstetrician regularly.* The usual schedule is once a month until your sixth or seventh month, then every two weeks until the ninth month, when visits are weekly.

11. *Select after a first visit a pediatrician with whom you feel comfortable, if you haven't already done so.* Discuss when she or he will evaluate the baby, and how.

12. *Consider amniocentesis between the fifteenth and sixteenth week if your doctor and you suspect certain genetic defects* (for more details, see chapter 1, p. 30).

13. *Arrange to be out of work about six weeks after the birth, and possibly a month before, especially if you must be on your feet.* Fathers can often arrange for paternity leaves. Check your work coverage. Remember that pregnancy benefits must now be equal to those for other medical problems.

14. *Prepare for transportation to the hospital that will be available at least a month before your due date.* The easiest way to calculate your birth date (date of confinement, as it is often called) is by using Naegle's Rule: take your last day of menstruation, subtract three months, and add seven days. For example, if you last menstruated on December 17, count back three months to September 17, and add seven days. Your due date would be September 24. This simple rule is accurate within ten days for two-thirds of all deliveries.

15. *Arrange for someone (father, mother, nurse) who is experienced with babies to live at home or at least to be there during the day for at least one to two weeks after the birth.* Make provisions to satisfy six major needs expressed by new mothers as they leave the hospital; you can anticipate and plan for ways of dealing with them well in advance.

sleep and rest
relief from discomfort
someone to provide body care to you
freedom from responsibility
freedom from anxiety
choice of whether to care for the baby

Perhaps the father can assume these functions. If so, be sure he can handle other children if there are any, manage the household chores, and is capable of caring for the newborn (perhaps he has learned how at the hospital). We don't mean to be chauvinistic, but many men don't ordinarily do these things and don't recognize that they take practice. By the second day home from the hospital they are on the phone, crying "Help!" while the new mother feels angry, helpless, and guilty. Scheduling practice days may be useful. After all, there is a vast difference between being pregnant and being a parent, and both parents need varying amounts of time, physically and psychologically, to make the transition.

16. *Contact potential child-care resources: babysitters, live-in-help, day care centers, other new parents.* Know your options.

17. *Arrange for a babysitter about two weeks after the birth so that you can go out together.* Give the babysitter an approximate date and check whether he or she will try to be flexible. Confirm the date when you come home from the hospital.

18. *Talk to other parents about infants.* Refuse to listen to scary stories that are of no help.

19. *Select names for a boy and a girl.* Don't neglect to consider relatives. Many parents find this to be a very political decision.

20. *Arrange for a diaper service if you wish to employ one.*

21. *Consider whether you want a son, if you have one, to be circumcised.* Recent data suggest that the health benefits are questionable and may not outweigh the risks and discomforts. Of course,

most American males have had the procedure, so your son would be unusual if he did not. You may want to read some articles on the pros and cons of circumcision (one is referenced at the chapter's end) and discuss them with your partner and pediatrician.

22. *Have a hobby or vocation worthy of interest.* Even if being a parent is a priority, it is not your sole function.

After Birth

The transition from pregnancy to parenting is emotionally and physically intense, and entails dramatic changes in your daily lives. The feedback, responsibilities and joys of an infant are qualitatively and quantitatively different from the pregnancy and birth experience.

> I would wake up in the middle of the night and go into the baby's room just to look at her, sleeping. Those were the happiest moments in my life.

> Every day new behaviors appear. He is endlessly exciting.

> It's a miracle. She's a miracle. We feel miraculous having given birth to her.

There is a joy and sense of wonder that accompanies the creation of a new person. There is also a sense of humility and vulnerability. For some people, love, even parental love, is slow to develop. They are more apt to feel the immediacy of the work, responsibility and limitations of infant care.

Most new parents experience some depression during the first few months after birth. Some of the precipitating factors are unavoidable, and the best you can do is to expect and recognize them. Other factors can be minimized.

1. *Physical and hormonal changes often follow birth.* The prevalence and intensity of postpartum depression (reported by two-thirds of all mothers) suggest at least some physical basis.

2. *Exhaustion and relief from the strong emotions associated with childbirth are common.* There is evidence that loss of sleep is subjectively experienced as one of the major stresses of the postpartum period. If it is at all possible to arrange ways of getting some uninterrupted sleep, at least in the first week after birth, do so. Would the father be able and willing to cover night-time problems? Or a live-in nurse or family member? Even so, there is likely to be disruption because of crying, feedings, and so on.

Many new parents are emotionally numb by the time they arrive home. This is a common aftermath to a long period of intense emotion, but parents who do not know this may feel undeservedly guilty.

3. *Sometimes infants are deformed, ill, homely, or fail to thrive.* Some parents fear that they are being punished for some horrible misdeed, either known or unknown. After all, the Bible tells us that the sins of the father will be passed on to the sons. In the past, deformed or retarded children inspired local gossip about the possible transgressions of the parents. While most of us rationally know this is not so, our emotions are not so reasonable. Most infants will have some health-related difficulty during their first year (the first year of life is the most dangerous until the age of 65), and as parents you will undoubtedly have to deal with this issue sooner or later.

4. *Newborns demand an amazing amount of work.* They scream, eat, throw up, mess their diapers. Studies have found that many new mothers feel "entrapped." There is a time commitment to parenting that seems abstract before and during pregnancy. After birth, it seems overwhelming.

First-time mothers feel inadequate and ignorant, and are often frightened about their baby's health and their competence as a mother. Fathers may feel neglected and overwhelmed trying to cope with a weakened wife and newborn. If a helper is in the house, the strain of someone else being with you (especially if it's a relative) can be pronounced. Most new parents may think, "Oh, my God, what have we done?" But it may help to appreciate that the first few months are the most difficult for many parents: it is the most work, you are the least prepared, and the baby is the least appreciative.

5. *Unrealistic expectations of the parent–infant relationship may develop.* Many articles and books on parenting (especially mothering) imply that after birth you have been changed by some magical biological process. No longer are you selfish, impulsive, lazy, or ambivalent. If you are tired, annoyed, and frustrated and feel anything other than surges of parental devotion, obviously you are inadequate! The truth is that you are pretty much the same person you were before. Yes, parenting means that you may have to behave differently, but these behaviors have to be learned and practiced.

In addition, newborns are not very interactive, even with their parents. Researchers until very recently believed infants didn't recognize their caretakers until they were six months old. Recent research, however, finds that babies can indeed distinguish their mothers from other women at about the age of two weeks. However, this recognition is so subtle that people who were looking for it didn't see it. This means that a lot of parents don't see it either. At no other time are children so demanding and so unrewarding (no week-old infant has been known to say, "Thanks, I needed that!" after a feeding). One father of two said, "I have no use for children until they start talking. Before that, they're just lumps."

6. *You may experience differences in feelings about babies.* Some people adore infants. They love to watch them and play with them. They feel busy and purposive and may even regret the fact that infants have to grow up. If the mother loves infants and the father sees them as "lumps," neither partner understands the reactions of the other. The baby may become a battle site. (Mother: "Alice discovered her hand today." Father: "I got to hand it to her! Isn't that nice? What's for dinner?" Mother: "Don't you care about your daughter?" Father: "Of course I do. What am I supposed to do? Cartwheels?")

Even more problematic is a little-discussed situation that we believe to be more common than you might suspect—when the father pays a great deal of attention to his infant and the mother resents it. She may want more attention, and the baby is getting it; she may feel unappreciated, by him *and* the baby; she may feel guilty because she can't share his enthusiasm, and she may feel his pleasure comes "cheap." Said one new father, "Am I enjoying my baby! He's the light of my life! But of course my wife is doing all the work."

The more common variation is the father's resentment of the time and energy demands of parenting. Many new fathers missed being the center of attention in their homes. They sometimes withdrew from their children and demanded that their wives spend less time on child care and more on them. The mothers then reacted by spending even more time on their babies, trying to compensate for their husbands' emotional withdrawal. Naturally, the fathers would withdraw even more, until both partners adopted incompatible and frequently hostile scripts. Avoiding this problem begins at conception and continues throughout pregnancy. After all, many fathers are expected to display a level of commitment after birth that may have been discouraged prior to birth. The best antidote is active paternal involvement in the decision, planning and caring of the baby.

7. *You will have to establish new roles.* With the increased time demands of parenting come problems of how the time will be divided. Sometimes this conflict is not verbalized, or even recognized, and only surfaces many years later. Listen to a conversation of a mother and father whose children are grown:

Husband: I loved the kids when they were babies. They were so cute.

Wife: Cute!

Husband: Well, they were.

Wife: Yes, but they were a lot of work.

Husband: They were worth it!

Wife: Oh? How would you know?

Husband: You know, I resent that! I did a lot, and you're dismissing it!

Wife: You did not! You were working all the time. If you changed a diaper, you thought you'd done a day's work with the baby. I'm the one who stayed home and did nothing but take care of babies.

Husband: There were plenty of diapers I changed! And midnight feedings! And if I wasn't home, I was out working to make money so you and the kids could eat!

Two common misunderstandings in this interchange are shared by many couples. The first is that people believe they have an accurate estimate of the extent of their partner's work efforts in the relationship. There is almost always a feeling that you are doing more than your share. When a baby comes, these feelings often intensify because both of you have more to do. A second area of misunderstanding is that staying home with a baby is *quantitatively* different from most people's work outside the home. The woman working at home may have a romanticized notion of her husband's job (which most men encourage, in order to increase respect). Most men work because they have to; their jobs are often boring, tedious, and often anxiety-eliciting. People above them power trip; people below are bucking for their jobs. The responsibility of a child may feel awesome; some bosses actually increase pressure on new fathers, knowing that they'll work harder, take more, and generally be less likely to leave their jobs than before. The father may envy his wife's "security," isolation, and environmental control. His wife, on the other hand, sees her life as tedious and isolated. She thinks he is "escaping" and earning all sorts of imaginary, and actual, goodies—attention, companionship, money, recognition. In truth, both are working hard and making sacrifices, and both are securing benefits.

8. *You may unknowingly project your own conflicts and fantasies on your partner and/or baby.* One such subtle interchange occurred while we were in a Boston maternity ward:

> Husband (gazing at newborn): Isn't he beautiful!
>
> Wife: Yes! He looks so much like you in your baby pictures.
>
> Husband: I hope not! Everyone said I was pretty ugly as a baby.
>
> Wife: Oh? Well, he has the same hair and features you did.
>
> Husband: Yeah, I guess he does.
>
> Wife (hurt): So you think he's ugly.
>
> Husband: No, I didn't say that.
>
> Wife: Yes, you did.

It's safe to assume that neither parent could see their baby objectively. Rather, they see all kinds of fantasies and fears and assumptions. They may see each other in the infant and react either positively or negatively to the image, rather than to the baby (frequently, when a child gets into mischief, one parent will say to the other, "Your kid did this and that").

Psychologists have convincingly demonstrated that it is difficult, often impossible, to separate what is being perceived from how we perceive it. An interesting example of this is the study done by Philip Zimbardo and his colleagues on how the sex of an infant influences the way in which adults perceive it. A picture of a baby named "Sandi," along with birth size and health data, was given to a group of men and women. When people were told Sandi was a girl, they saw her as being cute, innocent, feminine, and delicate. When Sandi was said to be a boy, they saw him as being alert, strong, active, and masculine. Of course, the baby was the same in both cases, although people (particularly men) perceived her (it really was a she) quite differently, depending on the sex they thought she was. All too often, people lay their own trips on babies that are destructive to the development of both parents and children. Our images of ourselves and our partners get all mixed up with the existence of a separate and unique individual.

9. *Other positive events in your lives may decrease.* Parents are very frequently ignored by people who once attended to them before the baby was born. People have a tendency to greet new parents with "where's the baby?" Parents are often ambivalent about their reactions—they usually feel a little guilty over resenting the

attention given their own baby. In truth, however, as soon as the baby is born, the number of "good" things parents receive drops precipitously. Attention from friends and relatives decreases; they have been through quite an experience, and yet most presents are for the baby; they generally don't get to go out very much, if at all, during the first few weeks, even months; sexual activity is usually restricted for several weeks; they may lose sleep and be less affectionate with each other. A woman is no longer pregnant, but it may take her a few weeks or months to get back into prepregnancy shape. Bills are coming in, and it is easy to feel economically strapped.

These consequences are only temporary, but they can depress parents if they are not prepared. ("Oh, my God—is this what parenting is like?")

10. *You may have difficulty in balancing romance and responsibility.* If possible, have a space for the baby out of your direct line of sight where you can place him or her when you want to be alone. Many parents keep their newborns in their bedrooms with them; we don't think this is such a good idea. It is important for parents to be able to minimize parenting behavior at times, no matter how much they love their children. The baby should, if possible, have a space that is convenient, easily visible, and from which she or he can be clearly heard. If this is not possible, at least remove the infant from your bedroom temporarily if you find him or her cramping your romantic style. We know of one couple who used an intercom (switched on to receive from the baby's adjacent room) to maintain close contact with their baby during the evening hours. Your partner is still a spouse as well as a mother or father. It is too easy for these roles to seem incompatible. Even if your baby is quiet, just seeing him or her can set the occasion for maternal or paternal worries from which all of us need a break!

As you can see, it is not surprising that many new parents feel overwhelmed and depressed following birth. We think it is helpful to recognize these issues beforehand and prepare to handle them intelligently when they do arise.

The Parenting Years

Birth is just the beginning to the many intense experiences of parenting. Many parents learn new things about themselves and their partners, even about life itself. Most of us want to be able to max-imize the joys and constructively handle the problems. How?

1. *Try to include each other in parenting as much as possible, even if it involves rearranging your schedules and withholding criticism.* Fathers can play an important role in child rearing, and parenting can provide men with a unique opportunity for personal growth. Too often fathers exclude themselves or are excluded from being more actively involved. You may also want to talk over and agree upon a parenting decision so that both you and your children will be less likely to divide and conquer.

2. *Try to arrange to parent with more adults (both men and women if possible) and more children, of different ages.* Few adults, and even fewer children, are well suited to isolated parenting. No matter how lovable and charming a child, adults also enjoy other adults. No matter how playful a parent, children also enjoy other children. Shared parenting is more interesting and benefits both parents and their children. You can maximize contact with family members, and/or initiate play groups, strolls, and park visits with others in your neighborhood. Join food co-ops, take turns shopping, and develop your neighbors as resources. Encourage yourself and others to view child rearing as an activity that benefits the entire community and in which all members have a stake. For those of us with and without children, youngsters can be the vehicle by which we reestablish community life. (Don't forget to talk with and include childfree couples. They can be ever so enthusiastic and helpful). With the average American family moving once every five years, communities have been unstable. But soaring house prices and fuel shortages may limit our future mobility and encourage us to become more committed to our communities. Children, and we think adults as well, can benefit from caring, long-term relationships with those living around them.

3. *Resolve and continue to discuss power issues between you and your partner while parenting.* Rhetoric aside, many primary parents suffer a loss of control in their relationships, especially over money matters. This is particularly likely if one of you gave up a job, or part of one, to assume nonpaid parenting responsibilities. It is essential that you both feel the work and pleasures of your part-nership are fairly divided and that the primary parent does not lose

ground in the relationship. Each couple has to work this formula out in different and changing ways. You may want to schedule family conferences every six months in which you, your partner, and your children (when they are old enough) can exchange feelings, discuss problems, and resolve differences. The meeting time sets the occasion for both talking and listening. These meetings can prevent a problem from continuing indefinitely. Care should be taken that everyone in the family gets an equal opportunity to communicate.

4. *Make a point of browsing through a good library or bookstore every six months or so and selecting some age-relevant books on parenting and children.* This practice will enable you to anticipate and prevent problems and avoid expecting unrealistic behavior from your child. Knowledge about how children develop will also allow you to reward good behavior more often than punishing bad, and often predictable, behavior. You will be less likely to become overly anxious or worried about problems when you are familiar with the many, temporary difficulties common to normal development.

5. *Make rules and their consequences clear.* Such a pattern will help you and your child to be more consistent. Inconsistent parenting appears to be a source of pronounced emotional problems in many families.

6. *Help your child's educational development by reading to him and having lots of interesting and colorful books and magazines around.* Provide a relatively unrestricted space, with a moderate assortment of challenging, manipulative objects. Try to encourage exploration, especially during the toddler years. Help your child when asked, but resist the temptation to do for her what she can do for herself, even if it takes her longer. When your child is school aged, take an active role in his education. Also, if you verbalize your thinking process, it will be easier for your child to learn how to solve problems and make decisions.

7. *Promote your child's self-confidence by delegating appropriate responsibilities as a member of the family and by openly expressing empathy and pride.* You can also help by assisting your child in developing strengths and interests. Explore, rather than assume, what these strengths are or should be.

8. *Establish good health habits and health care from the start.* Limit, rather than forbid, sweets, late hours, and so on.

9. *Don't automatically assume you can't do this or that because*

you are parents. Much of child rearing is drudgery and work, but you can plan ways of spending happier times together. Let the chores go if you have to make a choice. Try to stop yourselves before you make sacrifices in the name of your family and consider whether they are really necessary.

10. *Identify those goals that are important for you and plan on ways of attaining at least some of them while parenting, especially in the early years.* Parenting is often depressing because it does not secure the rewards presently valued by many Americans—money, prestige, influence, and attention. While we may prefer the less tangible rewards of child rearing, we do not live in a vacuum; we are going to be strongly influenced by our history and by those around us. List the sorts of activities that give you the most pleasure and satisfaction, and then plan on ways in which you can continue to do at least some of them. If you are a primary parent and if your economic situation is tight, considerable planning may be required. But we think it is worth the time and effort, because you will be less likely to be depressed, anxious, and looked down upon by others (including yourself). You will also be less likely to resent parenting and to expect unreasonable rewards from your child. You owe yourself, your partner, and your child an interesting parent who does not feel resentful.

Those of you who have decided to parent are going to embark upon an exciting, challenging and unique experience. You will find that parenting raises new joys, problems, and thrills. For many people, it is the most enriching experience of their lives. We hope that pre-parenting will help you have an enjoyable and positive parenting experience.

We Want to Parent Again

Some of you are already parents and have decided to have another child. The majority of parents still prefer two or three children. Parents report that the cost and labor involved in the second or third child is considerably less than in the first. However, noise levels and general chaos may increase dramatically with each child. Parents of more than one child find it easier if they have a high tolerance for noise and disorder and are good at settling disputes in ways that teach children to settle them independently as they get older. The optimum spacing between children, both socially and medically, appears to be two-and-a-half to five years apart. A second child can be very helpful in distracting an overly smothering, intense, or worried parent. Two or more children can play together and under good conditions develop close relationships.

As family size increases to over four children, the dynamics change considerably. A large family requires special considerations in housing, transportation, child-care arrangements, and so on. But responsibilities are often more evenly distributed and parental pressures less intense. As one mother of seven put it, "Most of your work is in assigning tasks, not doing them." Parents of large families are happiest when they are effective managers of people and resources and when they enjoy being part of a great deal of bustle and activity.

Most parents of more than one child report problems with children fighting. Researchers have found that preschoolers average one fight every three to five minutes! But, certainly, sibling arguments can be reduced considerably. You can do this in several ways:

1. *Tell your children that they are going to have another brother or sister to play with as soon as you know you are pregnant.* Sometimes children are understandably confused, even resentful, but they are also excited and eager. Expect both kinds of feelings, and pay a lot of attention to the good ones.

2. *Include your children in the preparations and caring for the baby.* One key to reducing jealousy is to focus on family interactions. Too often, parents treat the family as a work unit whose members have to compete for whatever resources they can secure for themselves. One family we interviewed labeled everything in the house, even in the refrigerator. Everyone hoarded their possessions and smirked over having things that others did not. And the parents couldn't understand why their children were always squabbling!

3. *Encourage the equitable sharing of work, fun, and possessions.* Teach your children how to help each other. Studies have found that children learn more by teaching than by being taught. The relatively high performance of firstborns, even better than only-children, may reflect their teaching their siblings. However, it can be a mistake to treat the eldest as the only teacher. There are many

things we can learn from younger people if we are shown how. The more of an exchange siblings can establish, the less rivalry and jealousy!

4. *Respect and appreciate differences.* One father of six told us the following: "All of us in the family are talkers. We shout and scream. Our dinner conversations could drown out a marching band. But our little girl was very soft spoken—she could never be heard above the din. So we gave her a little bell. If she had something to say, she would ring her bell, and she would have the next turn!" What a great alternative to trying to force her into a screamer! As you can guess, this family had virtually no squabbling because they respected differences, rather than pitting the children against each other.

5. *Be fair but don't try to treat your children as though they are identical.* "That's the challenge," said a father of five. "You can't give everyone the same thing, and then you're always thinking, 'should I have spent more time with X or demanded more of Y?'"

6. *Rotate chores and responsibilities.* One of the major shortcomings in a large family is that children can get stuck in a role. The family unit begins to depend on everyone playing a certain part in the script and the resistance to change can be considerable. Children can become crystallized and may find it impossible to change within the family. Sensitive parents can control for this by trying to keep roles flexible and by encouraging the children (and themselves!) to try new and different activities, both within and outside the home.

Having more than one child can provide great joy, as described by one parent: "Watching my children walk hand in hand is so beautiful it makes me laugh and cry at the same time." We wish you as exciting and rewarding an experience.

CONCLUSION

We hope this chapter has helped you consolidate and summarize the many complex issues raised in previous chapters. You have considered health factors and are aware of what is involved in having a positive, planned pregnancy and a healthy baby. You know how to influence the sex of a child, how to spot possible problems, how to tell when pregnancy has occurred, and what options are then available. You have considered information about the birth experience and how important it is for the father to be involved in selecting a birth style.

You have also given consideration to the economics of parenting, and you have a realistic picture of the expenses entailed and the style in which you can afford to parent. You have thought about the changes in lifestyle that occur if you were to parent. You know what it is that parents do, how much of it you are likely to do yourself, and with whom you would be willing to share the remainder.

You have considered interpersonal factors involved in parenting and how having a child would be likely to affect your relationships with your partner, other children, parents, and friends. You have thought about what having a child would be like emotionally. You have tried to look years ahead and take your past and present experiences into consideration.

You have addressed what it takes to raise a healthy, intelligent, loving, and confident child. You have considered whether you have problems that you may want to overcome before you decide to parent. If you have done the suggested exercises, you have observed parents and their children. You have spent hours with children of different ages, and seen how both you and your partner respond and interact. You have taken a child into your home. You have noted, in your daily lives, what you would find more difficult to do with children, and what you would find more difficult to experience without them.

In this, the final chapter, you have considered your options. We are sure that most of you will want additional time to consider and discuss what you have read. Despite all the lists, the reasons, the tables and the charts, the parenting decision is primarily an emotional one. This is not to say that rational, practical, and realistic assessments are not critical in making a good decision. But the prime rewards of parenting are to be found in your emotions, not in your medical charts, and certainly not in your pocketbooks. For some of you, the activities and feelings experienced in parenting will more than outweigh the aggravations. This is not so for others, and it may not be so throughout your lives.

We hope that pre-parenting has helped you to explore your alternatives, with insight and knowledge, and to share your feelings with each other. We hope that it has indeed been a guide to your planning ahead, and that is has been an interesting and useful one. Whatever your decision, we hope your preparation will help you to have an enjoyable and positive experience, to the benefit of us all.

ADDITIONAL READINGS

Ehrlich, Paul R., and Ehrlich, Anne H. "What Happened to the Population Bomb?" *Human Nature* 2, No. 1, January 1979.

"Is Breast-Feeding Best for Babies?" *Consumer Reports,* March 1977.

Lord, Lewis J. "Delayed Baby Boom: Its Meaning." *U.S. News and World Report.* February 20, 1978.

Paige, Karen Ericksen. "The Ritual of Circumcision. *Human Nature* 1, No. 5, May 1978.

Whelan, Elizabeth M. *A Baby, Maybe?* New York: Bobbs-Merrill, Co., 1975.

Whelan, Elizabeth M. *Boy or Girl?* New York: Bobbs-Merrill, Co., 1977.

Appendix

Will You Let Us Know Your Decision?

On the following page is a short questionnaire we have devised so that we can hear from you. The ultimate test of this book is whether or not you found it useful, informative, and interesting. We would appreciate your filling out the form and sending it to us. If you wish to sign your name and address, please do. With your permission, we'd like to contact you in a few years and find out if you are happy with your parenting decision and the role this book played in it. If you do not wish us to contact you, just don't check the box provided and/or leave out your name. Your feedback now can prove ever so helpful to others who are trying to decide, and to us, who are trying to help. Thank you!

Mail questionnaire to:

> Dr. Barbara Fournier
> Division of Behavioral Sciences
> Curry College
> Milton, MA. 02186

1. Why did you buy or borrow this book?

   ☐ Saw it on display
   ☐ Someone talked to me about it
   ☐ Heard or saw advertising or reviews about it

2. Who purchased the book?

   □ Wife
   □ Husband
   □ Single or divorced male
   □ Single or divorced female

3. Did both you and your partner read and discuss this book?

   □ Yes
   □ No

4. How many children do you have now?

   □ 0 □ 1 □ 2 □ 3+

5. Which chapter(s) did you find most useful and interesting?

   □ Health
   □ Birth
   □ Economics
   □ Lifestyle
   □ Interpersonal
   □ Competency
   □ Options

6. What decision did you reach at the end of the book?

   □ To remain indecisive for a while
   □ To be childfree
   □ To not have another child
   □ To have another child (number?   )

7. What did you like most about the book?

8. Least?

9. Do you have any suggestions for ways of improving the book?

10. Do you think the book is biased? If so, in what way?

Name: _____

Address: _____

_____

Please check this box if it is permissible for us to send a follow-up letter to you in a year or so.　□

Thank you!

Additional comments: